Baghdad
Without A Map

TONY HORWITZ

⋙ Baghdad ⋘
Without A Map

and other misadventures in Arabia

A DUTTON BOOK

DUTTON

Published by the Penguin Group
Penguin Books USA Inc., 375 Hudson Street,
New York, New York 10014, U.S.A.
Penguin Books Ltd, 27 Wrights Lane,
London W8 5TZ, England
Penguin Books Australia Ltd, Ringwood,
Victoria, Australia
Penguin Books Canada Ltd, 2801 John Street,
Markham, Ontario, Canada L3R 1B4
Penguin Books (N.Z.) Ltd, 182-190 Wairau Road,
Auckland 10, New Zealand

Penguin Books Ltd, Registered Offices:
Harmondsworth, Middlesex, England

First published by Dutton, an imprint of New American Library,
a division of Penguin Books USA Inc.
Distributed in Canada by McClelland & Stewart Inc.

First Printing, March, 1991
3   5   7   9   10   8   6   4   2

Portions of this book were previously published
in Harper's, Washington Monthly, *and* Playboy.

Library of Congress Cataloging-in-Publication Data

Horwitz, Tony, 1958–
   Baghdad without a map, and other misadventures in Arabia / Tony
Horwitz.
      p.   cm.
   1. Middle East—Description and travel.   2. Horwitz, Tony, 1958–
—Journeys—Middle East.   I. Title.
DS49.7.H67   1991
915.604'53—dc20   90-46653
                                                         CIP

Printed in the United States of America
Set in Janson

Designed by Steven N. Stathakis

To Geraldine, again.
"I think of happy days alone with you in desert places."

Contents

✦✦ Acknowledgments ✦✦

I would like to thank Sayed Hassan and Yousri Khier, for guiding me through the wiles of Cairo and Arabic; Linda Halsey, for her broad definition of travel; Jim Landers, Jack Hitt, David Hawpe, Keith Runyon, Jason Deparle, Karen House, Lee Lescaze and Barry Kramer, for deciphering smudged faxes and broken telexes, and sometimes publishing them. And Michael Ross and Barbara Slavin, for their friendship and butterball turkey at Sharia Abu Al Feda. *Alfi shokr.*

*Young men who like their comforts, and a dainty table,
or who wish to pass their time pleasantly in the company
of women, must not go to Arabia.*
   —CARSTEN NIEBUHR,
    Description of Arabia, 1774

I never saw a fat man in the desert.
   —RICHARD BURTON,
    nineteenth-century English explorer

Love at First Sight

I was driving alone, on a moon-less night, along the rim of the vast desert known as the Empty Quarter. The road was black and narrow, the occasional sign written in Arabic script I couldn't yet decipher. I turned and turned again and felt the back wheels spin in drifting desert sand.

Retracing my route, I stopped at a small oasis of palm trees and whitewashed villas. Arab houses, particularly those in the Persian Gulf states, reveal little to the outside world. Knocking on a plain metal door set in a high wall of stucco, I wondered if the home inside was a palace or a hovel.

The door creaked open a few inches and a woman peered out, her face concealed by a black canvas mask. It formed a beak around her nose, with narrow eye slits, like medieval armor. I asked in simple Arabic if she could direct me back to the town I had left to watch the sunset, three hours before.

She paused, glancing over her shoulder. There was a rustle of garments and the whisper of female voices. Then she invited me in and slipped behind another door to find someone who could help.

Five women sat on a carpet in the courtyard, sipping tea from tiny glasses. They wore masks like the woman at the door, and billowy black shrouds that fell to their toes, concealing hair and skin.

I smiled and offered the ubiquitous Arab greeting: *"Salaam aleikum."* Peace be upon you. Ten eyes stared back through their peepholes. It was difficult to tell if anyone returned my smile. Then one of the women stood up and offered me a glass of tea. She spoke in hesitant English, and her voice was muffled by the veil. "I love you," she said.

I looked down, embarrassed, and studied the red henna dye painted in swirls across the tops of her toes. Somehow, saying "I love you, too" to a Muslim woman in a face mask didn't seem appropriate. So I smiled and thanked her. We stood there, blue eyes to black eyes, until a man appeared at the edge of the courtyard. He wore a starched white robe and a white kerchief folded like a fortune cookie atop his head. "I love you always," the woman said, retreating toward the black-robed huddle on the carpet.

The man explained in a mix of English, Arabic and pantomime that I should follow the oil wells, vast laceworks of steel strung out along the highway. At night, wreathed in blinking lights, they looked like dot-to-dot drawings without the lines sketched in. Before Mohammed brought Islam to the Arabian peninsula, the bedouin worshiped stars and used them as guides in the night. These days, nomads navigated by a constellation of oil.

The drive was long and dull, and I passed the time by replaying the courtyard scene in my head. I'd noticed a satellite dish perched atop the villa; perhaps the women had been watching television. Wasn't "I love you" what men and women often said to each other in the West? I let my imagination drift out across the sand. Perhaps the women dreamed of strangers in the night—though probably not blond men in khakis and sneakers, sputtering bad Arabic. Perhaps the women were concubines, held captive in a desert harem. It was the sort of thing that often happened in movies about Arabia.

Most likely the meeting was meaningless, a linguistic impasse common to rookie correspondents. "My first few months out here, I felt like Helen Keller," a fellow journalist had confided a few weeks before, welcoming me to the Middle East. "Blind, deaf and also dumb—particularly dumb." He chuckled and took another swig of soapy Egyptian beer. "But I've stopped worrying. Your average reader, even your average editor, can't tell if you know what you're writing about or not."

So I shrugged off the strange encounter. Surely, as my Arabic and my understanding of Arab subtleties improved, I'd be able to make sense of such scenes, even use them as anecdotes in my feature stories.

But strange things kept happening. And in the two years that followed, I often found myself in dimly lit hotel rooms or dusty airport lobbies, trying to fathom notes I had scribbled just hours before. What was I to make of the teenager in Gaza, his face wrapped in a black-checked keffiya, who guided me through streets smudged with burning tires, then paused to ask, "Mr. Tony, there is something I must know. Are you Portuguese?"

Did he know somehow I was Jewish? What did this have to do with the Portuguese?

Months later, I arrived by boat in Beirut, amid heavy artillery fire. A lone sentry patrolled the dock, and I assumed he would ask for my papers. "Visa? Who said anything about visa?" he said with a shrug. Gesturing toward the shell-pocked shore, he slung his weapon onto his shoulder and melted back into the gloom.

Was this an invitation or a warning?

On a later reporting trip, to cover the funeral of Ayatollah Khomeini, I found myself stuck in Tehran traffic beside a taxi driver who kept grabbing my thigh and shrieking: "America! Donkey! Torch!" He refused to accept a single riyal for the hour-long ride.

After a time, I contented myself with scribbling in my notebooks and filling the margins with question marks. Islamic society, like the homes I had passed that first night in the desert, didn't open easily to Westerners. To pretend that I understood all that I saw and heard was folly.

But the mystery kept tugging, even after I left the Middle East. The margins were still filled with question marks. And some nights, when the rain raps hard against my window, I wander south to the Empty Quarter, to black masks and black eyes and red-henna toes, and wonder why it was she loved me.

I

We Must Go to the East

*Free lance . . . one of those military adventurers, often
of knightly rank, who in the Middle Ages offered their
services as mercenaries, or with a view to plunder . . .
a "condottiere," a "free companion."*
—*Oxford English Dictionary*

Some men follow their dreams,
some their instincts, some the beat of a private drummer. I
had a habit of following my wife.

This wasn't a problem, except for the places she chose
to go. First frostbitten Cleveland, where she had a job and
I didn't. Then Australia, her parents' home and ten thousand
miles from mine. Now, after three years Down Under, Geraldine proposed that we move Up Over again—to Cairo.

"It's seven time zones closer to America," she said hopefully. Her newspaper office had just called to offer her the
Middle East posting. "You like historical places," she added.
"It's awfully old, Egypt."

The thought of starting over again, in another strange
country, alarmed me. In a month I would turn twenty-nine,
an age at which most pharaohs were already drifting toward
eternity in their barges of the night. Tut didn't even make
it to eighteen. By then, he'd been ruler of Upper and Lower
Egypt for seven years. At twenty-eight, I was still struggling
to rise from the ranks of cub reporter.

I quit my job and traveled home to explore my journal-

istic prospects. They weren't very good. Several years of
reporting on koala care at the Sydney Zoo and school board
meetings in Fort Wayne, Indiana, hardly qualified me for a
foreign correspondent's job writing about Abu Nidal or the
finer points of OPEC negotiations.

Work as a stringer was the best I could hope for.
"Stringer" is a descriptive non-job title. It means you are
paid piecework, for occasional stories, usually when the regular correspondent is out of town or busy with a more
important assignment. Stringers are the double-A players of
journalism: pitifully paid, forced to travel on the cheap and
strung along with the promise of being called up to the
majors. Most never make it.

So I decided to take a job-hunting swing down the East
Coast, to make sure I wasn't missing a shot at big-league
journalism in America.

"We need someone to cover education, and you've got
experience at that," said Editor #1, at a big paper in Boston.
I moved to the edge of my chair. "Have you tried the *Quincy
Patriot-Ledger?*" he asked. "They beat us on a lot of suburban
stories. There's also a weekly in Braintree. You might try
that."

As the train chugged south, past Pawtucket and Provi-
dence, I perused *Seven Pillars of Wisdom.* "All men dream;
but not equally," wrote Lawrence of Arabia, on the opening
page. "Those who dream by night in the dusty recesses of
their minds wake up in the day to find that it was vanity;
but the dreamers of the day are dangerous men, for they
may act their dream with open eyes, to make it possible.
This I did."

Editor #5 glanced at my clips and said, "Good ear for
quotes. Fine writing." He stubbed out his cigarette, stared
me straight in the eye. "We may have an opening on the
business desk, covering metals. Are you sure that's what
you're looking for?"

I was looking for shortcuts, for adventure. On the train
to Baltimore, I daydreamed of dusty casbahs and caftaned
bedouin. The melody of Middle East cities began to enchant

me. Fez, Khartoum, Bengazi, Baghdad. I read *The Blue Nile*.
"We must go to the East," Napoleon declared, shortly before
heading off to conquer Egypt. "All great glory has always
been gained there." He too was almost twenty-nine at the
time.

Editor #8 handed me his business card, told me to
"think small," and suggested I stop in again—like sometime
in the twenty-first century. I told him I'd rather wing it as
a free-lancer in the Middle East.

"Mr. Horwitz," he cautioned, "you could end up with
a definite flake factor in your résumé. A year here, a year
there. Beware of that."

Stalking out through the crowded newsroom, I jump-
shot my résumé into the trash and booked two tickets to
Cairo.

Cairo. Mother of the World. In Arabic, Al-Qahira, the Tri-
umphant. Largest city in Africa, capital of the Arab world.
And on a stifling September night, the most awful and
bewildering place my jet-lagged eyes had ever beheld.

I'd never set foot in the "Third World." Nor had my
hurried reading on modern Egypt purged old stereotypes,
bred of *The Alexandria Quartet*, the mummy collection at the
British Museum and the Passover service, in which Pharaoh
commanded that Hebrew sons be cast in the Nile. I knew
that the Mother of the World was an overcrowded mess. But
I clung to the notion that ancient glory would still be visible
in the rubble.

It wasn't, at least not from the back steps of the Nile
Hilton at nine o'clock on a Thursday night. A hundred yards
away, on the opposite side of Cairo's central square, stood
the Egyptian Museum and its trove of antique treasures. But
between myself and Tut's tomb lay a dense moat of flesh
and combustion, swirling dizzily through the gloom.

There were trucks, taxis, trolleys, buggies and buses,
the latter so overloaded that bodies draped from the doors,
limbs stuck out of windows and a few brave passengers even
clung to the rooftops, their turbans unraveling in the wind.

There were men on bicycles, men on oversized tricycles, men on motorbikes—whole families on motorbikes, children crammed in the drivers' laps, sometimes two in a lap, clutching the handlebars. There were donkeys and burros and even a camel: toting firewood, toting fruit, toting garbage, toting ashes. There were two-legged men in wooden wheelchairs, one-legged men with crutches shaped like tree limbs, and a no-legged man on a wooden skateboard, propelling himself with rapid pawing motions across the ground.

There were also pedestrians, erupting out of the earth and swarming into the traffic from a newly built subway. Men in white robes and sandals, black Sudanese in foot-high turbans, men in frayed business suits, women in full-face veils, women in what looked like bathrobes, Africans with rings through their noses and tribal markings burned on their cheeks. And at the eye of the maelstrom, an old man selling melon seeds and stalks of sugar cane spread on a scrap of cardboard that served as his open-air shop.

A crowd clustered beside me, wading a few feet into the street and shrieking toward the traffic. "Shubra!" "Giza!" "Abdin!" From my guidebook I recognized the words as Cairo neighborhoods, but it took me a moment to realize that the crowd was hailing taxis. If a cabbie heard the name of a place to which he was already headed—over the honking and the atonal Arab music blaring on his radio—he paused just long enough for the lucky person to pile on top of his other passengers, then drove off, leaving the rest to continue their pleading chorus: "Dokki!" "Attaba!" "Bulaq!"

This was Cairo's hub, Medan Tahrir—Arabic for Liberation Square. Standing at its center, I gazed down broad boulevards laid out by Napoleon: dimly lit arteries pumping more cars and bodies into the clotted square. In Cairo, all roads lead to Tahrir.

I retreated back inside to collect Geraldine, and we headed out the hotel's other flank towards the Nile-side corniche and the wide, slow river winding behind it. As we picked our way through the closely packed cars, stepping onto bumpers, six men on the far shore began waving sheets of brittle paper. They were hawking papyrus. Or rather, "babyrus." The Arabic alphabet doesn't include a *p* sound and the letter almost always comes out as *b*.

"Blease, misyer," the first man said, merging "mister" and "monsieur" into one all-purpose address. "Babyrus for bretty madam."

"Just to look, not to buy."

"Very cheap, very real."

The papyrus was decorated with images of ancient Egypt: long-bearded pharaohs, smiling sphinxes, Cleopatra-like princesses with snakes entwined about their heads. A certificate accompanied each sheet, assuring the buyer that the cheap banana leaf was actually genuine Egyptian papyrus, freshly plucked from the banks of the Nile.

"Is like Moses from bulrushes!" cried one exuberant salesman, holding his banana leaf as delicately as Torah scrolls. "Is holy! Is ancient!"

The corniche looked considerably more timeworn, as though it had been excavated for a sewer line some years ago and then abandoned. Refuse gathered in the furrows, as did mangy cats. In one pothole, a boy had ignited the trash and was using it to barbecue ears of corn, fanning the flames with discarded papyrus. Parked or abandoned cars, it was hard to tell which, crowded onto the pavement, nudging pedestrians into the street. Only the young couples, discreetly holding hands on a low wall beside the promenade, seemed oblivious to the bleating of car horns and commerce.

As we shoved our way past the papyrus men, eyes trained to the ground, I felt something strange clinging to my throat and nostrils. It was the exotic air of the East, a greasy and malodorous broth of dust, dirt, donkey dung and carbon monoxide. The air was so dense that it brushed against my face, whole particles collecting in the creases of my skin and on the lenses of my glasses. "Cairo," a long-suffering correspondent once declared, "is the biggest upturned ashtray in the world."

We scrambled onto the riverbank and into the arms of men offering rides on wooden boats lining the water's edge.

"*Habibi*, my friend," a teenager said. We seemed suddenly to have many *habibi*, many friends. "I give you finest trip on the river."

The Nile was black and silent, and a few stars poked bravely through the smog. A trip on the river seemed a romantic way to celebrate our arrival in Cairo—and to escape the wretched corniche.

Geraldine asked our new friend how much his finest ride would cost.

"Ten bounds," he said, spreading both hands just to make sure we understood. He was missing two fingers.

"Okay, eight," I said, offering the equivalent of four dollars.

"Okay!" he cried. And then the news *tamenya guinea*—eight pounds—resounded along the Nile. Boatmen raced toward us from all directions, swallowing the eight-fingered teenager. It seemed two pounds would have been an appropriate counterbid.

"Misyer, madam, this way," said the pilot with the strongest stiff-arm, who announced himself as "Ahmed of Aswan." He helped us down a creaking gangplank and onto an even creakier boat. Then he shoved off from shore with a huge wooden oar. It wasn't until we'd glided thirty yards out that I realized our boat had no sail.

"*Malesh*," Ahmed said, producing a second oar. *Malesh* is an Egyptian phrase of surrender, meaning "never mind" or "doesn't matter." It is the most commonly used word in Cairo, usually when something matters very much but isn't going to happen.

Ahmed splashed one oar in the water, and then the other, turning us in wild wet circles. Peals of laughter drifted out from the boatmen on shore. It seemed that Ahmed of Aswan had never worked oars before. In his frenzy to win our business, he had commandeered the first boat at hand, not bothering to check its rig.

After flailing for a few minutes, he let go of the paddles and sighed. "*Malesh*," he said again. Meaning, I guess, that the current would carry us to shore before we reached Alexandria.

I offered to do the rowing, and Ahmed took my seat in the back of the boat, beside Geraldine. The oars were thick and clumsy, and the oarlocks quickly buckled. Water seeped through the boat's cracked floor, soaking my sneakers and making me uneasy. The Nile is rife with a microscopic parasite called bilharzia, which burrows through the foot and lodges in the liver, lungs, eyeballs.

Ahmed's anxiety centered on something else. "I do not want to take a bath," he said, glancing overboard as a motorboat roared past, tumbling us in its wake.

"*Malesh*," Geraldine said. Ahmed laughed and complimented her Arabic. Then he let go of the side just long enough to grab her thigh. She edged away, causing the boat to list still more.

I stopped rowing. We were in the middle of the river now, far from the noise and congestion. The water lapped gently against the oars, and the Muslim call to prayer wafted out across the river. It was the calm, contemplative moment I'd hoped for on shore—except that the boat was sinking, and the captain was groping my wife.

We reached the island of Gezira, midway across the Nile, and decided to abandon ship and return on foot, on one of the river bridges. As we struggled up the bank, clutching tall reeds, Ahmed shamelessly demanded, "Eight bounds." I rifled through my pockets. A ten-pound note was all I had. Ahmed kissed the bill and put it in his pocket, mumbling in Arabic that Allah would bless me for my charity.

We found a bench and gazed out at the skyline we'd be living with for the next few years. Just to the south rose a tall statue of a fat man in a fez, gazing determinedly into the smog. Behind him soared the Cairo Tower, a modern building of such ugliness that my guidebook described it as "an immensely elongated waste-paper basket." Farther back, somewhere in Gezira's thicket of tall, tattered apartment blocks, was the building we'd be moving into the following day.

The view across the river was equally grim. Crumbling concrete buildings lined the opposite shore, topped with squiggles of neon Arabic that advertised Fiat, Sanyo, Seven-Up. I couldn't see the traffic in Medan Tahrir, but I could hear it. The dun-colored city seemed to stretch forever.

Months later I returned to Tahrir to interview the Egyptian novelist Naguib Mahfouz, upon his award of the Nobel Prize. Each dawn, Mahfouz hiked from his apartment on the river's west bank across a Nile bridge and through Tahrir to a coffeehouse named the Ali Baba. The café was drab and dusty, opening right onto the swirling traffic. The fumes of stalled cars mingled with the reek of Indian tobacco from the tall water pipe that Egyptians call a *sheesha* or "hubble bubble."

Mahfouz sat at a second-floor table, stirring the silt of his Turkish coffee. Rather deaf, he leaned close to hear my questions over the roar of the morning rush hour. Why, I asked him, did he come for inspiration each day to the least pleasant spot in Cairo, perhaps in the entire world?

He smiled and cocked his head at the stalled tide of bodies, hooves, cars. "It is true Tahrir is not a pretty sight," he said. "But I am a novelist, not a painter. You can see the whole world from right here."

I understood then what it was to love Cairo. To revel in the grit, the noise, the press of flesh and pavement. To snort and gulp the bracingly foul air. And I understood then that Cairo was a city I could never come to love.

2

YEMEN
Confessions of a Qat-Eater

A habit peculiar to the Yemenis is the chewing of a mildly narcotic leaf called qat, mainly throughout the afternoon. Parties are held at which much business may be settled, and a foreigner honoured with an invitation should accept. . . . Addiction to the taste need not be feared. —The British Bank of the Middle East, Business Profile Series

We had stripped and chewed an entire shrub before the qat took hold. From my bed of pillows, the hose of the water pipe looked roughly the length of the Amazon, only longer. It started in a cloud of tobacco smoke at the far end of the room, snaked through a jungle of qat leaves and Pepsi bottles and ended in the pile of cushions beside me. Somewhere in there was Mansour. He'd shrunk out of sight in the course of the afternoon.

"Qat kwayes," he said. Qat is good. A dragon's puff of smoke rose from the pillows and a hand reached out for another glossy sprig.

Across the room, Mansour's uncle kept pointing at his head and flashing me a green-toothed grin. Like most Yemenis, he was small, dark and wiry, with a pinched face and furrowed brow. He looked like an old squirrel. I pointed at my head and returned his smile, unsure what the gesture signified. Then the qat shuddered through me again: whistling up my spine, ruffling the hair on the back of my neck and whooshing out both ears. Odd snatches of poetry wafted through my brain and I recited them aloud.

"The fog crept in on little qat feet. . . .

"In the room the women come and go, chewing Michelangelo. . . ."

Qat juice dribbled down my chin. Mansour giggled. I giggled. The old man grinned and pointed at his turban again. This time I understood. "Qat very good for the head," I said, breaking a fresh branch and offering him a leaf.

Qat explained a lot about Yemen. The tourist literature did not.

"He who blows into fire makes either flames or is covered by ash," read the proverb on page one of my *Traveller's Guide to Yemen*. I was thirty thousand feet over the Red Sea, en route to the Yemeni capital, Sanaa. I studied the proverb for a moment, then moved to another. "A lasting little is better than an ending lot."

It was either the worst tour book ever written or the worst translation. After a cursory swing through Yemeni history, the publication wandered into lists of "Under Construction Roads" and "Non-Religious Holidays"—Mother's Day, Revolution Anniversary and Corrective Movement Day—before drifting to a photographic spread called "Views from Yemen." Judging from the fuzzy box-camera snapshots, no tourist had viewed Yemen since 1937. And the proverbs became more obscure with each chapter.

"You may stretch your feet only to the length of your mattress," began a chapter titled "General Description of Yemen." The guide ended with this bewildering message: "Don't teach the bear how to throw stones."

Nothing about the place made sense. Geraldine, as a staff correspondent, had an invitation to visit Yemen for the opening of the country's first oil pipeline. I didn't. But since Yemen rarely admits journalists, I decided to sneak in under the hem of her dress-for-success suit. Arabs often seemed baffled by our odd Western relationship, but they always understood a husband's desire to keep a close eye on a traveling wife. While officials squired her from palace to palace, I'd melt into the souk and find something else to write about. Or so I imagined.

When I went to collect my visa in Cairo, an official at the Yemeni embassy said, very casually, "You did not answer the religion question." This was true. North Yemen, like most Arab countries, wasn't enthusiastic about Jewish visitors. Rather than lie on my visa application I had simply left the religion question blank. Now, assuming my visa had been approved, I saw no harm in telling the truth.

"I'm Jewish," I said.

"Your passport," the man said. "It needs another stamp. Come back later."

Later, say, after I'd converted. "No Jews allowed in Yemen," he said curtly on my return. I called the Yemeni embassy in Washington to complain and was told that visas were left to the discretion of the local ambassador. Unfortunately, the Cairo envoy hadn't been seen for days. "Come back later," my embassy friend said again, twelve hours preflight.

I phoned the ambassador's residence and reached a man who spoke not a word of English. I had been speaking halting Arabic for all of three weeks. The conversation that followed strained my vocabulary to its meager limits.

ME: I journalist. I Jew. Go Yemen. No visa. Passport me embassy of you.

YEMENI: Never mind. Come to my office at eleven tomorrow.

ME: No good. Plane go Yemen seven morning.

YEMENI: Okay, come to the embassy tonight.

ME: Time what?

YEMENI: One o'clock.

ME: One o'clock?

YEMENI: Okay, two. As you wish.

·   ·   ·

I hung up the phone convinced that neither of us had understood a word the other had said.

Heading out on foot in the middle of the night, I tiptoed
over my neighbors, sleeping beneath a bridge across the
Nile, and into the diplomatic quarter. Soldiers slumped
against submachine guns in guard boxes before each embassy.
Then, around a corner, I encountered an elfish man in an
overcoat and pajamas.

"Embassy Yemen?" I asked.

"Yes, good morning." He smiled and handed me my
passport and visa. "Have a nice trip." Then he vanished into
the night. It seemed we had followed normal procedures for
the issuing of visas to Yemen.

Later that day, stepping outside the airport in Sanaa, I was
greeted by ten men in colorful turbans and knee-length
skirts. A gaudy curved scabbard stretched from the belly
button to the middle thigh of each man, with a dagger handle
poking out the top. How picturesque, I thought. The
Yemeni National Guard.

Actually, I was at the taxi stand. These men were cabbies, clad in the Yemeni national dress. In the rest of the
Arabian peninsula, conformity is the keynote: white robes,
white headdresses, sandals, sand. The whole Persian Gulf
can seem a monochromatic shimmer, camouflaged by same-
ness. Here, nothing matched. From the waist down, the men
looked like fierce, dagger-toting tribesmen. From the waist
up, they resembled Bowery bums, clad in cast-off shirts and
cheap Western-style sports jackets. Nor did any man look
quite like his neighbor. Each had his scabbard angled just
so, his turban a tight-wound rosebud or a full-blown cauli-
flower, his qat bulging in right cheek instead of left.

"How much to the city?" I asked the lead driver, assuming that taxi rides here, as in Cairo, were subject to lengthy
negotiation.

The man named a price roughly equal to the per capita
income I'd seen listed in the tourist literature. I laughed and
offered one tenth as much. He rested his hand on the hilt

of his dagger and gazed off at the mountains. I went to the next cabbie and had no better luck. Each man looked different, but the price of service was the same, set by tribal cartel. I finally paid the asking price.

The cabbie drove to what he said was the center of Sanaa. It didn't look like any downtown I'd ever seen. Mud towers teetered all around, reaching eight and nine stories into the air. Each earthen skyscraper was crowned like iced cake with whitewashed extrusions; stars, zigzags, triangles, snatches of Arabic script praising Allah; whorls, swirls, waves and squiggles. Stained-glass windows swathed the upper floors in ribbons of red and blue. Lurching into the sky at odd angles, without a single plumb line, the whole city seemed tipsy.

"Mister, what you want?" a voice called from the dark.

"Is you English man?" called another.

"Mister, come smell beautiful essence!"

The peddlers stood just inside the city's thick mud walls, luring me toward a tangle of cobbled alleys. Each lane was devoted to tinkerers in trades long lost or forgotten in the West. Blacksmiths heated ore in hellish furnaces, then beat the metal on broad black anvils, their sledgehammers spraying sparks through the night. There were milliners, bookbinders, brass-beaters, veil-makers, Koran-sellers and spice merchants whose high baskets of cinnamon and nutmeg crowded beneath my eyes and nose. In one narrow lane, men sat crosslegged, sharpening the curved blades, called *jambiyas*, which I'd seen at the airport. Nearby, carpenters crafted small wooden daggers—training *jambiyas*—for boys too young to carry real ones. I peered into a dark stall and saw a camel harnessed to a giant pestle, walking in a tight circle around a huge vat of seeds, crushing them into oil. The animal had a rag tied around its eyes. Without the blindfold, the camel's keeper said, whirling his eyes in pantomime, the camel would become dizzy from walking around and around. I felt like asking him to fit me with a blindfold as well.

"Mister, this way!"

"*Habibi*, my friend! I sell you fine silver!"

"Mister, what your name?"

I turned a corner and wandered into what seemed a Halloween party. Strange specters in head-to-toe sheets scurried between the stalls. When the veiled women stood still, the direction of their toes was the only way to tell back from front.

"Mister, fine cloth," an embroiderer said, holding aloft a dress as I stared at the phantoms before his shop. Indeed, the dress was very fine, and I asked him how much it cost.

"For you, my friend, only one hundred riyals." About ten dollars.

I went through the bartering histrionics I'd learned since my first night's boat ride in Cairo: the eyebrows raised in mock surprise, the dismissive chuckle, the abrupt exit, the casual return.

The merchant watched my theatrics and shrugged. "Man in next shop, he will charge the same," he said, "You like dress, you pay." It was the routine I'd encountered at the airport. So I paid. The embroiderer folded the dress and handed me a twig with glossy green leaves. "Chew this and you will not care that you just paid too much," he said, returning to his needle and thread.

Chew qat and you will stop caring about many things. One day, a millennium or so ago, a sleepy goatherd noticed that his flock became lively after grazing on a roadside shrub. The boy sampled a few sprigs himself and felt much the better for it—and qat has been the national dish of Yemen ever since. Or so the legend goes.

Qat is the last of Yemen's bounty. It was here that the biblical Queen of Sheba loaded "a very great retinue, with camels bearing spice and very much gold" for the journey to King Solomon's court. Ten centuries later, the Romans imagined Yemen a land of such fabulous wealth that they dubbed it Arabia Felix, meaning happy or prosperous Arabia. The finest coffee in the world grew here, named for the Red Sea port of Mocha from which the beans were exported.

It was to celebrate this good fortune, and to guard it against marauders, that the medieval merchants of Sanaa built their fanciful towers and ringed them with ramparts of mud.

Yemen had stood almost still ever since. Slavery endured until the 1960s. Illiteracy stuck at ninety percent. Life expectancy still hovered at forty. Bedouin roamed through sand dunes spooned out by the wind where the Queen of Sheba built her Temple to the Moon God. And the fertile coffee fields had been resown with a spindly shrub that was without value beyond the borders of Yemen.

"I quickly became accustomed to using qat," confessed a nineteenth-century French traveler, "and ended up getting great pleasure from its gentle stimulation and the vivid dreams which followed." Reading this at a teahouse in the old city, I wondered whether qat explained Sanaa's strange skyline and the odd behavior of every Yemeni I'd met.

Across the café, a man was well into the stuff. Slumped against the wall, he crammed leaf after leaf into his mouth, working it into a dense green cud. Teeth stained, cheek bulging, he looked like a third-base coach on a last-place team in late September. Except that, like every other Yemeni male, the man carried a dagger that was broad and sharp enough to slice a man up like so much pita bread.

I returned to my reading, looking for story ideas. I'd come to Yemen "on spec," a polite term that editors use when they might want your stories but don't want to commit themselves in advance. Working on spec is the lowest form of journalistic life, a notch below stringer. No assignment means no expense budget, no letters of introduction and no worker's compensation for dagger wounds incurred in the line of duty. But so little had been written about Yemen that I figured it was worth gambling five hundred dollars or so to see what I could come up with. As I looked again at the qat-eater in the café, eyes glazed, dagger slung in his lap, the outline of a feature article suggested itself. Weed and weapons, mellowness and menace, the yin and yang of Yemeni society. A *Traveller's Guide to Arms and Qat*. Why not?

■   ■   ■

"You must understand that my country is not like other Arab nations," the young man said. "We want to be Yemen. We do not want to hurry up and be like the West."

It was two days after my arrival, in the waiting room of a government office, and I was chatting with an American-educated bureaucrat named Mansour.

"We must get to know each other," he said. "We must chew qat."

"When?"

Mansour smiled. "Monday, Tuesday, Wednesday, as you wish. All days in Yemen we chew qat."

"Today," I said, scribbling down his address.

After forty-eight hours in Yemen, I had picked up a thing or two about local customs. I knew, for instance, that qat is usually consumed after a heavy lunch, so as to buffer the stomach against the plant's acidic juices. I also knew that most qat chews are BYO affairs, so I headed off in search of an appropriate bush to bring with me to Mansour's.

At Sanaa's qat market, several thousand men in extreme good humor wandered from one open pickup to another, each vehicle loaded with what looked like piles of yard clippings. Farther back sprawled a covered bazaar, also devoted to qat, and behind that, a tired-looking vegetable and animal market, dwarfed by the commerce in shrubs.

I joined a jostling crowd at the most popular qat stall, figuring that eight hundred Yemenis couldn't all be wrong. After ten minutes of stiff-arms and toe-squashings, I reached the front and faced a towering pyramid of qat. Unnerved by the choice, and by the dagger hilts pressing against my spine, I quickly pointed at the closet bundle of boughs, about like your average suburban hedge. The seller wrapped the plant in pink cellophane and demanded eighty riyals, or eight dollars. Qat, like everything else in Yemen, wasn't subject to much haggling.

During the previous two days, I had noticed another odd thing about Yemen: the natives treated foreigners with total indifference. In Cairo, complete strangers would often demand, "Where you from? Is this wife? Have you children?" or peer into your shopping bag on the street and ask, "Food?" In Yemen, apart from a few merchants and peddlers, most people were either too proud or too stoned to even look a visiting Westerner in the eye.

But elbowing through the crowd at the qat stall, clutching my half-crushed bouquet, I felt everything had changed. Men pointed at me, laughed, raised their thumbs and nodded approvingly. Several came up to pat me on the back and fondle my qat, trying out their pidgin English.

"Qat nice, mister?"

"Chew with me?"

"Like you qat?"

They also wanted to assist me with another purchase, which made me suspect my sudden popularity carried the whiff of easy money. The crowd parted to let an old man with a cane hobble toward me. He was my chosen escort. I had joined the fraternity of qat-chewers, and the boys of Arabia Felix wanted to initiate me with the best stuff Sanaa had to offer.

The old man inspected my bush and didn't seem impressed. "Good qat we find for America," he said, leading me to a distant cranny of the qat market. He stopped at one stall and then another, inspecting the fullness and luster of the leaves. Finally, finding a shrub to his liking, he held up ten fingers. One hundred riyals. My limited budget was fast being exhausted to buy drugs.

"We call it Yemen salad," an onlooker said, sampling a sprig. "It gives you ideas all over the world." I nodded, making a mental note of which bundle I'd put under my left arm and which under my right.

Over a hot lunch, I digested some more history on the substance I was soon to abuse. As with everything in Yemen, the information was contradictory. "It makes you feel a devil of a dog as long as the feeling lasts," exulted a former English administrator in Yemen. One of his countrymen, a physician, disagreed. The habitual user, he wrote, resembles "a wild-looking, dull-witted automaton." Another doctor termed qat as nothing more than a "mild stimulant," while a third thought it an addictive amphetamine that caused high blood pressure and left the user feeling "lazy and sick."

Confused, I continued my research by quizzing the taxi driver, who noshed on a few sprigs as we drove to Mansour's. I asked him if he thought qat affected health.

"Oh yes!" he cried. "My uncle never used to chew, but then he got diabetes, so he started to chew every day. Now he is completely cured and works like ten men in the field."

And did he find qat addictive?

"Oh no," he said. "I have chewed every day since the age of fifteen and I am still not an addict."

The only acknowledged drawback of qat was the price. In one of the world's poorest countries, most males spent twenty dollars or more each day on the plant. And since alcohol was banned, they often spent as much again on bootleg scotch to knock themselves out after getting too wired on qat. "This is much money," the cabbie conceded. "But I am never hungary after chewing qat. So I save much money on food."

The Yemen salad diet. Slimming, and economical, too. So what if it turns your teeth green?

Mansour lived in the sprawl of run-down suburbs encircling the old city of Sanaa. At his office, he'd worn a suit and tie, but now he greeted me in a long white robe and slippers. "Qat clothes," he said. He led me into the small home's finest chamber, a carpeted expanse with stained-glass windows, pillows lining the wall and a water pipe perched in one corner. "Qat room," he said. Traditionally, Yemenis located their qat room or *mafraj* in the penthouse of Sanaa's odd mud towers so chewers could enjoy a panoramic view. Women held their own chews in separate, less luxurious quarters.

We took off our shoes and waited for the other guests. Mansour inspected my stash, as the men had done at the market, casting an expert eye on the firmness and gloss of the leaves. "This one from Taiz, not very special," he said, holding up my first purchase. Then, examining the other, he announced: "Shibam region, maybe farther north. Very fine qat." He guessed the exact price I'd paid for each.

I told Mansour about the fraternal embrace I'd felt that morning at the market. He said that he had once gone through the same experience—in reverse. During three years of studying computer science in America, he decided qat was a waste of time and vowed to abstain from chewing on his return to Yemen. But back in Sanaa, he felt as though "someone had taken my passport away. There was nothing to do, no one to talk to." In a country still centered on the home and village, qat-chewing was an enforced sociability— what afternoon tea is to some British, or a pub crawl to Australians. It was also the accepted way of settling disputes and sealing business contracts. Even Yemen's president held regular chews with his ministers.

Mansour, the son of a mystic Sufi healer, came back from America with another ill-fated notion. "I wanted to computerize my father's business," he said. It was a simple program. F2 for cough, F3 for fever, and so on. "That way he could just punch in a key and the right amulet would come up on the screen."

The idea went over about as well as Mansour's attempt to kick qat. "The old man just laughed," Mansour said. A year later, the father still dispensed herbs and prayers from memory, and his thirty-three-year-old son chewed qat every day after work.

At three o'clock sharp, the other guests arrived. There was Mansour's brother, who wore a robe and dagger; an aged uncle, who seemed to have just hiked in from the fields, with dusty feet, a dirty shift, and a dagger; and a young cousin who sat in a far corner and remained rather distant, inspecting the blade of his dagger. Each man dropped a bundle of qat at his feet and reached over to fondle mine, guessing its price. Despite these repeated inspections, I still couldn't tell my two purchases apart.

Mansour brought in bottles of Pepsi and several brass

spittoons. He stirred the coals atop the water pipe and puffed it alight. Then, without so much as a prayer or a nod or a *bon appétit*, each man plucked the smallest leaves from his bunch and stuffed them into his mouth.

Mimicking the others' motions, I stripped a branch and shoved one leaf at a time between my cheek and gum. The plant tasted bitter, making me gag and spit whenever a little juice began to flow. The others, meanwhile, seemed to have no trouble chewing, chatting, smoking and sipping Pepsi all at once, at high speed. I felt as though I were competing in some odd oral decathlon.

Mansour offered the occasional translation of the party chatter. It was workaday stuff: the weather, the price and quality of this year's qat crop, the lopping-off of a thief's hand in Sanaa's central square a few days before. Then, after about half an hour, the conversation became much more animated and the men addressed me in a mix of English and Arabic.

"America good," declared Mansour's brother, Abdul, apropos of nothing. A bulky and self-important man, he perched on a throne of pillows and sucked contentedly on the thirty-foot hose of the water pipe. His uncle, Mohammed, nodded and repeated the words in Arabic. "*America kwayes.*" Everyone laughed, as though he'd made a clever joke. Then they concentrated on their chewing. The old man had brought the smallest supply of qat, and the others made periodic contributions by tossing a sprig or two at his feet.

Soon the pace of the babble quickened and Mansour's English deteriorated. I had some catching up to do. I crammed a dozen leaves in my cheek, sucked hard through my teeth and reached for the spitoon. As soon as I spit, the small wad in my cheek felt dry and stale, like used-up bubble gum. I stoked myself with fresh leaves. Meanwhile, the others worked effortlessly on the same glob they'd begun chewing an hour before.

I was so busy chewing and hacking and spitting that I didn't notice at first that the carpet was massaging my toes. *How long has this been going on?* I stopped chewing for a moment, feeling a sudden urge to leap to my feet and stretch. But someone had glued my back to the cushions. *When did that happen?* I slumped back and closed my eyes. The tingling in my toes worked its way up my calves and along the back of my thighs and flooded into my spine. I noticed for the first time that Arab music was playing on a radio in the next room, mingling with the steady, soothing bubble of the water pipe. It sounded like a brook tumbling over smooth, small stones. Burble burble went the hubble bubble. Bubble hubble went the hurble burble. . . .

I opened my eyes and felt at once tipsy and hyperalert, as if I'd knocked back two good Irish coffees, or eight good Irish coffees. I wanted to blurt out something special to each person in the room—all at once. Either that or go ask Mansour's wife for a long and languorous massage.

"I can see from the stupid smile on your face that you have discovered the wonders of qat." It was Mansour, prone on the pillows to my right, with a rather stupid grin plastered on his face, too.

"As a matter of—" I clamped my mouth shut as a torrent of green spittle gushed onto my shirt. Mansour handed me a spittoon. I reached for it and toppled a Pepsi bottle. The room erupted in laughter.

"Actually, yes," I resumed. "I feel like a million bucks and I want to know just exactly how you feel in your fingers and toes." This gibberish was delivered in a rapid-fire burst, as though my tongue couldn't keep pace with the thoughts racing through my head. Fortunately, Mansour felt rather expansive as well and we vaulted right over small talk and straight into politics, religion, qat, culture, dreams, qat, fears, fantasies, qat. It was all I could do to let Mansour finish a sentence before launching into a fresh thought of my own.

"I agree with you completely but there's a whole nother way to look at this issue," I jabbered, convinced that I was about to deliver the most perceptive comment ever made on the topic. The topic, which was—what was it? Mansour smiled. We giggled and kept on chewing leaves, like a pair of dopey koalas.

"I tell you a hidden truth about Yemen," Mansour said conspiratorially. "Everything in the world, it comes first from here." It was a typical flight of qat-fancy. Turkish steam baths were invented in Sanaa and stolen by the Ottomans, he said. The Santa Fe style of architecture originated with Sanaa's mud-brick skyscrapers, not New Mexico's adobe. ("My people travel a great deal," Mansour hypothesized. "Maybe there was a Yemeni conquistador in America.") Even the few thousand Jews of Yemen were "the real ones" because they had fled Jerusalem in biblical times.

"William Shakespeare came from here, too," Mansour said, reaching the punch line. "His real name was Sheik Zubayre, very common in Yemen. The English changed it to Shakespeare."

I laughed and reached for the spittoon again. Mansour said his brother was an Islamic scholar, so I turned to Abdul and blurted out a question: how was it that Islam, which forbade alcohol, could allow something as pleasant as qat to flourish? It was blunt and in rather poor taste, but under the circumstances perfectly okay; the sort of exchange, between Arab and Westerner, Muslim and Jew, that would have been difficult outside the collegial cloud of qat.

"Actually, Islam has two minds about qat," Abdul said, puffing professorially at the water pipe. When qat first became popular in the fourteenth and fifteenth centuries, he explained, Arab mystics claimed it was a visionary substance that brought the chewer closer to Allah. Traditionalists countered that qat was an intoxicant, like alcohol, and should be declared forbidden or *haram*. Scholars in Mecca were called on to mediate the dispute, and they ruled that qat-chewing should be permitted but not encouraged; they termed the plant a "doubtful substance."

"Doubt is okay," Abdul said, picking the last few leaves from the bottom of his cellophane package. "Qat is not like marijuana. Now *that* is a drug."

When the conversation was relayed to Mohammed, the

old man mumbled in Arabic and Mansour translated. "He says qat is not like alcohol because if you chew alone, nothing happens." Other Yemenis had told me they felt no withdrawal symptoms when they traveled abroad. It seemed that the nation's addiction to qat wasn't so much physical as social; each time people chewed, they became part of the tribe again, part of Yemen.

Still, something strong was unsettling my body chemistry, and I asked Mansour why he thought the drug hadn't ever caught on in the West.

"I think Americans like drugs that hit fast and hard and then wear off, such as whiskey and cocaine," he said. "They could never get used to something that makes you sit around all afternoon doing nothing."

For the moment, at least, I wasn't so sure he was right.

After a few hours the loquacious, fidgety high ebbed away and a meditative glow flowed in to replace it. The room went quiet. Abdul puffed thoughtfully on his water pipe, studying the smoke rings curling out of his mouth. The old uncle gazed out the window at streaks of purple and orange forming on the mountain horizon. Mansour turned on the television news, without sound. The screen showed a Western woman standing with a pad and pen, interviewing Yemen's president. The image startled me. It looked just like Geraldine. Then I realized it *was* Geraldine, not a qat hallucination. I was glad to see she was getting on with her itinerary. Getting on with mine, I slumped deeper into the pillow and nibbled at a last green sprig of qat.

When the qat was finally finished, Mansour's *mafraj* was a mess. Soda bottles lay on their side, ashes coated the carpet, and smoke hung thick in the air. Mansour turned on a lamp and the light bounced back, like high beams in fog.

We sat there for another hour as dusk gathered outside, wrapped in our warm cocoons of silence. Then the magic melted away. For the first time in hours I wondered what time it was. I had to urinate. My stomach was telling me with a growl that it never wanted to eat anything, ever again.

"Don't be surprised if you can't sleep tonight," Mansour said. "You might want to have a whiskey at the hotel to relax you. Lots of Yemenis do." Apparently, when it came to a qat hangover, a certain doubt about alcohol was okay as well.

The qat chew ended as unceremoniously as it had begun. One by one, the guests gathered up their shoes and daggers, retied their turbans and headed into the night. The air tasted thin, the sky was starry and bright. And standing in the courtyard, gazing out at the ancient city with its mud walls and mud towers girdled round, everything real seemed unreal, and everything fantastic seemed, at least for the moment, worth seriously considering. Even the Yemeni bard, Sheik Zubayre.

3

YEMEN
For You I Make a Special Deal

Nothing but evil comes through here.
—Governor of Sanaa,
closing the city's
northern gate in 1860

I fell into a fitful sleep convinced that I would chew qat for the rest of my stay in Yemen, perhaps explore the prospects for overseas cultivation (one of the giddier notions Mansour had floated in the course of the afternoon). I awoke four hours later with a loose piston clanging away in my cerebellum. Someone had emptied an ashtray down my throat. My jaw ached from too much chewing. Focusing slowly through bloodshot eyes, I saw in the bathroom mirror the "wild-looking, dull-witted automaton" I'd read about in the medical literature.

I needed either a day in bed or another round of qat to kill the pain. What I had scheduled instead was an eight-o'clock interview at a Western embassy to gather background for the rest of my Yemeni reporting, on weapons and mayhem. Creaking into a chair opposite the defense analyst, I managed to string together enough monosyllables to form a question.

"What arms are out there?"

The diplomat doodled something on his notepad. "At a guess," he said, "I'd say there are more weapons per capita in Yemen than in any other country on earth." At a guess, he estimated two rifles and two daggers per adult male. "Slightly less for teenagers." And that was just small arms. "You've got your submachine guns, your hand grenades, your mortars—maybe even your flamethrowers," he said. Some tribal sheiks stocked big-ticket items as well: bazookas, tanks, surface-to-air missiles.

I nodded dumbly. "Why?"

"You've got to understand the basic instability of the place," the diplomat said. "The last two presidents weren't too fortunate with their retirement programs." Indeed. One was shot and killed during a coup. His successor lasted eight months before a man walked into his office with a briefcase that blew up and killed them both. The current president had survived several assassination attempts and now prudently packed a pistol beneath his business suit.

The source of most of the violence was the mountainous north, where tribal sheiks still resented central government. Some of these outlaws even had mafia-style monikers, such as Sheik "Two Fingers" Hantash of Wadi Hadad, who earned his nickname after tossing a grenade a little too slowly at an enemy clan.

In the old days—up until the early 1960s—swarming south and sacking the capital was the sheiks' favored means of political expression. These days, tribesmen contented themselves with killing each other, or the occasional Western oil worker. This was lucky for the government. One sheik commanded a private army of 30,000. Yemen's entire armed forces totaled a mere 37,000.

In an effort to contain the killing, the government had launched an advertising campaign attacking the custom of *kharab wa-turab*—the right to "lay waste" to an enemy who breaks the peace without paying blood money.

"The campaign's called Revenge Awareness Week," the diplomat said. "I don't know for sure, but I suspect it's unique to North Yemen."

To see the weaponry up close, the diplomat recommended that I travel a mountain road to a northern town called Saada. Transportation, though, was a problem. What I needed was an armored personnel carrier. What I got was the only rental car in Yemen.

"Car good, very good," the rental agent said, tapping the hood rather gingerly. The dented sedan was so stripped down it was almost naked. I could do without a radio, heater, lighter and functioning gas gauge. But the car also lacked a turn signal, an inside light, back lights, one headlight, brake pads, a door handle, springs and second gear. The seat belt looked as though it had been hacked to pieces with a dull *jambiya*.

"Horn works very good," the agent said, giving the steering wheel a savage blow that produced one barely audible bleat. With that, he demanded a cash deposit of fifty dollars, enough to replace this flagship of his meager fleet.

"Where you go?" he asked.

"Up north. Through the mountains to Saada."

He raised his eyes in the Islamic equivalent of crossing oneself. "Go very slow," he said, as if there were any choice in the car he'd just rented me. "Mountains bad. Road very bad. People too much bad."

Car more bad. Ten minutes from the rental office, third gear grinded and gave out. I had to race in first gear to twenty-five miles an hour, then jolt into fourth and putter along until I reached my maximum speed of forty. Sanaa at midday was a high-speed free-for-all, clouded in dust. When traffic slowed, cars scaled the median strip and sped down the oncoming lane until that side gridlocked as well. Parking consisted of finding a wedge of open street and abandoning one's car or donkey. There were screams, threats, the thud of bumpers and the braying of trapped beasts. It seemed only a matter of minutes before someone reached for his *jambiya* and ran amok, cutting a swath through the thicket of cars.

In this sort of lunacy, questions such as "Can you turn right on red?" and "Is this a one-way street?" seem stunningly irrelevant. So I was astonished to find a policeman waving me over for one of a dozen traffic felonies I was committing along with every other driver in Sanaa.

"Your papers," he said, climbing into the backseat. I handed him my passport and international driver's license.

"Where is Yemen license?"

I pointed at my permit, which listed Yemen as one of the countries included.

"No good," he said. "You need Yemen license."

"Where do I get it?"

"Here," he said. "Three hundred riyals."

"What if I don't buy one?" I asked. I was weary of being hustled.

"We go police station," he said.

"Good. Let's go." I turned on the ignition.

He grabbed my arm and twisted. "Two hundred riyals."

We settled at one hundred, about ten dollars. He scribbled something in Arabic and tossed it into my lap. Yemen license. In a feeble attempt at payback, I took out my notebook and asked for his name and badge number. Then I noticed he didn't have a badge.

"I am Ahmed Mohammed," he said, giving me the name of perhaps a quarter of the male population of Yemen. Then he reached through the window, opened the door from the outside and vanished into the traffic.

The scenery at least, improved at the edge of town. Sanaa sits in a mile-high plateau, ringed by terraced peaks that climb in broad green stairs to twelve thousand feet or more. High above the road, on fields cut like shelves into the hillside, peasants nudged wooden plows across narrow fields of qat. Deep green and wreathed in mist, the mountains had the sharp, rugged beauty of the Andes.

Half an hour out of Sanaa, I reached the first military roadblock: four bullet-riddled oil cans guarded by the tallest Yemeni I'd yet seen. Standing seven feet at least, immobile in his helmet and fatigues, the soldier was cut from cardboard. The real soldiers were laid out in a roadside booth, chewing qat. One of them raised his head and lazily waved me through.

Soon after, just outside the town of Raydah, I hit another traffic jam: a long line of donkeys, their riders perched on saddles of qat. They were headed in to sell their produce at a bustling street market, which also offered slabs of liver, bunches of grapes and huge leaves of cured tobacco. I parked and walked through the bazaar, trying to avoid the evil green shrub.

"Best qat in Yemen—it grows near here." There was a teenager at my elbow, following me through the bazaar. "You like buy?"

"No, thank you."

"You like tour Raydah?"

Abdul was seventeen and anxious to practice his English. I was anxious to practice mine, and to get away from the qat. So we headed off through the village.

"This Raydah main street," he said proudly. We stood before a jerry-built slum of mud brick and concrete, with metal sheets and odd bits of wood tacked this way and that. It looked raw and unfinished, on the way to being old and unfinished.

A black woman with nose rings and neck rings walked a camel down the middle of the road, balancing a basket on her head. Abdul said she was a Tihama, from the Red Sea coast where the Arab world meets the African. I couldn't take my eyes off her face—one of the few exposed females I'd seen in Yemen. Then I spotted another unveiled woman and two others with half-veils.

"Village not like city," Abdul explained. "Every person know every person. Why need hide?"

The men, at least, wore the usual accessories: turban, *jambiya* and cow's cud of qat. Mindful of my mission, I asked Abdul why everyone carried a dagger.

"Yemen not safe," he said. "And Yemen is very proud history, we learn always in school." From the vantage of Raydah's main street, with its tumbledown buildings and qat-wasted fields, things didn't look so proud. But Arabs

have long memories. Yemen was one of the few pockets of
Arabia that was never fully conquered or colonized. The
Romans came, saw and left. The Ottoman Turks managed
a beachhead, as did the British, and they divided the country
into North and South Yemen before being driven out. Only
qat had successfully subdued the population.

The *jambiya* was a symbol of that defiance. Why, I
asked Abdul, didn't he wear one?

"It is at my home," he said, blushing. He'd taken it off
that morning before school, where weapons are forbidden.
"Also not allowed at courts and hospitals," he said. On airplanes the weapons had to be checked in before takeoff.
Everywhere else, Yemenis carried daggers the way Western
men carry wallets.

Abdul had one other sight to show me. We hiked down
a dusty lane to a mud house at the edge of the village. Two
men sat in front, banging small tacks into the soles of leather
sandals. They wore skullcaps rather than turbans and tight
ringlets of hair drooped down around their ears. Like Abdul,
they didn't wear *jambiyas*.

"This is Ezra and this is Ibrahim," Abdul said, intro-
ducing me. "They are *Yahoodim* of Raydah."

"*Yahoodim?*" Jews? I stared a the two men. I had read
that there were still a few thousand Jews in Yemen but I
hadn't expected to find them here, on the muddy back lane
of a highland village. Nor had I expected them to look as
they did. Except for their headdress, these dark-skinned,
Arabic-speaking, qat-chewing cobblers in grubby shifts and
sandals were indistinguishable from their Muslim neighbors.

I didn't fit their image of a Jew, either, despite my
repeated statements that this was so. The two men stared at
this fair-skinned stranger in khakis. "*Yahood? Mish mumkin.*"
Jew? Not possible.

I tried to sketch some Hebrew letters in the dust. Ezra
studied the crude dust doodles and shook his head. "*Mabiki-
lemshee ingleesie,*" he said. I don't speak English.

One of Ezra's boys went inside and returned with a
thick tattered book. Inside it were pages of Hebrew prayers

and the address of a congregation in Brooklyn. Ezra said it had been sent to a Jew in Sanaa some years before. When I began reading aloud in Hebrew, his eyes opened wide. *"Kamen,"* he said. Again. I read another verse, and a third. Women in odd veils that covered only their mouths were called out of the house to bear witness.

"Hoa Yahood!" one of the young boys cried. He is a Jew.

Ezra spit qat juice in the dust. *"Mumkin,"* he said. It is possible.

I asked the brothers if they wanted to go to Israel. They stared at the ground, uneasy. Going to Israel wasn't *mumkin.* The government forbade it. I learned later that several thousand Jews were held behind when Operation Flying Carpet airlifted fifty thousand others from Yemen to Israel in 1950. Yemen wanted them for their skills as craftsmen, and also as a bargaining chip with the fledgling Jewish state.

After fifteen minutes, we'd exhausted our common stock of Arabic and Hebrew and reached the limits of Abdul's talents as a translator. I took a photograph of the children. The children took my pens. And Ezra handed me a few sprigs of qat, insisting that I come celebrate the Sabbath with his family next time I happened to be passing through Raydah.

North of Raydah, the road climbed steeply between saw-tooth crags topped with turrets of mud. Crude huts with tiny windows clung to the mountainside. They looked like small family garrisons, built for defense rather than for comfort. The road also appeared battle-worn. Cracked and thin, the tar wound up and around the ridges without even a metal rail between the road and the thousand-foot plunge into an adjoining ravine. Qat-addled drivers screamed past on blind hairpin curves, kicking up hails of gravel and dust. Pulling off the road to let a few pass, I peered over the cliff edge and saw heaps of twisted metal lying at regular intervals along the floor of the ravine. Tiny at this height, the ruined cars looked like so many crushed beer cans tossed from the windows of passing trucks.

By the time I reached the next village, Khamir, it was clear that I'd left the semicivilized plateau and entered the uncivilized mountains of the "people too much bad" the car agent had warned about. At a roadblock just outside Khamir, there were two men in uniform and six others out of uniform, all well armed. The six were apparently local tribesmen, sharing watch with the army for unwelcome visits by enemy clans.

The village itself seemed outside the orbit of central government. Few cars and trucks had license plates, and there was no arms control at all. In addition to carrying *jambiyas*, most men had assault rifles slung over their shoulders, pistols jammed in their belts and bandoliers slung across their chests.

Nor was it hard to locate the source of all this firepower. Sidling up behind a dozen men window-shopping on the main street, I gazed through the glass at a display of Kalashnikov AK-47 assault rifles. Curiously, the sign above the shop advertised it as a money changer's; weapons were either a sideline or the money changing was a very transparent fig leaf for the brisk trade in arms.

Inside, a man sprawled languidly across several burlap sacks, smoking a water pipe and grinning, like a fat Cheshire cat. Behind him on the wall was a poster of an alluring woman with faraway eyes, her veil pulled completely away from her face. Yemeni pinup.

The merchant addressed me in German, then, when I looked at him blankly, in English. "I am Mohammed, at your service," he said, straightening his turban. "You want change money? You want sugar?" He paused. "You want bayonet?"

I smiled noncommittally. His question provided a structure for my reporting. Posing as a shopper, I would tease out information without actually buying anything.

"Something big, maybe?" Mohammed asked. He opened a cabinet to reveal a small arsenal of automatic weapons. "One thousand two hundred riyals," he said, gesturing at a Belgian FN rifle. Then he reached under the counter for a

Turkish musket that looked as though it had done service in the Siege of Constantinople. It weighed roughly a hundred pounds. "This one very cheap, only three hundred riyals."

"Very nice." I gave Mohammed the gun and another noncommittal smile.

He nodded knowingly and opened a drawer. "These just in from Iran," he said, dropping a plump green grenade in my hand. "For you I make a special deal."

Mohammed's prices did seem rather special. Only $20 for the grenade, $5 for a bayonet and $120 for an assault rifle. A man could play Rambo for less money than he paid for a week's worth of qat.

I asked Mohammed where all the weapons came from.

"Libya, Djibouti, Egypt, Iran—we like all country. It go bang, it go boom, we buy." He flashed me another Cheshire-cat grin. "You like grenade. What is two hundred riyals to a rich man?"

I still had the explosive in my hand, afraid even to hand it back to him. "Maybe another day," I said.

Mohammed shrugged and plucked the grenade from my palm. "Other villages, you find grenades only at Friday market. At Mohammed's, every day."

At this point I half expected him to hand me a promotional flier. Free Bayonet with Every Sack of Sugar! Grenades Every Day! These Just in from Iran! I changed twenty dollars at a favorable rate, climbed back in the car and headed deeper into the hills.

The road north from Khamir led through villages with names that sounded like dog barks: Huth, Hamra, Harf. Mohammed was right, grenades only on Fridays. But at Huth there were M-14 submachine guns smuggled from Afghanistan, on sale in the hardware section of a general store. At Harf, a man took me to his house to show off World War II–vintage artillery shells. At Hamra a man tried to peddle land mines from Ethiopia, though he said I had to order them a few days in advance. It seemed that weapons from every insurgency over the past fifty years had washed up in the mountains of Yemen, on special. Nor did anyone seem particularly curious about a Westerner rolling into town and asking where to buy a *bandook* (rifle), a *genable* (grenade) or even a *dababat* (tank).

"One *dababat* in this region belongs to Sheik Salah Hindi," said the mine merchant in Hamra. "He keeps it at home. Not for sale, I think."

The landscape north of Hamra was poorer and more threatening. At some roadblocks there were no soldiers at all, just ragged men in skirts and turbans, hunched over submachine guns in the rear of open trucks. The only other traffic was the occasional teenage goatherd, coaxing his flock across the road with tossed stones or the nudge of a rifle butt. One shepherd appeared to be no older than twelve, standing roughly the height of the assault rifle he dragged along the ground. As his goats blocked the road, I climbed out and tried to make chat in kindergarten Arabic.

"Beautiful gun, very beautiful," I said, giving my one Arabic adjective a workout. He looked at me strangely. Pale dude in beat-up car, grinning madly and mumbling something about guns. I offered him a Pepsi and he popped off the cap with the muzzle of his Kalashnikov.

"Beautiful gun," I said again. "It work?" Then, to make my point clearer, I pressed an imaginary trigger and went "Bang bang." I was trying to establish if it was possible that a prepubescent goatherd was toting a loaded automatic weapon.

The boy shrugged, raised the barrel and pumped several rounds into an abandoned roadside hut. Dried mud chipped off and scattered in the air. The goats skittered across the tar, clearing the highway. I skittered back to my car shouting "Beautiful gun, very beautiful" and shifted from first gear to fourth gear as quickly as I could.

It was dark by the time I reached the city of Saada, 150 miles north of the capital. A mud-walled settlement at the country's northern frontier, it was known as the Dodge City of Yemen, a lawless place where tribal spats sent lead singing through the streets.

"My first year here, there was gunfire all the time," said a young man named Ali. We were sitting in a teahouse on Saada's main street, talking about his decision to leave the capital for a government job in the north.

"Have you seen anyone killed?" I asked him.

"Only six. But many more injured."

The worst shootout he'd witnessed occurred one day after work, when he offered a colleague a ride home. A truck pulled alongside Ali's car and two man began shooting rifles through the window. Ali's passenger returned the fire. Before it was over, six people had died, three of them unarmed passersby.

"I think this is too much," said Ali, who, unlike his passenger, survived the exchange. "Now I give rides only to people I know well."

Ali said things were getting better. Tribesmen used to travel each weekend to an open-air weapons market in the nearby village of Al-Tuhl, also known for its handwoven baskets. There they could buy grenades by the kilo, like tomatoes, and also pre-order tanks and shoulder-held missile launchers. But the government had recently closed the souk. And tribesmen visiting Saada now had to check their bullet clips at roadblocks outside town, though they were permitted to carry empty rifles through the street.

"It is a way of letting them keep their dignity while taking away their danger," Ali explained. Even so, two hundred people had been gunned down or stabbed to death in the Saada region the previous year, a rather astonishing figure for an area with a total population of about ten thousand.

After chatting with Ali, I wasn't sure I wanted to hang around town and risk becoming innocent victim number 201. But driving back to Sanaa in the dark, with one headlight, seemed out of the question. So I asked Ali where I should stay for the night. He recommended Saada's finest, the no-star Rahban Hotel. "It is more like a camping ground than a hotel,' he said. "But the other places, well . . ." He left it to my imagination.

The Rahban was as advertised. I had a choice between

a two-dollar room with a swampy communal toilet at the end of the hall, or a three-dollar room with a swamp *en suite*. I treated myself to the latter, which came at least with a toilet bowl and seat.

The toilet didn't flush, however, and judging from its contents, hadn't for some time. I wandered out into the hall and found a sitting room with geological maps spread on the floor and a Yemeni bedded down on the couch. He spoke a little French and explained that foreigners with trucks and drills had left the maps there that morning. They were either Italian or German or English, he wasn't sure. They were searching for either gold or silver or gas, or maybe something else. He went back to sleep.

It wasn't hard to fill in the blanks. Oil had just begun flowing through pipelines farther south; now even distant Saada was awash with prospectors as well.

I awoke late the next morning to the sound of automatic gunfire. With the special sickness of the scoop-hungry journalist, I heard in the rat-a-tat the rhythm of a headline: SHOOTOUT IN SAADA. Rushing to the window, I located the gunslingers just below. A boy of about ten was tearing pages from a magazine and pinning them to the mud wall of the old city. Then he and a middle-aged man took turns pumping lead into the pages with a huge automatic pistol. It was a touching scene, in a Yemeni sort of way; father and son, on a bright Sunday morning, out for target practice in Saada. The father seemed particularly pleased with a series of head shots drilled into what looked like a photograph of the Yemeni president.

Downstairs, I dug into flat bread and *ful*, the ubiquitous Arab breakfast of slow-cooked fava beans. Mashed and marinated with hot spices and lime, the *ful* tasted like a week-old burrito. "If your friend is as sweet as honey, don't taste him all at once," read the proverb heading the chapter on Saada in my *Traveller's Guide*, which I perused over breakfast. The book didn't mention that Yemen is home to thirty-four types of stomach parasite. Living dangerously, I washed

down the *ful* with lukewarm tea that seemed not to have
boiled, then pushed open the saloon-style doors leading into
the street.

By day, Dodge City was disappointing. Its straight and
dusty main street looked the part. But at high noon the only
dueling was between a pair of mangy dogs, humping in the
road. A merchant paused to watch, then resumed scrubbing
a stain of qat spittle from the sidewalk in front of his shop.

The main road ended at the gate to the old city. At first
it looked like a miniature Sanaa, with clay walls and fanciful
mud towers topped in stained glass and gypsum. But most
of the towers seemed to squat rather than soar. Urine trick-
led from holes in the upper floors, a primitive sewage system
that relied on the hot sun to dry waste water as it dribbled
down.

From atop the ramparts there was still a glimpse of
former glory. A cleft in the mountains marked the site of an
ancient trade route, along which passed caravans of myrrh
and frankincense on their way to the Mediterranean port of
Gaza. Muslim pilgrims also followed the road north to visit
Mecca, just over the mountains. Their gravestones, covered
in calligraphy, massed outside Saada's walls, facing the holy
city.

These days, thousands of Yemenis made the pilgrimage
to Saudi Arabia for worldlier gain. They went to do the
kingdom's dirty work, returning with enough petrodollars to
buy a home, a wife, a higher grade of qat. The old city of
Sanaa seemed resilient enough to survive the onslaught of
modern ways. But here in Saada, the mud towers were
neglected, the dirt streets littered with paper, polystyrene
and crushed aluminum cans. From atop its eroded walls,
Saada had the precarious feel of a city that the next hard
rain might wash away.

Descending into the old city's bazaar, I spotted men
with skullcaps and ringlets of hair, hawking silver jewelry.
More of the chosen people. They squatted at the fringes of
the market, displaying their earrings in the dust. Other Jews
labored in dark stalls, crafting scabbards for the daggers they

were forbidden to wear. Yemeni Jews also had traditionally been barred from building their homes higher than Muslims', or even from riding a camel, which might elevate them above their donkey-riding neighbors. "Jews are not permitted to ride astride animals," declared another obscure statute, "but must keep their feet to one side."

Jews had nonetheless prospered in Yemen. As in other Arab countries, they were a protected minority called "people of the book," a classification that referred to the Bible and included Christians as well (the Koran, Muslims believe, is an improvement on the two earlier religions, not a complete rejection of them). In Saada, local tribes protected the unarmed Jews and exploited their skills as silversmiths, weavers and embroiderers. This created an odd disjuncture, now that Yemen had joined its Arab brothers in opposing the Jewish state. While the government news I watched on the hotel television railed against "the Zionist entity" fifteen hundred miles away, the few hundred Jews of Saada went about their business crafting *jambiyas* and silver baubles for their Muslim protectors.

The only sign of tension was the Jews' reluctance to speak with me. Visiting Westerners had caused trouble by discussing migration to Israel, a touchy subject for the Yemeni government.

So after a dozen abortive chats, I contented myself with camping outside the stall of a particularly able silversmith. Stooped in the dirt, he picked at tiny bits of silver with a pair of tweezers, and laid them between wire borders to form a finely wrought arabesque. He turned out one small square after another, spending about an hour on each. He'd pause, smoke a cigarette, add a few leaves to his qat cud, then resume work on a design identical to the one he'd just finished.

When I asked what the designs were for, he gestured at a sack in the corner and returned to his tweezers. Inside the bag were dozens of *jambiyas*, their decorative handles dented or peeling away. It was the Jew's job to repair them.

The silversmith worked through the afternoon while the

other merchants lunched and chewed and chattered. He
worked into the evening, laboring by lamplight. He was still
picking at his silver early the next morning when I returned,
shifting qat from right cheek to left cheek and fixing one
dagger after another. There was something in his mute,
unstinting labor, repairing weapons he himself couldn't
carry, which said all that needed to be said about centuries
of silent submission.

On my way into town the previous day I'd seen a sign with
the name of a hospital. I'd been struck by the irony of the
hospital's name: Al-Salaam, Arabic for "peace." The hospital
seemed like the logical place to continue my reporting on the
least peaceful place in Yemen. Going to Al-Salaam at nightfall, and settling in for a frankfurter and sauerkraut at the
hospital cafeteria, I got more than I'd bargained for: the distinguished Dr. Peter Drake.

"I'm interested in gross pathology—in the fantastically
gross things that happen here," the English physician said,
sinking his fork into lemon meringue. "Cancer of the pla-
centa is common as dirt here. A gyno will go his whole
career in the U.K. without seeing that." He stabbed his
dessert. I put down my hot dog. "Yesterday, I saw a bayonet
in the throat," he went on. "Day before, a bloke came in
with beriberi. Beriberi—can you imagine? We see leprosy,
snake bites, camel bites, rabies. The U.K., it's an awful dull
place compared to the Yemen."

The sixty-two-year-old doctor had left the dull U.K. in
the 1950s, first to work with Britian's colonial medical service
in Nigeria ("gone to the dogs since we stopped ruling it")
and from there to Saudi Arabia ("they don't wear veils
between their legs, but they would if they could"). For the
past eight years he'd been in "the Yemen," surviving on
smuggled brandy, three-week-old copies of the London
Times, and the fantastically gross cases he saw every day at
the hospital.

"The other week, I had a real beauty," he said, attacking
a second piece of pie. "Bloke brings in his missus, says he

married her that morning. She's bleeding all over the place, half dead. Know what happened? She was too tight, he says. So he opened her up a bit with his *jambiya*." He wiped lemon filling from his lip. "Can you imagine? Opening her up on their wedding night?"

An Irish nurse joined the conversation from the other end of the table. "Today I go to take some blood from a woman," she said, in a lilting accent, "and her arm is all covered with burns. Says the witch doctor did it to cure her. Then when I take her blood, she starts screaming. 'Give that back to me! You're going to sell it!' "

Dr. Drake cackled, swallowed his coffee in one loud gulp and invited me to follow him on his evening rounds. We stopped first at his flat so he could put on a tie and tweed jacket—"keeping up standards"—then walked into a waiting room filled with veiled women and men in skirts and jackets. It was the first gathering of three or more Yemenis I'd seen that showed no evidence of either qat or *jambiyas*.

"Qat's forbidden and we make them check their weapons at the door," the doctor explained. Sure enough, a nearby guard booth held a small arsenal of daggers and rifles, not unlike the collections I'd been pricing during my tour of the north.

"My first year here, they brought in some fellow who'd been shot in a tribal punch-up," Dr. Drake continued. "He must have killed someone first, because the other tribe decides to come get its revenge right here in the parking lot. So in the end we had four of them coming in the door, all dead as dodos. You can see the bullet marks on the wall outside. Can you imagine?"

Listening to the doctor, and looking at the unarmed men in the waiting room, I was struck by the precariousness of Yemeni machismo. Until now, the north had seemed a threatening territory of heavily armed natives, made manic by qat. Suddenly, surrounded by tiny men with sparrowlike features, anxiously clutching sick children and spouses, I felt like a giant among munchkins. Stripped of their guns and denied the consoling powers of qat, the men looked as vulnerable as fathers and husbands in hospital waiting rooms anywhere in the world.

The women also seemed changed, if only because some were too sick to cover their faces. They lined the corridor, many holding feverish babies and pleading with each passing doctor and nurse for attention.

"Don't think this one's going to make it," Dr. Drake said, lifting the eyelids of a jaundiced infant limp in the arms of its mother. Alongside sat a young girl with the rasping cough of a lifetime smoker. Stooping to press a stethoscope to her wasted chest, the doctor said to the girl's mother, "She'd better pull through or I'm not going to speak to her again." The woman, who obviously understood not a word, reached into the folds of her robe and offered the doctor a bag of raisins.

At the end of the hall several nurses huddled around a bed surrounded by curtains. "If you want to give your coronary arteries a blow-through," the doctor said, "look in there." A woman lay on her back, blood streaming down her thigh as a female doctor put stitches between her legs. Catching my eye, the patient used her last ounce of strength to pull a veil across her face, even though the rest of her was fully exposed. Ashamed, I pulled the curtain shut.

Dr. Drake checked her chart. The woman had spontaneously aborted after a six-hour trip down the mountains on the back of a donkey. "Husband can't be found," he said. "Off chewing qat somewhere." He shook his head. "Qat makes them bloody daft, you know. One minute their heads are clear. Next moment it's like London up there. Socked in completely."

His rounds finished, the doctor walked me to the parking lot. "Sorry we couldn't arrange a gunshot for you, or at least a stabbing," he said, sounding genuinely apologetic. "Got any plans for tomorrow?"

"Bit of shopping. Then back to Sanaa."

"Pity. Where are you staying?"

"The Rahban."

He grimaced. "Don't drink the water, don't eat the food and be sure you don't chew qat, here or anywhere."

"Too late," I told him. "Done all of those already."

"Good God." He chuckled to himself, no doubt thinking of something fantastically gross. "If you're feeling off in the morning, you know where to find us."

I drove back through the silent streets. Rabid-looking dogs lurked in the vacant lots. A demented motorcyclist raced back and forth down the main drag. But there wasn't another sound in the night, not even a car backfiring. The Rahban was also quiet, except for the toilet. I lay awake for a long while, reviewing the past days' adventures and listening to the putrid water drip from toilet to tile to carpet, thinking what a bloody dull place the world is compared to the Yemen.

In the morning I made a last tour of the bazaar, this time inquiring about the availability of deadly weapons. I'd already gathered most of the information I needed on the drive from Sanaa, and the purchasing charade had become rather weary. "*Andak bandook?*" Do you have a gun? You do? An AK-47 with retractable clip? And grenades too? How much for the lot? And so on, until I'd talked my way out the door and slipped into an alley to scribble the details down in my notebook.

"You like be strong?" a young man whispered, following me down a narrow lane. He was Jewish, about my own age, and rather biblical-looking with his dusty sandals, stringy beard and brown shift tied at the waist. "I see you look for something strong," he said, tugging my arm. "Come with me. I find you finest *jambiya* in Saada."

He led me into a dark corner of the casbah where an older Jew sat perched atop a heavy carpet. The man glanced both ways, then unfurled the rug to reveal a dozen *jambiyas*. It occurred to me then that none of the Jews had proper shops, possibly because this too was forbidden. Instead, they operated portable stores, opening and folding up shop at a moment's notice, like West African street hustlers in New York.

The man held up a stunning dagger, inlaid with minute bits of silver, much like the weapons I'd watched the Jewish silversmith laboring over. For the first time in three days of mock shopping, I was tempted to make a purchase.

The younger Jew—now self-appointed translator and middleman—leaped up and strapped the dagger around my waist. "You now very strong soldier," he said. A crowd of boys, some Jews, some not, nodded in agreement. It seemed the whole crowd was working on commission.

I put the dagger down and feigned interest in several others. Then I glanced again at the first dagger and asked in an offhand manner what it cost. The two men consulted in Arabic and the younger one said, "Two thousand riyals." About two hundred dollars.

"Two thousand?" I got up to leave.

There was another whisper of Arabic, and the young man grasped my sleeve. "Make my friend an offer," he said. "Perhaps today he is in need to sell." It was the first time I had heard bargaining words from a Yemeni merchant. It was also the first time I had felt some common blood flowing between me and these mocha-colored men with their beanies and ringlets.

I picked up a stick and scribbled "500" in the dust. The old man began rolling up his carpet. I handed him the stick. He wrote "1500." I got up to leave again. He held my arm, then wiped out the dust with his sandal and wrote "1000." I scribbled "500" again. He turned away, as if to catch the eye of a passing shopper.

"You have dollars?" our go-between asked. After all, dollars were worth one thing to me and quite another to them, traded on the black market. I laid a fifty-dollar bill in the dust, which equaled five hundred riyals at the official rate and perhaps seven hundred at the unofficial. The young man held it up to the sun and made some quick calculations.

"It is good money but need more," he declared. I emptied my pockets: a ten-dollar bill, one hundred riyals, a return plane ticket to Cairo and a few lint-covered Egyptian stamps. I draped the riyals and the stamps across the dagger's handle. The old man considered the offer for a moment. Then he reached into a corner of his carpet and dug out two enormous worn coins like some I'd seen at a museum in Sanaa. They were Maria Theresa dollars, Austrian coins once used by the Ottoman Turks and apparently still legal tender in Yemen. He tossed them atop the dagger, then pointed at the ten dollars I was still clutching.

I added the bill to the loot and the man nodded his consent. He pocketed the dollars, riyals and stamps. I scooped up the *jambiya* and Maria Theresa coins. The young man helped strap the dagger around my waist.

"You make very big bargain," he said, standing back. This seemed dubious. "You look like very big sheik," he continued. This seemed even more dubious. But marching out of the market, past the silversmith and down the dusty main drag, my hand resting calmly on the hilt of the fine *jambiya*, I thought it likely that I was the first armed Jew to parade through the streets of Saada.

4

PERSIAN GULF
The Straight of Hoummos

If one goes into Arabia, he should carry his shroud under his arm.

—A friend's advice to Arabian explorer Charles Doughty

Late one Friday night in Cairo, I was watching a scratched videotape of *Dr. No*, dubbed into Arabic, when the call came through from New York.

"Tony? Jack."

"Jack!" I switched off the video. Jack was a former classmate and one of a dozen or so magazine editors I'd written to before moving to Cairo, in the hopes they'd throw an assignment my way. None had yet called.

"Did I catch you at a bad time?" he asked.

"No, just finishing off a story."

"Look," he said, "there's been some great TV footage over here on the tanker war in the Persian Gulf." He paused. "We'd like you to get out on the water and put the story into words."

I'd seen the same footage earlier that night, on the English-language news. Iraqi warplanes and Iranian gunboats, drilling oil tankers with Exocet missiles and rocket-propelled grenades. Flaming hulks skidding across the TV screen. Half-charred sailors leaping overboard, into shark-infested waters.

49

"Sounds great, Jack." After weeks of stringing, it was good to be tossed some rope, however frayed. "What's my budget?"

"A thou for expenses, three thou for the finished piece, and a thou kill fee." He chuckled. "That's if the piece gets killed, not you." He had another call waiting; he wished me luck and rang off.

There was one other Westerner on board the flight to the United Arab Emirates, the best jumping-off point for coverage of the Persian Gulf war. He was slumped in a window seat across the aisle, reading the *Emirates News*.

"Reporter?" he asked. I nodded. "Gulf-warring it?" I nodded again. "Me too," he continued. "Bloody dull business." He glanced out at the twilit sky as we banked over the Persian Gulf for the plane's first stop, at Qatar. "If there's any heat tonight you'll see it out the left side of the aircraft." With that, he handed me his newspaper, yawned, and drifted off to sleep.

I devoured every inch of newsprint. In Cairo, the only English-language daily was the *Egyptian Gazette*, a six-page chronicle filled with out-of-date AP stories, grainy photos of East German factories (available to the *Gazette* for free) and newsy nuggets on the domestic scene, such as "President Mubarak yesterday received a cable of thanks from Sultan Qaboos of Oman in reply to the President's greetings cable marking the 17th anniversary of the Sultanate's National Day."

The Emirates paper was encyclopedic by comparison, and crammed with curious glimpses of the society I was about to enter. The daily "prayer timings" were prominently displayed, alongside the arrival and departure schedule at the Emirates' four international airports—this in a nation with the population and habitable area of Rhode Island. Two of the airports were only ten miles apart. An advertisement on the opposite page offered "brief but intense shopping sprees in London" and "slimming vacations in West Germany."

At the airport in the Emirates' capital, Abu Dhabi, I climbed into a Mercedes taxi and tore down an empty six-lane causeway, past cloverleafs, shopping centers and lush strips of green pasted neatly onto the desert. Gleaming sky-scrapers rose on both sides. The whole city looked like an architect's model, a toy town, still under glass.

In Cairo I'd been surprised to hear Egyptians speak dis-paragingly of Persian Gulf Arabs, to whom they gave the diminutive nickname "Gulfies." The Gulfies had oil but they didn't have a civilization to rival that of the Egyptians, who were tossing up pyramids five thousand years before the Gulfies moved out of goat-hair tents. "When the chips are down, there is only one real place in the entire area—Egypt," a Cairo diplomat once declared. "All the rest—forgive me—are tribes with flags."

There was a kernel of truth underlying this arrogance. There was also a great deal of envy. Egypt had a per capita income of $560 a year. In the Emirates the figure was $24,000. At the height of the oil boom, the tiny nation had been the richest in the world.

But a traditional culture could still be glimpsed through the shimmer. At the Abu Dhabi Sheraton, there was a room-service menu offering fresh lobster flown in from Canada, and the in-house movie schedule rivaled that of a suburban cineplex. But kisses and cuddles were edited out of the films, to avoid offending Muslim guests. There was a notice by the bed that prayer rugs were available at reception. A decal on the night table pointed the way to Mecca.

Opting for the hotel bar, I found myself seated beside a Fort Worth oilman named Larry. "Change those Arab dishrags for ten-gallon hats and this place could be Dallas," he said, sipping Budweiser. He was watching the Texas Longhorns play the Arkansas Razorbacks, live via satellite on a twenty-two-inch television screen. "Biggest, tallest, richest, they love that shit." He lowered his voice. "If you've got it, flaunt it. And let me tell you, son, they've got it."

By day, Abu Dhabi was blinding. White sky. White build-ings. White-robed men in white Mercedeses, calling each other on car phones. Imported laborers provided the only color: red-turbaned Sikhs, laying green turf on the median strips. Staggering through the sunstruck streets, I took refuge in Abu Dhabi's only historical edifice: a mud-and-coral fortress that had, until the 1960s, dwarfed the huts of what was then a pearling and fishing backwater. The fortress was now a pygmy amid thirty-story towers of steel and glass.

The mud had been covered with whitewash and the fortress converted to a government center. Inside, an amiable English archivist, Edward Henderson, invited me into his air-conditioned office. "This building used to lack certain amenities," he said. "Glass, electricity, potable water, that sort of thing. But by the standard of the day it was quite grand."

Henderson first came to Abu Dhabi in 1948, by wooden sailboat, to win oil concessions from the local sheik. The sheik invited Henderson onto the fortress rooftop to feast on dates, camel's milk and a whole sheep lying on a bed of rice. Bedouin retainers recited poetry as they dined. "One had the feeling that life hadn't changed for centuries," Henderson said.

Forty years later, Henderson was now among the legion of Westerners in the principality's employ. "One must learn to move with the times," he added, smiling wryly at the irony of his situation.

It was a Friday, when most Arab offices close and reporting is difficult, so I rented a car and drove inland to a camel race I'd seen advertised in the *Emirates News*. The causeway swept me out of the city and into an arid plain dotted with signs for camel crossings: red triangles with humped silhouettes at the center. Thirty minutes out of Abu Dhabi there was nothing: a vast soup of oil, crusted with sand.

It was my first real view of desert, and I searched in vain for the majestic vistas I'd seen in *Lawrence of Arabia* and countless other films. A nineteenth-century traveler, Alexander Kinglake, described the desert much better: "Sand, sand, still sand, and only sand, and sand, and sand again."

The wealth here had to be mineral, because there was nothing else, animal or vegetable, for miles.

Gazing out at the bleak expanse, it was easy to understand why Islam had caught on so quickly among seventh-century Arabs. For the faithful, the Koran promises a paradise "watered by rivers. It's food is perpetual, and its shade also" (heaven also offers its guests "beauteous damsels . . . whom no man shall have deflowered before them"). It was also easy to see why the oil-rich Gulfies had quickly discarded their camels and tents for Mercedeses and modern villas. At noon the temperature was 109 degrees. Turning on the air conditioner, I eased up the tinted windows and listened to Casey Casum play American top forty on Abu Dhabi radio.

The oasis of Al Ain announced itself with a billboard offering an unlikely bit of Mohammed's paradise here on earth: an indoor ice rink. There was also a squat villa shaped like a flying saucer, which had touched down on a lot so vast that it would have been zoned industrial in any other land.

Driving through town and into the desert on the other side, I couldn't find a trace of the camel race. The directions in the newspaper were vague, and there was no one out in the blazing midday sun to ask. About to give up, I spotted a dozen men seated in the shade of a cedar tree. They wore traditional garb: a white robe with a white headdress held in place by a ring of black cord, which had once doubled as a rope to tie camels' legs so they wouldn't stray. A few camels and goats milled nearby. It seemed I had stumbled on a genuine bedouin encampment.

I wandered over to ask directions. One of the men spoke English and told me that the races had ended a few hours before. But with typical Arab hospitality, he invited me to stay for lunch. The men were about to dig their fingers into a communal mound of meat and rice, and they indicated politely that I should take the first bite.

A southpaw, I instinctively reached my left hand toward the—

"*La! La!*" twelve voices cried in unison. No! A man put

his left hand on his backside, reminding me of its proper use. The others laughed. I'd forgotten the first commandment of desert etiquette, but my hosts seemed good-humored about it.

Proceeding clumsily with my right hand, I bit into a piece of sinewy flesh. It tasted like overcooked sandal. I must have made a quizzical face, because the man beside me nodded his head toward the animals milling nearby. I had missed seeing camels run and was now eating one instead.

"Do you live here?" I asked Mobarak, the English-speaking young man who had invited me to eat. "Or do your people still roam through the desert?"

Mobarak smiled. "Today I am a bedouin,' he said. "Tomorrow I study business administration."

He pointed to another cedar tree where a row of Toyota Land Cruisers was parked in the shade. The men, it turned out, were students and government workers from Al Ain. They came here only on Fridays to race their camels and picnic in the desert. Even the food had been prepared beforehand in Mobarak's kitchen. "It is nice sometimes to live in the old way," he said, sipping Pepsi.

There was an older man seated beside Mobarak. His face was the color and texture of scorched almonds. Mobarak said this was his father, born near here and raised herding camels across the vast desert known as the Rub al Khali, or Empty Quarter. In those days, the Bedouin lived from well to well, relying on their camels for food, milk and hides for tents and water bags.

The older man spoke poor English, so I asked Mobarak what his father now did.

"Business," he said. "Mostly he buys properties and builds on them. I cannot think of the English word."

"Developer?"

The older man smiled, his mouth full of camel and rice. "*Aywah*," he said. Yes, that was the word. Then he said something in Arabic I didn't understand.

"He says that this war between Iraq and Iran is very

bad for business," Mobarak translated. "It takes many years to grow a tree and only a minute to cut it down."

After lunch, after a group snooze under the cedar tree, Mobarak led me a few miles across the desert to a place where other camel breeders were running heats in the waning sun. The track was a long spit of hoof-beaten sand, beginning at a cedar tree and ending at an oil rig. Bangladeshi grooms hoisted saddles made of toweling onto the camels, then hoisted on the jockeys, Bangladeshi boys of seven or eight. The boys were barefoot and secured to the saddles with Velcro straps across their calves. The owners, elegantly robed men like Mobarak, sat in their four-wheel-drives, windows up and air conditioning on.

When three mounts had been readied, the grooms hit the camels with bamboo crops and the awkward beasts humped their way through the sand. A moment later, three of the cars pulled out of the shade and took off after the camels, cruising alongside the track. Windows down, the passengers yelled encouragement to their riders. *"Emshee!"* Move it! Fifty yards from the starting line, cars and camels disappeared in a cloud of desert sand.

"This is quite a primitive race," Mobarak said, rather apologetically. Usually, the owners coached their jockeys through walkie-talkies, which were wired to radio transmitters strapped to the young boys' chests. The best camels eventually raced in a stadium with a five-mile track and seating for thousands. "It is like your Kentucky Derby," he said.

I asked him if the jockeys were ever Arabs.

"These days, no," he said. "It is a dangerous sport, and most families would not allow their sons to race. It is much safer to hire boys from Pakistan and Bangladesh."

We stood there watching the camels and cars take off, three by three, until the sun became a dull red flame, sinking into the desert.

That evening I accepted Mobarak's invitation to visit him at his home near Al Ain. The villa was tucked into a tidy

subdivision with its own small mosque. Two white Mercedeses were parked in front, alongside the Toyota Land
Cruiser I'd seen that afternoon.

A Filipino servant led me into what seemed a ballroom,
with carpet and walls merging into a vast ocean of baby
blue. The room smelled antiseptic, as if the furniture had
just been unpacked or sprayed with disinfectant. An over-
stuffed sofa ran the perimeter of the room, with a small
coffee table forming an atoll at the precise center. The space
was so vast that our voices echoed and I had to lean forward
to hear Mobarak's words.

"You see, we can live here or in the desert, it makes no
difference," he said, as the servant poured sweet tea from a
waist-high pink pot into tiny glasses. Mobarak wore a freshly
pressed robe, or *dishdasha*, and seemed as much at ease in
air-conditioned splendor as he had that afternoon squatting
in the sand.

"How many people live here?" I asked.

"Three. Myself, my brother and my father."

"And none of you are married?"

He paused. "Of course, we have all taken wives." He
rearranged the folds of his robe, offering no further details.
I had shown bad manners for the second time that day. In
traditional Gulf homes it is impolite to inquire directly about
womenfolk. Queries about family, I later learned, are
phrased in a way that translates "How many sons do you
have?" or "How are those that stand behind you?"

But Mobarak was broad-minded, and curious about
"women's liberty" and other peculiarities of Western culture.
I obliged by giving a thumbnail sketch of life in urban
America, touching only lightly on drugs, AIDS, crime and
other blights.

"Forgive me, but I think your culture is too free," he
interrupted. "Man is not a perfect creature. He must live
under certain rules."

Everything Mobarak read and saw on television confirmed what his own culture taught him. Westerners drank
too much and went on shooting sprees; much better not to

drink at all. Men gambled away their earnings—even their wives, he had heard. Here, gambling was forbidden. He had seen a television program on New York that showed walls topped with razor wire and buildings guarded by snarling Dobermans. Here no one needed to steal, as everything was provided: free medical care, free education, a free plot of land and a job for any university graduate.

The balance and civility of Mobarak's vision was appealing, at least for the men. The only women I'd yet seen were black ghosts in head-to-toe veils, herding children through the streets. I asked Mobarak if women resented the obvious restrictions on their dress and activity.

He smiled. "In the West, you are obsessed by our women. Do not worry. This too is changing." Islam allowed a man to have up to four wives, but marrying more than one was frowned on by the younger generation. And though technically a husband could divorce a wife by saying "I divorce thee" three times, this too was discouraged, unless the wife was barren. "Women must be protected and cared for because they are controlled by emotions," he said. "Surely man is not woman and woman is not man."

We finished the tea, and the cardamom coffee that followed. Then Mobarak explained that he had to retire, because classes began early the next day. "I must work on my accounting," he said. "In the West you have learned to use Arab numbers. But we must learn to use your computers. After all, this is a modern country."

In fact, the United Arab Emirates hadn't been a country for long; like everything else, the state itself was newly minted and rather insecure. Before uniting in 1971, the seven shiekdoms often took up arms against each other, usually over land, and the map of their confederacy remained a crazy quilt of neutral zones and lines marked "border disputed" or "boundary undefined." One of the emirates covered an area of only one hundred square miles. Here, in microcosm, was the Arabia of "tribes with flags" the Egyptians so disparaged.

Abu Dhabi, the biggest and richest of the city-states,

was the center of power. But Dubai, ninety miles down the coastal superhighway, was the country's brash commercial hub. It was to Dubai that I headed to find some way out onto the Perian Gulf.

The official at the Dubai Chamber of Commerce had tinted glasses and six pens clipped to the breast pocket of his *dishdasha*. "We are the black camel of the Emirates family," he said, grinning broadly. "We love the West. We love capitalism." He stuffed my shoulder bag with glossy promotional literature, each page of which assured the prospective businessman that Dubai's port was duty-free, regulation-free, everything-free. Dubai hadn't let the Gulf war get in the way of its longstanding trade ties with Iran, whose territory lay just fifty-three miles offshore. There were daily flights to Tehran, shell-pocked Iranian tankers limping into Dubai's drydock for repairs, and Iranian traders pulling up in graceful teakwood sailboats, called dhows, as they had for centuries.

"We love business, we love tourism, we love everybody!" the Chamber of Commerce official exulted, seeing me to the door. I found myself grinning stupidly back at him, saying, "I love Dubai, too!"

And I did, though its real appeal was diversity. Outside the scrubbed white skyscrapers and gleaming white Mercedeses, the white-robed natives were lost in a subcontinental stew of Indians, Pakistanis, Bangladeshis, tall-turbaned Sikhs and a host of others whose homelands I would have been hard pressed to find on a map: Tamils, Baluchis, Pathans, Keralans, and Singhalese. Caste signs were more common than veils on the narrow alleys of the souk; Hindi and Urdu more commonly spoken than Arabic. At the oil boom's peak in the late seventies, imported "guest workers" outnumbered natives five to one.

There were also Westerners, most of whom hung out at a mock-Mexican bar called Pancho Villa's. It was there that I found Jim and Johannes, well into their third pitcher of beer and second basket of double-cheese nachos.

"About the only thing I've never met in this city,"

said Jim, an oil worker from Oklahoma, "is a native Dubai-ite."

"Dubain," Johannes corrected. "Rhymes with Hawaiian."

"Dubain, Dubaier, Dubai-ite—who gives a fuck?"

The two men laughed. Even their giggles seemed to slur.

"Hombre!" Jim yelled, calling the waiter. A Filipino barman clad in sombrero and bandolier scooted up with another pitcher of beer. It was "ladies' night," but there wasn't a lady in sight. Men outnumber women in Dubai by three to one.

"Money honey," Jim said, rubbing his thumb and forefinger together. "That's the only reason anyone lives in this hole." He gestured at the wall, which was adorned with two bumper stickers: "If you don't smoke, I won't fart" and "Beer drinkers get more head."

"The last time I got any of that, jeez, it's been centuries," Jim moaned, staring into his beer. "Must have been Bangkok. About '74."

" '76," Johannes corrected. "I was the one who gave it to you."

Jim giggled and reached over to fill Johannes's mug, spilling most of it on the floor. I asked Johannes what kind of work he did. "Sit here and wait for hell to break loose," the Dutchman said, handing me a business card that read "Tugboat owner and salvage operator." His boats tugged tankers out to sea, then tugged them back in after they'd been riddled with missiles and mines.

"I am like a wrecker driver on the highway," he said. "I make money from other people's distress." American destroyers had flattened an Iranian oil platform earlier that day; tension was the highest it had been for months. "At the moment," Johannes said, flashing gold incisors, "business is very good."

I told him I was a reporter, looking for a little distress myself. Could he get me out on the water?

Johannes shook his head. Lloyd's of London had recently

raised its war-risk premium by fifty percent, and insuring another passenger was costly. But he knew someone who might help and scribbled the agent's name on the back of a soggy napkin. "Say you're a friend of mine." He laughed. "And if you get into trouble, you know who to call."

The shipping agent from Bombay worked by the Dubai Creek, the narrow channel that snakes through the city and into the Persian Gulf. Teakwood dhows were moored three deep along the dock, jostling for space with a workaday fleet of trawlers, tugs and supply boats. Most of the dhows were manned by Iranian traders who stuffed their hulls with pistachios and carpets, forbidden exports from Khomeini's Iran.

The shipping agent gazed out at the creek, then lowered his teacup and whispered, "I know a vessel that leaves tonight. If the Persians cause no trouble, you will reach the Strait of Hormuz after dawn."

He waited for a colleague to take a radio call, then slipped a piece of paper across his desk. "You have never met me and do not know my name. I do this for you only, as a favor." He nodded his head toward the door.

The rendezvous was set for three in the morning at the Dubai Creek. Sleeping Iranians now littered the decks of each dhow, bundled like mummies in the aisles of their seaborne bazaars. Outgoing traders were already awake and piling their teakwood ships with Marlboros, Levi's and Panasonic boom boxes for the sixteen-hour run back to Iran. The water was thick with smugglers.

I was scanning the dark for the Bombay man's boat when an Arab official stepped from the gloom, demanding identification. He weighed my passport and visa in his hand, barely glancing at their contents. "Your papers," he said, "I think maybe they are not in order." He looked as though he might bite one corner to test for counterfeit.

I forced a nervous smile. "Perhaps I have caused some inconvenience by arriving at this late hour." Overblown language is the Musak of Arab officialdom. So is *baksheesh*, at least in Cairo. "Certain arrangements of a—"

"Please, no," the man said, recoiling. Here in the world's richest country, offering a bribe was insulting. He handed back my papers and disappeared into the dark.

I spotted the name of the Bombay boat on the back of a sixty-foot workhorse, snub-nosed and broad across the beam. On the deck stood a muscular young Indian with curry on his breath. "I am Lawrence of Goa," he said, helping me on board. "Do not be afraid. The captain knows where the mines are. Maybe."

A dim light showed from the bridge, and a fine-boned man with black curls and a pierced ear sat cross-legged before the wheel. "I am Captain Kochrekar," he said. Still chewing on Lawrence's "maybe," I asked the captain if there was much danger traveling through the Persian Gulf at night.

"Wherever there is darkness there is also light," he said, staring into the night. "A man must make his own map for the shadows."

Lawrence of Goa untied the boat and Captain Kochrekar steered us toward the shallow black water of the Persian Gulf.

Lights blinked from a container terminal towering at the mouth of the Dubai Creek. Offshore oil terminals blinked back. Then we were swallowed up by the night. Faint points of green blipped across Kochrekar's radar screen. Otherwise he navigated without lights. The Persian Gulf wasn't the sort of place where mariners sought attention.

Not that there was much of an audience. Except for a lonely coast guard boat swishing past us in the dark and a few container ships lying at anchor, we sighted no other traffic for the first two hours at sea. But the quiet was deceptive. The gunboats and missiles I'd watched on TV posed little danger to Kochrekar's small craft, a supply boat that provisioned tankers with spare parts and food. It was Iranian mines strewn haphazardly across the shipping lanes that threatened destruction.

"A mine is like a snake," Kochrekar said, peering over

the wheel at a dark patch of water. "It does not think before striking."

The captain's engineer, Jesudasyn, appeared from below, munching a chapati and studying a nautical chart. On the map, the Persian Gulf was shaped like a headless figure, reclining comfortably in a La-Z-Boy chair. The Emirates formed the figure's buttocks and thighs, with Iran sitting heavily in its lap. The figure was covered in pencil marks stretching from Dubai to the Strait of Hormuz.

"These dots are mines we have spotted before," Jesudaysn explained. "Of course, the Persians always put new ones."

I asked him what would happen if we hit a mine.

"Like this," he said, brushing chapati crumbs from his trouser leg.

I decided to add my own eyes to the night watch. There was a momentary flare as gas burned off at a distant oilfield. Then black sea and black sky, stretching all the way to Iran. We could have been sailing through an inkwell.

The last time Kochrekar had made this run from Dubai to Fujairah, just south of the Strait, the supply boat patrolling ahead of him struck a mine. Kochrekar reached the scene in time to haul his fellow captain out of the sea. "The man was not broken but he was swollen with water, like a fish," he said. The others came ashore in pieces.

Every war has them; little people, caught in the crossfire. But for Kochrekar and his crew, the Gulf conflict was especially cruel. Like other Gulf proletariat, they had come to Dubai in the vast subcontinental drift that brought millions of Indian workers to the oil-rich Arabian shores. The wage in the Emirates was three times laborer's pay in Bombay. But tending Arab gardens and grooming Arab camels was one thing; dying in someone else's war was quite another. In the three years since the tanker war had flared in earnest, Iran and Iraq had already destroyed a third the merchant tonnage that went down in all of World War II. Most of the 350-odd dead were Indian, Pakistani, Korean or Filipino.

"I chose the sea because it is a peaceful place," Koch-rekar said. A fifth-generation sailor, he'd shipped out of Bombay at eighteen and had been on the water for the thirty years since. "But this, this is—what do you call it? I believe it is Russia roulette."

To Lawrence of Goa it was mostly tedium. While his mates stood watch in the wheelhouse, the handsome bronze Goan shelled crabs in the galley, peppering them from make-shift spice jars with labels that read "Tang," "Nescafé" and "Super Chunky Peanut Butter." When he wasn't stirring curry, Lawrence added line after line to an already epic-length letter to his wife in Goa, on the west coast of India. "This is she," he said, pointing to a picture taped at eye level, just above his writing table. It was a small, poorly focused snapshot of a sari-clad beauty in a tropical paradise of blue water, white sand and waving palm trees. "This is my dream, day and night," he said.

Like his mates, Lawrence squirreled away his earnings for the three months each year that he returned home to spend with his family. Even in port, the crew slept on board, cooking curry in the cabin, watching Indian movies on video-tape and listening to sitar music on the radio. It was as though they'd never really landed in the Emirates at all.

"I am not interested in these Arabs," Lawrence said, returning to his Homeric letter. "Only in their money."

I asked him what he had to tell his wife about these long empty days at sea.

"Nothing," he said. "So I write how much I miss her and how I count the days until we are together in Goa again."

This day's count was 210.

Above, on the bridge, Jesudasyn's imagination drifted along a parallel plane. He was an earnest dark Tamil, about forty-five, who spoke with the unflinching bluntness of a four-year-old.

"There is something I must ask you," he said after staring at the sea for several hours. "Is it true that men and women in America live together without marriage?"

"Yes, that's true."

"How is it then that they are still virgins when they marry? Please explain."

"They aren't."

Jesudasyn pondered this for a moment, then shook his head. "This could not be in India. A woman must be a virgin."

We studied the water for a few minutes before he resumed his interrogation.

"How is it then that they have no children when they marry?"

"Some do," I told him. "But mostly they use precautions. In marriage, too."

"And what precaution do you prefer? Please explain."

I paused. "Well, there are many options."

"Do you like the condom?" he interrupted. "Myself, I do not think it can be so effective." Then he reached into a drawer and pulled out the previous day's newspaper from Dubai. He'd circled a story that told of an Arab man who had thirty-two children and three wives—and wanted more of both.

"This man," Jesudasyn said, "I think he needs a precaution."

Kochrekar, who had been silent till now, joined in the conversation. "A woman is not to be used up and then thrown away," he said solemnly. "In India a man takes only one wife and they are one until the funeral pyre."

The conversation was wandering off course, but I was happy to go with the flow. It was taking my mind off the mines.

"And what happens after the pyre?" I asked Kochrekar. My cartoon image of Hinduism showed a lot of people lined up to come back as cows.

"Only the old still believe in reincarnation," Kochrekar said, "because such things cannot be with science. After the pyre burns, what is left? Dust and ashes only."

It seemed a sad creed for a man who spent his life dodging mines in the Persian Gulf.

"And what gods do you worship?" Jesudasyn asked.

"I was raised as a Jew."

The two men turned to stare. For a moment there were no eyes at all on the water. In three hours at sea, we'd broached two topics—Judaism and sex—that would have remained untouched for a year on Arab land.

"I have always wanted to meet this thing called Jew," Jesudasyn said softly, "and to hear about your messiahs. Please explain."

At daybreak the Gulf became a whitish haze and we churned across it as if through a giant bowl of milk. As the mist cleared, the water turned a brilliant cobalt blue, the way a child paints ocean. And the sea remained astonishingly empty. I'd imagined the Gulf as a cluttered bathtub with ships packed so tightly that they barely had room for incoming missiles. The reality was an azure expanse, twice the size of New York State, stretching from the Hormuz Strait to the swampy confluence of the Tigris and Euphrates in Iraq. There were a lot more sea turtles than frigates.

The tension on board our craft eased with the night. In the shimmering morning light, a mine would be obvious at one hundred yards or more. Jesudasyn closed his eyes and slumped against one corner of the wheelhouse. Lawrence's voice wafted up from below with the aroma of something cooking. "Captain,' he said, "how would you like your eggs?"

Kochrekar tilted his head toward the cabin. "It is as you decide, Lawrence. A cook must be his own master."

When the breakfast was ready, Kochrekar peered through binoculars for a moment, then asked if I'd take the wheel and continue on the same course while he ducked below. It seemed easy enough. I grasped the wheel and trained my eyes on the island toward which the bow was pointing. Steady as she goes. When the boat shifted a little to starboard, I swung the wheel the other way. Now we were too far left. I swung again and the bow began bobbing like a compass needle. Suddenly the island was nowhere in sight. By the time Kochrekar finished his eggs, I was trying to pull us out of a skid straight toward the Iranian coast.

Kochrekar allowed himself the first smile of the long boat ride. "You must let no current move you from the path you have chosen," he said, taking the wheel. Even his simplest statements seemed lifted from the Upanishads.

Nine o'clock was rush hour on the Persian Gulf. First one tanker and then a second and third sprouted on the horizon, followed soon after by another trio. The supertankers, some the size of several football fields, seemed indecently exposed in waters so open. Except that each convoy was tailed by a gray battleship bristling with cannons and radar. The scene reminded me of walking to kindergarten with my older brother.

If tanker convoys and radar were new to the Persian Gulf, naval warfare certainly wasn't. For centuries the coastal sheiks had sent their fishing and pearling boats into the Gulf to plunder European ships bound for India and the Orient. By the nineteenth century, the entire shoreline of what is now the Emirates and Oman had become known as the Pirate Coast. The pirates took no prisoners.

"After a ship was taken, she was purified with water and perfumes," reported a British naval officer. "The crew was then led forward singly, their heads placed on the gunwale, and their throats cut, with the exclamation used in battle of *Allah akbar!*—God is great!"

British gunboats eventually imposed treaties titled "Cessation of Plunder and Piracy by Land and Sea" and "Maritime Peace in Perpetuity." On maps, the Pirate Coast became the Trucial States. But the truce was uneven, and peace in perpetuity lasted five years. When the British captain Felix Jones made his peacekeeping rounds in 1858, his business with one sheik included "restoration of a slave girl" stolen in battle and reparations for a British merchant "plundered of his whole venture." Jones sailed out with no more than a "pledge" of future payment and returned a year later, only to become "a butt for the gun practice" of warring clans.

A similar script was now being acted out with supertankers, destroyers, and Silkworm missiles.

"This is U.S. warship 993," came a Tennessee drawl on Kochrekar's radio. "Ship on starboard, please identify yourself and what are your intentions?"

Another voice cut in, "Brown Hotel Roman Zebra. Supply vessel on port bow, please keep clear."

"Italian warship, this is Brother Charlie Gulf, do you read?"

Nearby, one show-and-tell was concluding in more genial fashion. "British warship, this is Soviet warship. Thank you for identifying yourself. We wish you a *bon voyage.*"

"Cheers," a British voice replied. "A safe journey to you and your crew."

But the Tennessee drawl on warship 993 was still questioning its starboard stranger. "Who are you and what are your intentions? You have one-zero seconds to respond."

There was an uneasy silence. Then a high-pitched cackle screeched onto the radio waves.

"It's the Fil-i-pino *mon*-keeee. Who wants some of my Fil-i-peeeno ba-*naaan*-a?"

Kochrekar laughed, nudging Jesudasyn awake. "It is our monkey friend," he said, as the radio filled with screams. The voice belonged to a renegade radio hacker, code-named Filipino Monkey, who liked to break in at tense moments with obscenities and animal noises.

"The monkey is horn-eeeeeeeeeee!!!! Who wants some bananaaaaaaaa!!!!"

Another voice shouted, "Monkey, we will find you and you will die!"

Shippers had been trying to trace the monkey for several years, without success. "I have given this matter much thought," Kochrekar said, serious again. "I do believe there now may be more than one monkey."

When the warships passed, Kochrekar picked up the radio to chat with a few of his fellow captains, usually in Hindi. There were also captains from Korea, the Philippines and Pakistan. It was the same as on shore; everyone but Arabs was doing the Arabs' business.

As the morning wore on, Kochrekar draped his arms across the wheel, staring lazily at the water. Lawrence came up from below and sat flipping through an Indian tabloid with a headline that read: "Housemaid Recalls Freud's Daily Life." And Jesudasyn, a recent convert to Christianity, studied a fundamentalist text, written in Tamil. The cover showed a crowd of copper-colored people moving toward a flaming pyre. A few survivors emerged on the far side of the blaze to ascend a tall flight of stairs towards a shimmering crown. Fire and brimstone, Hindu-coated.

Jesudasyn began reading aloud, and Lawrence told him to stop. "Jesudasyn, please," he said through clenched teeth. It was an old spat, deepened during long empty days at sea. Jesudasyn glanced up and said curtly, "Go to your curry, man." Lawrence ducked below, and Jesudasyn resumed his reading. I closed my eyes, afraid he might ask me to "please explain" some aspect of Christian theology. We had spent the hour before dawn discussing whether Mary was a virgin, and why it was that Jews did not believe Jesus was one of the messiahs. The morning heat made me groggy, and I drifted off to the lilting cadences of Tamil.

It was midday when Kochrekar shook me awake at the entrance to the Strait of Hormuz. The captain knew this was the highlight of his passenger's journey. It was through this narrow channel that a third of Europe's oil passed, and half of Japan's. It was here, too, that Iranians held the West ransom, training their guns on passing tankers, laying mines and threatening to close the channel. On tense days, an armada of destroyers, minesweepers and gunboats lurked in and around the strait, waiting for trouble. Shippers had dubbed this end of the Gulf "Silkworm Alley."

Like every news story that drags on too long, the Strait of Hormuz was also angling for some kind of record in the cliché department. In one week, screaming headlines had told me that America was Engulfed, in Dire Straits and Steering into Rough Water because Iran might mine the Oil Chokepoint, Straitjacket Hormuz, Turn Off the Tap on the Free World's Energy Lifeline. The Strait of Hoummos, one colleague called it. I had to see the real thing before I drowned in the metaphorical one.

What I saw, gazing into the brilliant midday sun, was an orange sea snake slithering past our bow and a dolphin poking its head above water. The rugged pink cliffs of Oman rose on one shore, the softer Iranian hills were shrouded in haze on the other. And in the thirty miles between lay an untroubled stretch of aquamarine.

A lone gray supertanker chugged through the strait, spitting black smoke. Sandbags surrounded the bridge. Silhouetted against the tanker was an Omani fishing dhow with a rectangular white sail and an upturned prow, like a miniature Viking ship. As I watched through binoculars, six men in white robes and turbans draped hand-held fishing lines into the water and calmy hauled in one red snapper after another. Each time they reeled a fish in, they smacked its head against the wooden rail, unhooked it and dropped the newly baited line into the water again. The men smiled as they worked. It was the most contented labor I'd ever seen.

"At night they burn paper fires in the stern so ships will not run them over," Kochrekar said. Otherwise, the boats carried on as they had for centuries, oblivious to the turmoil around them. When I looked through the binoculars again, the boat had moved off and all I could see was a flash of white robe and red fish against blue water.

I stepped onto the open deck and unbuttoned my shirt. The breeze tasted fresh and salty, the sun was warm and soothing on my chest. The Gulf looked clear enough to drink. A sea gull circled overhead. And I felt a sudden urge to dive in and swim through the World's Most Dangerous Waterway.

There was a shout from the bridge. I turned and saw Jesudasyn waving frantically at the water, just ahead. Kochrekar swung the wheel hard left as Lawrence rushed to the starboard rail. A circle of light flashed just below the surface.

"My God!" Lawrence cried. We were on top of it now. "Sardines, thousands of them! Oh what I'd give for a net!"

We came ashore in Fujairah at dusk, just as a small fleet of fishing dhows headed out to sea. I ducked below when the coast guard pulled alongside and again as the harbormaster steered us into port. The Bombay agent hadn't included me in his paperwork, and the ship's log only listed three men having traveled through international waters.

The crew tied up at the dock and settled in for another evening aboard their odd little capsule. Jesudasyn flicked through a collection of videos and chose *The Ten Commandments*. Lawrence put the finishing touches on the curry he'd been cooking all day. "Next time you are in Goa, you can meet my beautiful wife," he said, spooning incendiary broth into my mouth.

Kochrekar sat in the cabin, just as I'd found him the night before, studying charts beneath a twenty-watt bulb. In eight hours, after delivering supplies to a tanker due later that night, he would run the gauntlet again.

"Another map for the shadows?" I asked.

He smiled. "A man must be careful of the night."

There was much darkness and little light as I walked away from the water. Ahead lay a low concrete hut marked "Immigration" and another evasive chat with Arab officials. Then the long trip back overland to Dubai. It had been an oddly peaceful day on the water.

I turned to watch the sun sink into the Gulf of Oman. In the gathering dark, the sea and sky washed together in an even canvas of blue. Then the last bit of light drained away. And one by one the fishing boats ignited their paper flames, fanning out like fireflies across the night.

■   ■   ■

Two weeks later, back in Cairo, I came home to a message blinking on the telephone machine.

"Tony, it's Jack. Great story. Just a couple suggestions. Gimme a buzz."

I let the sweet taste of success wash around in my mouth. Three thou and a glossy magazine spread. Free-lancing, nothing to it. I dialed New York.

"Jack, Tony."

"Tony! Hot stuff!"

So hot it needed a rewrite. "Minor surgery," he said. The problem was that the boat ride was a "tease"; sardines in the water weren't drama enough. "Not a lot actually happens out there," he said.

This was true. Of course, if something had happened—a missile strike, say, or a close encounter with a mine—I would have had a much better story, pieced together from whatever notes floated ashore. But I promised to punch the story up and have it to him in a few days.

There was one quick call from Jack after that, warning me that the Gulf conflict "has kind of disappeared from the news over here," then nothing for several weeks. I didn't need a coroner to tell me the story was dead; or, as they say in the trade, "spiked" (though computers have eliminated the need for editors to impale reporters' copy on desktop lances).

Then one day there was a message from Jack, asking me to call again. Of course! They've changed their minds!

They had. But it wasn't the story they'd reconsidered. "Remember I promised you a thou for a kill fee?" Jack said. He paused. "Well, it seems I overstepped my authority. . . ."

I settled for five hundred, which about covered my over-run on expenses. Hanging up the phone, having just renegotiated my first kill fee, I wondered how much lower my free-lance career could sink.

5

CAIRO DAYS
Ozymandias Slept Here

> Why try to call up the traditions of vanished Egyptian
> grandeur? Why try to think at all? The thing was
> impossible. One must bring his meditations cut and
> dried, or else cut and dry them afterward.
> —MARK TWAIN,
> The Innocents Abroad

Sayed took the corner reck-
lessly, scattering chickens and swerving to avoid a water buffalo blocking the road. Traffic was bumper to bumper, the
buffalo backed up behind a donkey cart whose rear wheel
was stuck in the mud. The donkey brayed, the buffalo bel-
lowed, the chickens cackled madly. We'd escaped the snarled
streets of downtown Cairo for a gridlocked barnyard instead.

Sayed glanced over his shoulder and flashed me a loopy
grin. "Home, sweet home," he said. His goggles were spattered with mud. He kick-started the motorbike and roared
off through the animal jam, and into the tangled back alleys
of Shubra.

I had met Sayed a few months before, in Australia,
where he'd tutored me in Arabic. Our lessons foundered on
the gagging "ah" sound that has no equivalent in English—
or in any other language. "You sound as if you're choking
on spaghetti," Sayed would say, correcting me. "Just choke.

Forget the spaghetti." He usually gave up after fifteen minutes and tutored me in the wiles of Cairo instead.

"Carry heaps of one-pound notes, because no one will ever give you change in Egypt, even if they've got pocketfuls of it."

Or: "Always walk close to the curb, well away from the buildings. Otherwise you may find water or something worse raining down on your head."

The chubby, impish Egyptian promised to continue my education during a visit to his family in Cairo later that year. And so I found myself on the back of a motorcycle, clutching Sayed's waist as he bent the bike around the corners of the neighborhood he'd fled eight years before.

Shubra was once a rural quarter at Cairo's edge, a tree-shaded suburb where the nineteenth-century ruler Mohammed Ali built his summer palace. It was now one of Egypt's densest slums, with three million people poured into a space smaller than Central Park. The buildings clung so close to each other and to the narrow streets that they seemed to touch at the tops, like overarching boughs, crowding out the thin winter sun.

Still, like so much of Cairo, Shubra retained a village air. It wasn't just the donkeys and buffalo. It was also that someone at every corner recognized Sayed as he tore past on his motorbike, dodging potholes and pedestrians.

"Ya Sayed!" a woman cried from four floors up. She was hanging veils and the long Egyptian robes called galabiyas to dry in a narrow patch of morning sun. Sayed sputtered to a halt and blew her a kiss. "One of my cousins," he said.

At the next corner, a man beckoned from a sidewalk café. He sipped thick Turkish coffee and took languorous puffs from a water pipe as tall as himself. "Another cousin," Sayed said, pulling over for his fifth free coffee of the day.

The men kissed each other on both cheeks in the affectionate manner that is obligatory between Arab males, and forbidden in public between men and women. Then they sat holding hands and blowing smoke rings, chatting about family, about work, and about the women walking past to the market. When a buxom teenager sashayed by, Sayed's cousin let loose a low whistle and said something in Arabic that I recognized from my trips to buy food.

"She's got onions?" I ventured.

Sayed frowned. "Third lesson, you've forgotten." The word was garlic. "She's got garlic. Meaning she's hot. Spicy."

Two men, one tall, one very short, rode up on bicycles and cadged cups of coffee from the café's owner. "In honor of Sayed's visit!" the short one cried in a strange, high-pitched giggle. Sayed leaned over and whispered, "Hashish speaking. When he's not so high, he uses the bike to snatch purses."

"Another cousin?"

Sayed smiled. "I have lots of cousins. Last time I tried to remember them all I lost count at three hundred."

The tall man had milky eyes and a sly, gap-toothed grin. Sayed introduced him as Port Said, a nickname that referred to his skill at smuggling goods past customs officials at the Mediterranean port. Port Said stood up and proudly pantomimed his technique. Several jackets, worn over ten or so shirts—each pocket crammed with calculators and camera gear—and a bowlegged walk that concealed the small television set wedged between his robe-covered legs. He had a female accomplice who was always nine months pregnant with electronics strapped to her belly.

"Do you need anything?" Port Said asked.

"Yes, desperately," Sayed said. "Someplace to pee."

The men laughed and we climbed back onto the motorbike. Sayed kicked the accelerator and enveloped us in dust and fumes. We made it as far as the next corner before the owner of a produce stand rushed into the street, kissing Sayed and stuffing his pockets with bananas and cucumbers. "You see why Egyptians are so fat," Sayed said, thumping his ample belly, "and why Egyptian storekeepers are so poor." At the next corner, a one-legged woman approached, holding a crude wooden crutch with one hand and using the other to balance a basket on her head. A duck poked its bill above the rim and squawked. Sayed slowed down, slam-dunked the bananas into the basket and sped around the corner, into the street where he'd been raised.

"Nothing's changed," he sighed, parking beside his fam-ily's motorcycle shop. Chains, carburetors and dented cans of diesel lay strewn across the unpaved road. Men with grease on their faces came out to greet us, offering the backs of their hands to avoid blackening our palms. "Runs like a dream," Sayed lied, wheeling the bike inside. The garage was cluttered with motorcycle designs I'd never seen, except in old movies. Clunky machines with huge hooded fenders. Blunt-nosed sidecars. Wheels big enough to fit on snow-plows.

"I bet some of this is leftover junk from El Alamein," Sayed said, referring to the World War II battle site near Alexandria.

At the back of the shop, a man clutched a dented spray can and frantically spattered a new white car with blue paint.

"That car's got garlic," Sayed said slowly, in Arabic, so I'd catch the joke. Then in English: "It's so hot the cops will probably be here by lunchtime."

It was the Cairo I'd glimpsed from taxi windows and during walks through the city, but failed to penetrate for lack of a guide. Perched in my twentieth-floor apartment on an island in the Nile, I'd read Naguib Mahfouz novels about Cairo slums crowded with opium addicts and con men like "Zaita the cripple-maker," who rearranges the limbs of aspiring beg-gars—and takes a cut of every cent they earn. I'd taken Mahfouz's city for a Cairo that had long vanished, or perhaps had never existed. But here it was, hot and dusty and close, and here they all were: the car thief, the smuggler, the hash head.

There was honest labor as well, though it wasn't hard to see why so many hustled instead. A pile of logs sprawled at the end of Sayed's street, beside a weed-covered rail line. Brawny men hewed furniture and split firewood with rusty axes as women stooped before each workshop, collecting sawdust in baskets. Sayed said the sawdust was used to soak up the dirt on the floors of their homes—jerry-built sheds of scrap timber, chinked with mud. Children gathered out back, competing with goats to salvage whatever they could from a mountain of smoldering rubbish. They worked intently, pausing only to fling orange peels and rotten tomatoes as the occasional locomotive chugged past.

I had seen the same industry applied to garbage all across Cairo. Each dawn, Coptic Christians in donkey carts wound down from the desert hills to gather the city's rubbish, carrying it back to pick through and recycle. What they couldn't use, they fed to their pigs. The donkeys knew the way so well that they hoofed through the dark without harnesses while their drivers, often children of six or seven, slept in the cart's front seat.

Whatever the Copts didn't take, the doormen in our lobby did. To dispose of anything, we simply set it on the stairwell or fire escape; within minutes it was gone. In the street sometimes, as I walked sipping a Pepsi, children trailed after me to see if I'd discard the bottle. In Cairo, littering was a philanthropic act.

Sayed strolled over to greet one of the women—another cousin, apparently—and children swarmed around him, thrusting their palms into his face. Sayed handed out twenty-five-piaster notes, one at a time, feigning shock at their begging. "They think because I was on top of things here that I must be big in Australia," he said. "They'd do better learning a few tricks from Port Said."

I had visited Sayed at his home in Sydney, a bare semi-detached house with the bathroom out back. He worked at a government welfare office, earning just enough to support his Australian wife and two kids. Even so, by Shubra standards he'd "made it," which is to say he'd made it out of Egypt, an unlikely feat for any but the best-connected Cairenes.

Sayed's mother came to Cairo from a small Nile village and married his father at the age of eleven. She bore her first child at twelve, and twenty-five years later she went into the bathroom and gave birth to number seventeen—Sayed. "She was taking a shower when she felt labor pains," Sayed said. "I popped out on the bathroom floor. After sixteen kids, she didn't think anything of it."

Sayed's father was a journeyman: sometime mechanic, sometime truckdriver, and sometime ill-tempered brawler who landed several times in jail. Sayed wasn't interested in fixing motorbikes—or in snatching purses—though his first job wasn't much better. A hustler in the bazaar taught him to buy polished bluestones for a few piasters, then to resell them for ten times that much as "golden scarabs." Scarabs—dung beetles—were a symbol of resurrection in pharaonic times, and stone scarabs are talismans in modern Egypt.

"We had a complicated price structure, depending on the customer," Sayed said, chuckling at the memory. The highest rate was *tamen saye*, or "tourist price," an unabashed rip-off. Somewhat less was *tamen habibi*, or "friend's price." Cheapest of all was *tamen yahood*, or "Jew's price." Egyptians hated Israelis but held to the stereotype that Jews were clever bargainers, able to buy things for less.

Sayed memorized the scam in French, German and English, to capture the tourist trade, and discovered he had a talent for languages. He secured a student's visa to France, and it was there, while picking grapes to earn some cash, that he met an Australian woman named Jo. Two years later, he migrated with her to Sydney.

"I love Shubra," he said, as we sipped another cup of coffee at the motorcycle shop. "But there was nothing for me here, except family."

Sayed's parents had since died, but one of his sisters still lived in the family's apartment above the motorcycle shop. There was no elevator and no bulb to light our way up the five flights of stairs. The dark steps smelled of urine. Sayed shoved open a door, and we entered a cramped chamber that appeared to double as a living and dining room, with a sofa made up for sleeping as well. There was a picture of Mecca on one wall and a Bruce Lee poster across from it, alongside a photograph of a smiling teenager with a lustrous mane of black hair.

A stout woman in a housedress appeared in the doorway with a baby on each arm. Her hair was covered by a scarf, and the dark circles under her eyes had been hastily daubed with makeup. As she walked across to embrace Sayed, she barely lifted her slippered feet from the floor.

"My sister," Sayed said, lining her up beside the picture on the wall. "Still the most beautiful woman in Shubra." At twenty-nine, she already had eleven children.

She smiled shyly and disappeared into the kitchen, returning a moment later with steaming plates of rice and a basket filled with the puffed pita-like loaves that Egyptians eat by the dozen. It wasn't yet noon, a good two hours before the usual Egyptian lunch break, but she'd kept something cooking, just in case. Sayed tried to beg off eating, insisting that he'd had a big breakfast just a few hours before. His sister answered by bringing out a plate of roasted pigeons, garnered from a birdhouse she kept atop the building. In Arab homes, as in Jewish ones, overeating is an obligatory expression of love.

The rice was covered with a gooey green stew made from a vegetable that tasted like spinach but had the consistency of okra. "It's name is *molokiya*," Sayed said, letting some ooze off a serving spoon. "But we like to call it pharaonic slime." *Molokiya* was such an addiction in Egypt that one cruel and insane ruler named Al-Hakim had prohibited its consumption. The ban, and the mad caliph who imposed it, didn't last very long.

As soon as we finished, men and boys began drifting in from school, from work, or from the tea houses where I'd seen them loafing. Each time a male arrived, Sayed's sister appeared with another plate, another mound of rice and *molokiya*. Daughters were ushered into the kitchen to help with the food and to have a nibble themselves, apart from the men. There must have been a dozen shifts at the table before the afternoon was over.

The men ate quietly, keeping a lazy eye on the television, which broadcast the most popular show in Egypt: a Friday prayer session, led by a man named Sheik Sharawi. Pounding on his Koran, the sheik expounded on the evils of dancing, a hot issue in fundamentalist Egypt.

Sayed slumped on the couch. "Give me a break, sheik," he said, turning down the volume. When visiting Egypt, Sayed let his beard grow, along with his mustache and frizzy black hair. Scruff was a sign of piety among Muslims—and a convenient cover for lapsed souls like Sayed. "If I've got a beard, I don't get lectured about how I should spend more time in the mosque," he said.

Sayed glanced at his watch. It was four o'clock, the siesta hour. "Time to go for dinner at my other sister's," he said. "You're expected."

I looked at him incredulously. The pharaonic slime had formed a dense green sludge somewhere in my upper intestine. I'd been eyeing the couch before Sayed beat me to it.

"What's wrong with you, man?" he said, smiling broadly. "This is just a warm-up. I haven't even started in on my cousins."

Sayed hadn't lied when he tallied his relations; his extended family was a cast of thousands. In the poor confines of Shubra, fathers and brothers provided whatever work could be scavenged, mothers and sisters promised food and shelter when none else could be found. But the obligation cut both ways. For someone who aspired to more, there was the expectation that if you succeeded, you would carry half of Shubra with you.

Each time Sayed visited from Australia, he packed several trunks of clothes, small appliances, and even food for his relatives. And in Cairo he stayed up late each night filling out immigration forms for brothers and cousins who wanted to follow him out of Egypt. "Most of them will never make it," Sayed confided. "But they keep filling out the forms and saving. It gives them something to hope for."

Between translating forms and slurping plates of *molokiya*, Sayed offered to show me the sights of Cairo. I had spent most of my time in Egypt under self-imposed house arrest, plotting stories that would get me out of the bewildering city. Playing tourist for a few days was just what was needed to cure my Cairophobia.

"We'll do it properly,' he promised, "not the way its done in guidebooks." For Sayed, raised on the Arab socialism of Gamal Abdel Nasser, this meant accompanying each sight with footnotes on the greed and cruelty of Egypt's rulers, from the "self-indulgent pharaohs" to the "decadent Turks" to the "parasitic classes" who prospered under Anwar Sadat.

"Most of this is imperial rubbish," he said, racing through the Egyptian Museum. We hurried past the rooms of exhumed mummies, the exquisite sarcophagi, the dimly lit chambers bursting with friezes and obelisks. Sayed broke his stride only once to inspect the miniature tombs encasing King Tut's mummified viscera. "Lungs, liver, stomach, yuk," Sayed recited, reading the labels beneath the tiny gold-plated coffins, each one containing a different organ. Behind us, a French tour guide explained that the only item not embalmed was Tut's food supply for eternity: forty jars of wine, a hundred baskets of fruit, bread, and roasted duck. "A whole village could have lived for a year on what that fat pharaoh took with him," Sayed said, still staring at the pickled innards.

From there we caught a taxi to the Pyramids. The Great Pyramid of Cheops lies just seven miles as the dust flies from downtown Cairo. On a clear day you can see the Pyramids from the tops of city buildings. Postcards artfully obscure this proximity to Cairo, showing the monuments against a backdrop of boundless desert. And it is true that the arid expanse just west of the Pyramids stretches with little interruption to distant Libya. But point the camera the other way and the Pyramids are framed against a sprawling, smog-shrouded megalopolis of fifteen million. The city now reaches all the way from the Giza Plateau, on which the Pyramids stand, to the Moqattam Hills twelve miles away, where the giant building blocks were hewn and then floated across the flooded Nile.

When Gustave Flaubert visited Egypt in 1849, the trip from Cairo to Giza was still an all-day affair, beginning on donkey-back, continuing across the Nile on a small boat ("A corpse in its coffin is borne past us," he wrote) and ending with an afternoon's ride across the floodplain. Finally, he wrote, the Sphinx "grew larger and larger, and rose out of the ground like a dog lifting itself up."

Modern times have compressed the journey, and increased its peril. Egyptians undergo an odd personality change behind the wheel of a car. In every other setting, aggression and impatience are frowned upon. The unofficial Egyptian anthem *"Bokra, Insha'allah, Malesh"* (Tomorrow, God Willing, Never Mind) isn't just an excuse for laziness. In a society requiring millennial patience, it is also a social code dictating that no one make too much of a fuss about things. But put an Egyptian in the driver's seat and he shows all the calm and consideration of a hooded swordsman delivering Islamic justice.

As soon as our taxi sprang clear of the clotted city center, the driver began ducking and weaving through the traffic, looking for daylight. He swerved from right lane to left lane and back to right, then, spotting a space the width of a bicycle between the two lanes, he bulled his way forward and created a third. Clear once again, he resumed his sickening weave from right to left to right. I felt as if I were traveling inside a wandering eye.

Whatever lane lines once existed had been rubbed out by dust, rubber and hooves. Cairo was also the first city I'd seen where policeman stood at intersections simply to enforce the traffic lights. Unfortunately, there weren't any police on the Pyramids Road. Our driver raced through one red light and then another, honking to warn cars on the cross street against plummeting into the intersection just because *their* light was green. At green lights he honked again, to ward off anyone running the red. He even honked at a street-car motoring slowly across his path.

But then, Cairo drivers honk even when the road is empty. "It makes the car go faster," Sayed explained. The horn is the one piece of Egyptian taxis that always works, long after the doors have rusted, the window levers have snapped off, and the meter has been hit with a hammer, or fed wooden slugs. Egyptians also are fond of driving at night without headlights, keeping them in reserve to use as a spare horn when a simple honk won't do. Honk-honk-flash-flash, honk-flash-flash-flash; they burrow like moles through the night.

Not surprisingly, Egyptian drivers are the most homicidal in the world, killing themselves and others at a rate twenty-five times that of drivers in America (and without the aid of alcohol). Motorists in other Arab countries are almost as driving-impaired. The only insight I ever gained into this suicidal abandon came from a speeding Kurdish driver, after he'd recklessly run over a bird.

"Allah wanted it dead," he said. The same fatalism applies to passengers.

We reached the Giza Plateau in the time it took a team of Egyptian slaves to haul one block of limestone across ten feet of desert sand. "The Pyramids," Sayed sighed, sucking in the desert air. "One of the seven wonders of Egyptian greed." Hustlers enveloped us the moment we climbed from the taxi, offering rides on mounts so decrepit that they could have been dragooned from the Egyptian Museum. There were mules, ponies, buggies, and camels of every size and shape. "One hump! Two hump! No hump!" cried one young boy. There were "guides," "not guides" (who offered to fend off the former) and "watchmen" who promised to beat back both).

It is difficult to gaze in awe at the wonders of ancient Egypt with modern Egypt tugging so insistently at your sleeve.

"*Habibi*, my friend," asked one camel driver, following my gaze up Cheops' pyramid. "You looking for me?"

"Actually, no. I'm looking at Cheops." I buried my head

in a guidebook: 455 feet tall, for 4,500 years the tallest edifice in the world.

"*Habibi*, my friend," the voice nagged again. "You get much better look from my camel."

"Thank you, no. I'd rather look for free." Over two million stone blocks in Cheops' pyramid, its base covering eleven acres.

"*Habibi*, my friend." The driver dropped his jaw in a convincing facsimile of shock. "Who said anything about money?"

The Pyramids hustle is horizontally integrated. It begins with the cabbie, who happens to know the cheapest camel driver in all of Egypt, who happens to take tourists on a long detour to visit a boy on a burro selling Pepsis and papyrus, who happens to know a man with a Polaroid, who also happens to be an expert guide, offering, for an undisclosed sum, to reveal deep funeral chambers adorned with pharaonic graffiti. This last service was tempting. Ramses Loves Nefertari? Ozymandias Slept Here?

"Whatever it says, you can be sure he put it there himself, probably this morning," Sayed said, shooing the man away. Scaling a few steps of the pyramid, Sayed delivered his own expert lecture instead; on the geometry of Old Kingdom architecture ("all lines, no curves, because Egypt is so flat"), on the significance of death in ancient Egypt ("people didn't live long in those days, so death was a very big deal") and on the decadence of the pharaohs ("they slept with animals, which is why we have the Sphinx"). With that, he skipped back down to the ground and held out his hand, declaring, "Who said anything about money?"

Con artistry at the Pyramids represents the most dynamic sector of the Egyptian economy and certainly one of the oldest. When the Greek historian Herodotus stopped off to see Cheops' pyramid in 450 B.C., he asked the meaning of certain inscriptions and was duly informed that they recorded "the quantity of radishes, onions and garlic consumed by the laborers who constructed it." Herodotus didn't say how much he paid for this dubious intelligence.

By 1849, when Flaubert arrived, hieroglyphics had lost much of their mystery. "One is irritated by the number of imbeciles' names written everywhere," he complained after finding, at the very top of Cheops' pyramid, the signature of a fellow Parisian, "a certain Buffard, 79 Rue Saint-Martin, wallpaper manufacturer, in black letters."

But it was left to the acid wit of Mark Twain, seventeen years later, to describe the true curse of the pharaohs. "We suffered torture no pen can describe from the hungry appeals for bucksheesh that gleamed from Arab eyes," he wrote. "We were besieged by a rabble of muscular Egyptians and Arabs who wanted the contract of dragging us to the top. . . . Of course they contracted that the varlets who dragged us up should not mention bucksheesh once. For such is the usual routine. Of course we contracted with them, paid them, were delivered into the hands of the draggers, dragged up the Pyramids, and harried and bedeviled for bucksheesh from the foundation clear to the summit."

Islam attaches no shame to begging and much virtue to charity; to Egyptians in particular, baksheesh is a birthright and a blessing. In eighteenth-century Cairo there was even a beggars' guild, so wealthy that it presented the city's governor with a mount and saddle.

But at Cheops' pyramid the pleas for money know no bounds. Exploring the frontiers of Egyptian greed, Twain offered one of his tormentors a hundred dollars "to jump off this pyramid head first.

"He pondered a moment, and would have done it, I think, but his mother arrived, then, and interfered. Her tears moved me—I never can look upon the tears of a woman with indifference—and I said I would give her a hundred dollars to jump off, too."

Western avarice has left its mark on ancient monuments as well. Every European visitor to Egypt, from Napoleon onward, made sure to return home with his very own obelisk or mummy. One nineteenth-century vandal even wrote in his journal that he found the huge sculpted head of Ramses II "near the remains of its body and chair, with its face upwards, and apparently smiling on me at the thought of being taken to England." It was considered good fun in Victorian days to unravel mummies at fairgrounds, and the powder of mummied flesh was a staple of London druggists.

Now the Egyptians have full custody of their monuments—and full freedom to destroy them. A slum sprawls less than a hundred yards from the Sphinx, almost lapping at the man-lion's paws. Raw sewage and fetid canals seep beneath the Giza Plateau, unsettling the ancient monuments. A few months after my visit with Sayed, a six-hundred-pound piece of the Sphinx's shoulder separated and tumbled to the sand, its most serious injury since Ottoman musketeers used the Sphinx's nose for target practice (or so the legend goes). There were also dire predictions that the Sphinx and the Pyramids—even the vast Temple of Luxor—might soon succumb to smog, sewage and rising ground water, eroding to dust in the space of fifty years.

Modern Egypt inherited many things from the pharaohs—regal good looks, papyrus, bureaucracy—but a talent for building isn't among them. Egyptians have the opposite of a Midas touch; everything they set their hands on turns to dust. Even spanking-new skyscrapers seem, after a year or two, fragile and filthy lean-tos. It isn't just a question of money or expertise; fatigue and fatalism have so corroded the culture that Egyptians have simply stopped caring. Buildings collapse for lack of basic maintenance. Sewer lines explode, flooding whole neighborhoods. Dead horses lie rotting on the beach at Alexandria. And Egyptians muddle on, as they have for millennia, muttering *malesh*—never mind—and gazing toward Mecca in prayer.

Soon after my visit to the Pyramids, the supervisor of the building Geraldine and I occupied wrote a brief summary of the structure's condition. The building, one of the newest and reputedly one of the nicest apartment houses on the Nile island of Gezira, was described as follows:

1. The marble is falling off from pillars inside and outside the building.
2. The main stairs are collapsing.
3. The walls and ceilings are in poor condition, filled with dust and spiders.
4. There are constant breakdowns of the electricity, the lighting in the apartments, and the elevators.
5. The three water pumps do not work because maintenance was stopped a year ago. The room which contains the three pumps has no floor tiles and has become a lake full of water.

None of this was news to us, except the fact that the building had a supervisor at all. Still, that someone had bothered to catalogue the building's woes was in itself remarkable. The response was not. Nothing happened. What was worse, I found myself not caring. The water main burst? *Malesh*, I'll shower with bottled water. There are eleven tenants trapped in the elevator again? *Malesh*, I'll walk the twenty floors. The mail's being tossed in a forgotten storeroom filled with dust and spiders? *Malesh*, I doubt there was anything important. And I'd been in Cairo only a few months. In another year, I feared, Egyptian inertia would so overwhelm me that I'd be clambering over mummified residents as I scrambled through the unlit stairwell.

It doesn't take long in Cairo to realize that the only way to survive is by commandeering fixers who can cut corners (read "bribe") and keep things ticking feebly along. And it wasn't long before I met the ablest fixer of them all, Hassan Risk, a sweaty man with a carefully clipped mustache.

Hassan held a salaried job for which he no doubt earned the same hundred pounds a month—about fifty dollars—as every other Egyptian employee. But he also appeared on the payroll of every journalist in town, earning a hundred pounds a month from each of them as well. His only apparent function was delivering the monthly phone bill.

This in itself was not unusual. Hand-delivering bills is

yet another scheme for creating employment in a country
with an exploding birthrate and a collapsing economy (Egypt
must feed 55 million people from an arable area the size of
Holland's). It is also a way to make sure the bill doesn't end
up in a pile of dust and spiders, with the rest of the mail.
On some days, the lobby of our building was crowded with
able-bodied, well-educated men waving electricity bills,
newspaper bills, delivery bills—often totaling no more than
a few piasters, not counting baksheesh.

Hassan Risk's bill-delivery service came with a twist:
you paid him an outrageous sum to deliver the bill so that
you had him on call when you really needed him. Cairenes
could wait months, even years, to have a phone installed and
to have it repaired when a breakdown occurred. A computer
installation could take forever. Hassan could make it happen
overnight—for a price.

"Mr. Tony," he would patiently explain, holding a
frayed computer line in his palm, "I must have five hundred
bounds for the Telecommunications Ministry." He would
assume a serious expression and pantomime a man dealing
cards around a table. It wasn't hard to imagine a dusty office
in one of the Kafkaesque government blocks downtown,
filled with supernumeraries slumped on desks strewn with
papers and empty cups of tea, suddenly stirring awake as
Hassan arrived with the cash. It was, of course, understood
that Hassan would be dealt in as well.

It was also understood that if you didn't deal Hassan in
each month, choosing to pick up your phone bill instead,
things might happen. Phone calls fading out in midsentence.
Service mysteriously cut. No one available to fix the phone
for weeks or months. Journalists often bitched about Hassan
Risk and his monthly handout—subject to self-declared
raises—and insisted they could do without him. In two
years' time I never met anyone who did.

And so at the end of each month, I waited for the call
that always came.

"Mr. Tony? This is Hassan Risk. I have here your May
bill for thirty-six hundred bounds. Also, there is my salary

for this month. May I come? *Insha'allah*, I be there in fifteen minutes."

Insha'allah is the phrase ending all statements about the future in Egypt. It means "if God wills it." Hassan Risk was the only Egyptian I knew who put *insha'allah* in front of future plans instead of after, as though God's will were secondary to his own. Watching from the balcony as he double-parked his fancy Mercedes in front of our building and opened a trunk packed with cables and videos and telephone bills, I often wondered if Hassan Risk was the richest man in Cairo.

6

CAIRO NIGHTS
Dancing Sheik to Sheik

All Mohammedans love a spectacle.
—FYODOR DOSTOEVSKY

The New Arizona nightclub announced itself with a broken window and a sign that read: "europins and jabanese welcome."

"Don't worry," Sayed said. "No self-respecting tourist would be caught dead here." That was why he had chosen the club, to show me "real Cairo culture." We had done the Egyptian Museum, the Pyramids, the Khan-el-Khalili bazaar. Belly dancing was the last of Sayed's "must sees," and no venue but the New Arizona would do.

There was a picture gallery just inside the door, hinting at the enticing dancers awaiting us upstairs. The snapshots were arranged according to size, as in an elementary-school portrait. Towering above the others was a whale who went by the name of Ashgan. "My favorite," Sayed chuckled, grandly offering to pay the cover charge. On a Thursday night, the start of the Arab weekend, admission at the New Arizona was eighty cents.

Upstairs, in the dimly lit club, moldering wallpaper peeled from the bar and week-old balloons drooped from pillars surrounding the stage. Though the club was empty, it was impossible to find a table with an unobstructed view. "More poles than in Warsaw," grumbled Terry, an Austra-

lian friend of Sayed's who had arrived in Cairo that day. As
we waited for our beers, a small man in a turban crept out
from behind a pillar, slipped a plate of nuts onto our table
and vanished. I idly nibbled at a peanut. The man in the
turban darted out from behind his pillar again.

"Two bounds," he said.

I looked at him blankly and said, "Just add it to the
bill."

The man shook his head. "I not work for New Arizona." He was a free-lancer, like me, hustling peanuts under
cover of the club. There was also a free-lance flower seller,
a cigarette peddler, and a photographer who snapped our
table and returned with a picture so spotted that we appeared
to be sitting in a sandstorm. He pointed at a ceiling fan
circulating dust and lukewarm air, and shrugged apologetically. The club was a miniature bazaar and we its only
patrons, bleeding piasters.

"Don't let them help you out of your chair," Sayed
warned. "They'll make you pay for that, too."

At eleven P.M. the bar began to fill, mostly with visitors
from other parts of the Arab world. After several months in
the Middle East I had made a hobby of identifying nationality by the cut of a man's robe, the shape of his headdress,
the way he said certain words. The two slim men in blue
jeans and black-checked scarves were obviously Palestinian.
The small, dusky man with a furrowed brow and a cheap
jacket was Yemeni; his *jambiya*, apparently, had been left at
the hotel. Even darker—African-black—were the Sudanese,
with their enormous, sloppy turbans. But I wasn't sure about
two white-robed men in red-checked head scarves, who took
a table at the front. Even in winter, in cosmopolitan Cairo,
they carried a whiff of the desert with them. One man kicked
off his sandals and sat cross-legged in his chair, as if on the
floor of a goat-hair tent. The other had a dark, handsome
face, seared by wind and sand.

"Kuwaitis?" I ventured.

"Saudis," Sayed said.

"How can you tell?"

"The scarves." Saudis swtiched from white to red in winter, while most other "Gulfies" didn't. "And the way they're being treated."

Sure enough, their beer arrived in a bucket of ice. The waiter even shooed the nut-seller back behind his pillar and told the photographer to piss off. It was the New Arizona equivalent of red-carpet treatment, the same slavish devotion that the debt-ridden Egyptian government showed Saudi officials visiting town.

Once the newcomers had settled in, a jovial brown-skinned man appeared on the stage, waving a microphone. His threadbare suit matched his skin, giving him the look of a well-worn teddy bear.

"*Ahlan wa'salan*," he said. Welcome, most welcome. Then, spotting us, he added in English: "Good night to you. What country?"

Terry immediately yelled "Australia!" and the m.c. broke into song, offering "special greetings" to the land Down Under. Between verses, he looked suggestively in our direction. He repeated the lyrics five or six times before Sayed finally elbowed Terry. "You're supposed to tip him, mate."

Terry dug in his pocket and produced a five-pound note. "Anything to stop him singing," he grumbled. The m.c. pocketed the bill and moved across the stage, offering "special greetings" to the "land of Mecca." The barefoot Saudi quickly coughed up a ten-pound note. Then the m.c. began singing "black is sweet as sugar" to the Sudanese and "Egypt loves Iraq" to a visitor from Baghdad. Each matched the Saudi contribution.

As the m.c. milked the crowd, band members crept onto the stage and tuned their instruments. It was a weird ensemble. One man banged listlessly at a tambourine, pausing every few minutes to pop what looked like an antacid pill into his mouth. Beside him sat a cross-eyed accordion player. There was also an electric guitarist in shaded glasses, a man with one cymbal, and a piano player missing three fingers on his right hand.

The guitarist plucked his first chord and sent feedback screeching through the club. The m.c. ducked behind a stained wine-red screen, and three acrobats appeared: a lithe boy of ten or so, a sullen girl of about fifteen, and a middle-aged man, apparently the acrobats' father, who did nothing but shift a card table upon which the boy and girl performed some of their stunts.

Most of the routine was tumbling-class stuff: cartwheels, somersaults, headstands. Then the girl attempted a difficult and bizarre maneuver. Bending back her head, she raised one foot and nibbled at a piece of feta cheese, impaled on a fork held between her toes. As she closed her teeth on the feta, the fork shot across the floor, taking a bit of cheese with it. The girl spat the rest of the feta into her palm, scowled at her father and hurried off the stage, followed soon after by the other two, leaving the card table.

The m.c. reappeared and began prattling in Arabic.

"What's he saying?" I asked Sayed.

"Special greetings to the Saudis." This was to become the night's monotonous refrain, and never failed to entice another ten-pound note from the barefoot sheik's bottomless billfold.

"This is why we despise the Saudis," Sayed said, sympathizing with his impoverished countrymen. "We must go begging to the bedouin."

The band was joined now by a man with a bongo drum who thumped a steady, droning beat. Boom, boom, tac-a-tac. Boom, tac-a-tac. Then a dancer named Fifi sashayed onto the stage, though "dancer" wasn't the first word that came to mind as she bumped into the acrobats' card table. Baby fat bunched around the teenager's shoulders. An elastic bandage covered one wrist. Shuffling across the creaking floorboards, Fifi had the stage presence of an amateur wrestler.

Belly dancing, when expertly done, is a series of isolated quivers in which the performer vibrates her stomach or chest while the rest of her body remains sculpturally still. Traditionally, it is unabashedly erotic.

"Kuchuk's dance is brutal," Flaubert wrote of a private show during his journey down the Nile. The Frenchman became so carried away that he promptly escorted the women off the stage, performing a "coup" with one dancer ("she is very corrupt and writhing. . . . I stain the divan") and another with Kuchuk, holding her necklace between his teeth ("I felt like a tiger"). The women then resumed their dance, so sensually that the musicians had to be blindfolded so they wouldn't become too aroused to strum their instruments.

There was little danger of that at the New Arizona. As Fifi clunked through her moves, timing her pelvic thrusts to the bongo's boom tac-a-tac, the musicians looked about as titillated as mummies. The dyspeptic tambourine player even forgot about his antacid pills and drifted off to sleep.

Fifi also wasn't showing any belly; a gauzy veil concealed the space between her sequined bra and spangled skirt. Sayed explained that ex-president Nasser, who regarded belly dancing as colonial and corrupt, had decreed that dancers cover up. A quarter century later, Islamic fundamentalism had picked up where Nasserism left off. There was now a special squad, called the "politeness police," moving covertly from club to club and arresting dancers who showed any belly or whose bump and grind was too licentious.

"I don't think Fifi has anything to fear," Sayed said, as she thudded across the stage, occasionally glancing at the watch on her unbandaged wrist. The performance was also interrupted every few minutes by the cross-eyed accordion player shouting into the microphone.

"What's he saying?"

"Special greetings to the Saudis."

The barefoot sheik approached the stage and stuffed a ten-pound note into Fifi's bra. She gave him an extra wiggle before scampering off the stage.

I felt bad for Fifi and clapped as loud as I could. This brought a return visit from the nut-seller, the photographer and the flower man.

"That wasn't so bad for openers," I said hopefully. Surely Fifi was just a warm-up for the expert dancers still to come. Sayed shook his head. "It's all downhill from here."

Dancer #2 looked like the fat woman at a circus freak show. Fat bulged from beneath her shoulder straps and cantilevered over her low-slung skirt. Even without the midriff veil, her navel would have been obscured by rolls of flesh. Belly dancing, it seemed, was not a slimming occupation.

Her dancing was even less enthusiastic than Fifi's. She also had the disconcerting habit of blowing her nose mid-dance and stuffing the used tissue into the ample cleavage of her spangled bra, beside the ten-pound notes offered by the Saudis. "Good God," Terry groaned, staring into his beer. "I came eight thousand miles for this?"

Dancer #3, a gorgon named Geyla, wore a skin-tight dress with huge sunbursts exploding on her bottom, breasts and crotch. She didn't dance at all, preferring to strut across the stage, twirling a baton in the shape of a giant candy cane and poking it in patrons' faces. It was in the middle of her act, as she leaned down to tweak the nose of the now blind-drunk Saudi, that I made a disturbing discovery: the more obese and abusive the dancers seemed to me, the more alluring they were to everyone else.

Geyla bounced her candy cane off the Saudi's brow. Then she grasped a handful of peanuts from a nearby table and hurled it in his face. He squealed with delight and stuffed another bill in her dress. The free-lance nut-seller appeared from behind a column to plant a fresh plate of peanuts.

Geyla was offering "special greetings" to some late-arriving Kuwaitis when the club's electricity gave out, mercifully plunging the stage into darkness. A minute later the lights returned, another dancer took the stage—and police burst into the club. They headed straight for the table of Palestinians, rifling through the men's pockets and emptying packs of cigarettes and Chiclets. Then they left, taking two of the men with them. The dancing quickly resumed.

I asked a man at the next table what the search was about.

"It is usual," he said. "They are checking identifications."

"In Chiclet packs?"

The man shrugged. "I am just the manager here. It is best not to ask too many questions of the police." The man's name was Samy Salaam, and he invited me to join him for a beer. The New Arizona was beginning to look like a feature story, and I was curious about the manager's perspective.

"How do you rate the quality of tonight's dance?" I asked.

He frowned. "Poor to awful," he said. Ashgan the whale had just taken to the stage. "But it does not matter," Samy continued. "My customers drink, they joke, they say bad words. They do not know good dance or bad dance."

Ashgan tripped over her microphone cord and fell. For a moment it seemed the stage might collapse. "She must be feminine, that is all," Samy said. "Otherwise the men do not like her."

"And big," I said.

Samy looked at me quizzically. "Big? These are not big girls."

The floorboards shuddered as Ashgan hopped from right to left. Was I missing something? Could there be bigger women still to come?

"No, Ashgan is the last for tonight," Samy said. "But she is still young. There is room for some growth." He said it the way a football coach sizes up a freshman nose tackle. "Arab men like women they can get their hands around," he added.

Samy obviously knew his clientele. All around us, men pounded their tables and screamed as Ashgan continued her Richter-scale gyrations. But Samy feared for the future of his business. The government now required that dancers be licensed by an agency called the Department of Artistic

Inspection. To placate the fundamentalists, the department had recently stopped issuing permits.

It was the Egyptian way of dealing with sensitive issues. Desperate to cut the national budget, the government wanted to raise the price of bread, but feared this would spark riots. So it had solved the problem by coarsening the state-subsidized loaves—with sand, it was said—so that Egyptians had to buy a more expensive grade. Officially, Egyptians could still get loaves for five piasters, just as belly dancers could still get licenses. In practice, neither was a realistic possibility.

"Someday all these dancers will be old and fat and then I will have no more club," Samy said. "There is a limit to what customers, even my customers, will pay for."

Looking around at the tumultous crowd cheering Ashgan on, I wasn't so sure he was right.

Sayed left for Australia a few days later, but not before buying a dozen drums to sell back in Sydney. He gave us one, coaching me to bang out the monotonous boom-tac-tac to encourage Geraldine's nascent career as a belly dancer. He thought she had potential. "Eat plenty of *basbousa*," he advised her, recommending a favorite Egyptian dessert, a cholesterol nightmare of nuts, oil and fried dough. "In a few months, a year maybe, you could have a very nice figure for belly dancing."

Before going, Sayed also introduced me to another Egyptian who would become a close friend: a slim, dark Nubian named Yousri. The romance of Yousri's origins intrigued me. Shortly before coming to Cairo, I had visited the British Museum and stared at a frieze pilfered from a pharaoh's tomb called "Scenes of the Conquest of Nubia." It showed African-looking men swathed in leopard skins, fleeing before the chariots of Ramses II. They became, I imagined, the first of the Nubian slaves. Until I met Yousri, I hadn't realized that a people called Nubians still existed.

Nubia is an Egyptian province near Sudan, in Upper Egypt, so called because it lies upstream on the north-flowing Nile. Several millennia after Ramses swept south with his chariots, the conquest of Nubia was completed, first by crop failure and then, irrevocably, by the flooding of farms by the Aswan High Dam. The temples of Abu Simbel were moved to higher ground, and thousands of Nubian peasants swarmed north to the slums of Cairo.

As rural folk, accustomed to tight-knit village life, Nubians brought with them a reputation for trustworthiness, and they quickly took up residence as *boabs*, the ubiquitous Cairo doormen who live on the baksheesh they collect for opening elevators, hoisting bags and just generally keeping an eye on things. Perched before every building, sitting on bits of cardboard or on creaking wicker chairs, Nubian *boabs* in robes and turbans lend a leisurely, almost countrified air to the otherwise hectic metropolis.

Yousri's father graduated from *boab*dom to caretaker of a city mosque and sent his children to school so they could aim higher. Yousri's mother, like Sayed's, knew little beyond the complexities of raising seven children. "She couldn't even read numbers," Yousri told me. "We kids were her eyes and ears."

Yousri met Sayed at school, and together they studied languages, particularly Hebrew, which enabled them to spend their mandatory military service in a radio room, eavesdropping on the Israelis, instead of in a trench. By the time Yousri finished university, he spoke fluent English as well as a smattering of Turkish, Farsi and French. He had also picked up—through close study of movies, I suspected—a smooth, aristocratic bearing to complement his aquiline nose, and skin that glowed like well-burnished copper. Yousri's face wouldn't have looked out of place on the lid of a pharaoh's coffin.

In America, a man with Yousri's assets would have completed his father's ascent up the social ladder, becoming, perhaps, a businessman or professional. In Egypt, he found himself at thirty still living in an apartment with his parents and working the graveyard shift at the reception desk of a hotel near the airport.

"This is the most a man of my background can hope for," he said, without melodrama, flicking ash from the Cleopatra cigarette he held daintily between long fingers.

Like millions of other Egyptian men, Yousri had tried the alternative—lonely servitude in the hot, joyless cities of the Persian Gulf—and returned home after three years. "I do not like being a second-class citizen," he said. Though a man could earn three times the Egyptian wage in Kuwait or Saudi Arabia, the Gulfies were known for treating their imported labor with condescension.

Yousri also couldn't abide the drudgery of working for the Egyptian government, stamping papers in some outstation of the Cairo bureaucracy. The hotel paid no better than the state, but it offered Yousri the hope that someday, some way, he might do what Sayed had done and meet a woman with whom he could migrate to the West.

"I'm choking here," he told me one morning after a long night's shift at the hotel. "Just work and sleep and more work. This is the life of a donkey, not a man."

The only escape I could offer was a sympathetic ear and the occasional decent meal. By Cairo standards, my modest free-lance income made me a pasha, and I enjoyed treating Yousri to dinner at a Western-style restaurant near my home. He always ate slowly and made sure to leave some steak on his plate, lest anyone think he was ravenous.

But after three outings, Yousri turned down my invitations, saying he had to be at work early or that he wasn't feeling well. The subtext wasn't hard to ferret out. Yousri wanted to reciprocate, but taking me to a restaurant of similar standard would have cost him twenty dollars—half his monthly wage. Taking me to someplace less was, for Yousri, unthinkable. He was the proudest man I'd ever met.

So we began meeting instead at the sprawling Khan-el-Khalili bazaar, where we could take turns picking up the tab for sipping tea and smoking water pipes—and rarely spend more than two dollars. Our favorite haunt became Fishawy's, a back-alley teahouse that had been open twenty-four hours a day for two hundred years, without evidence of a single renovation. One-bladed fans clung precariously to the ceiling, looking as though they might descend at any moment to decapitate unwary patrons. Century-old dust coated the mirrors and the unflattering portraits of the café's former owners: portly men in Ottoman fezzes, perched on tiny burros. Rickety chairs and tables spilled into the alley, already crowded with peddlers selling papyrus, Korans and hashish. It was there, stirring the coals atop three-foot-high hookahs, that we plotted and replotted Yousri's flight from Egypt, and talked long into the night about women.

"See that one there?" he said one evening, pointing into a crowd of women in modest Islamic dress, promenading through the medieval streets.

"She's religious," I said. "Off-limits, right?"

Yousri smiled. "Look again. See how tightly her dress clings? And the braid holding her veil? She does not dress this way for Allah."

Yousri wasn't interested in devout women—or their counterfeit—and he didn't go for makeup and Western coiffures, either. "These women are not real," he complained. "If they wash their faces you do not recognize them."

Even the occasional woman who caught Yousri's eye was quickly dismissed as beyond his reach, usually because they looked wealthier than he was, an imposing barrier in class-ridden Cairo. "No middle-class woman will marry the son of a Nubian *boab*," he said. Women of similar rank posed a challenge as well. To propose marriage he would need an apartment, furniture, a dowry. His brothers had achieved this by returning to work in the Gulf, spending only one month each year with their families in Cairo.

"I do not want to waste the best years of my life in the desert, just so I can marry a woman I will never see," he said with characteristic dignity. The only other option was to take up residence in the City of the Dead, a Cairo necropolis whose above-ground tombs had become cheap housing for half a million people, many of them newlyweds.

Yousri was, in a word, trapped; too poor to live as he wanted, too proud to live any other way. All the things I took for granted—a wife, my own place, work I enjoyed— were denied Yousri for no other reason than the lots we'd drawn at birth. I made it my mission to equalize the stakes.

With Geraldine, I canvassed single women in America and Australia, thinking of any who might find Yousri a suitable mate, or who might consent to a marriage of convenience. When several of them visited Cairo, we invited Yousri over, on the off chance that some spark would strike. It never did. Each time, Yousri's charm and manners deserted him. He'd either retire shyly or come on much too strong.

"She likes me," he giddily confided one night on the landing outside our apartment, waiting for the elevator that never came. "I can tell already." But he was, unfortunately, wrong.

One night, after a particularly awkward encounter, I attempted a bit of coaching. "Ask about her work. Talk about politics. Anything but her legs."

He nodded. "Maybe she does not like me because I am Nubian."

"Nonsense. It sounds exotic."

"Yes, but all anyone knows is that Nubians were slaves."

"Maybe she's into bondage."

Yousri smiled, but I could tell he was angry. He was still angry when I met him a few nights later at Fishawy's.

"It is easy for you to get to know women," he said finally, staring into his tea. "It is not so easy for me."

Or for any single man in Cairo. Few Egyptian families would consent to have their daughters go out alone with a man. Ushers patrolled movie theaters, shining flashlights in the face of any couple daring to hold hands. It was part of Yousri's job at the hotel to make sure that Egyptian couples checking in for the night could give some proof of marriage. If they couldn't, Yousri booked them into separate rooms and another worker made "virtue checks" through the night to confirm that they remained apart.

The most an unmarried man could hope for was a furtive kiss and "brushing"—rubbing genitals with a woman while fully clothed. "Some girls expect a proposal of marriage, even for this," Yousri said. Then he confessed what I'd already suspected; though handsome and well-spoken, Yousri remained, at thirty, a virgin.

We gave up on matchmaking and tried to get Yousri a

visa through other means. This proved equally fruitless. Every Western embassy in Cairo—as in other Third World capitals—was a thinly disguised fortress against visa-seekers. Even tourist visas were unobtainable; it was widely assumed, with good reason, that an Egyptian would overstay a tourist visa and remain illegally. Some Western embassies charged two hundred pounds—twice the average monthly wage in Egypt—just for the privilege of filling out an application. The risk wasn't just monetary. A stamp in your passport saying that a visa had been denied all but destroyed your chances of successfully applying to that or any other Western embassy in the future.

So Yousri tested the alternatives: bogus applications, and bribes. He tried claiming medical cause, saying he had a back problem that could only be treated abroad. When this failed, he turned, inevitably, to fixers: shady men who promised that a visa could be "arranged," for a price. This was the Egyptian way, I knew, and I lent him the money to go ahead.

Soon after, Yousri began calling me from work and whispering over the phone line, "The man says my visa to Australia is coming any day." Three months later, the visa was still coming, any day.

After a time I began resisting Yousri's bleak vision of Egypt, both for his own sake and for mine. Unlike Sayed, whose cynicism was leavened by humor and by a genuine affection for Egypt, Yousri had an unremittingly grim outlook. I found it depressing to dwell on Cairo's faults, and I found it even more depressing that Yousri, who would probably remain there forever, found so little to sustain him.

"You need a new job," I told him one night.

"I need a new country," he replied.

"How about asking for a raise?"

"I did. They said in another year I might get ten percent more." That would bring his wage to sixty-six cents an hour, up from sixty.

Events conspired to alienate Yousri still further. One day his father woke up feeling sick, went back to bed, and died. Soon after, his mother took ill and went to a hospital. She lasted two weeks. "The doctors told us her organs were enlarged," Yousri said. "They said this was common for a woman in her fifties." It was the sort of mysterious ailment that often carried away Egyptians, frequently before they reached middle age. One of Yousri's sisters had died at twenty-four from what he called a "poisoned pregnancy." Most of Egypt's well-trained doctors had long ago fled to higher-paying jobs in the Gulf or the West, and hospitals in Cairo weren't much more sanitary than the streets outside.

I tried to cheer Yousri up with a trip to the Roy Rogers restaurant at the Marriott Hotel. But the sight of young Egyptians like himself, clad in kerchiefs and cowboy hats, serving up french fries, only made him more depressed. The restaurant's manager had "Dr." on the name tag pinned to his red-striped shirt. "You see," Yousri said, "Egypt is full of people like me. Too much education and too little to do."

We toured the lobby until just before midnight, when Yousri had to go to work. Then, at the door, two security guards pounced on Yousri, grasping his elbows and bombarding him with questions. Who are you? Where is your identification? What are you doing here at midnight with a foreigner? I explained that Yousri was a friend and the interrogation finally ended, but only after a warning to Yousri that he never return there in my company.

Egypt, though much freer than most Arab countries, keeps close watch on its citizens. Egyptians are barred from hotel casinos. Soldiers stand guard on the Nile bridges each night, stopping cars and quizzing drivers. And Yousri was suspected of unspecified offenses simply because he was Egyptian and I was not.

"It is a way to remind us that we are not free," he said, hurrying into the night, humiliated. I didn't hear from him for weeks. Then the late-night phone calls resumed. "The man says my visa is coming," he whispered over the hotel phone. "Any day."

7

BAGHDAD
In the Land Without Weather

If man has not heeded my words which I have inscribed on my monument, may the Lord kindle disorder that cannot be put down and despair to be the ruin of him in his habitation, may he allot unto him as his destiny a reign of sighs, days of scarcity and years of famine, thick darkness and death in the twinkling of an eye.
—THE CODE OF HAMMURABI, ARTICLE 250

On a midsummer's night in Baghdad, soon after an Iraqi triumph in its eight-year war with Iran, Mohammed Abid stood outside his restaurant by the Tigris River, poking a net at the last fish circling in a tiled tub of water.

"Tonight Iraq celebrates victory and eats a very great deal," he said. "But in the morning, maybe we find that peace is like this fish, a slippery thing that swims round and round and sneaks away."

Snaring the river fish, Mohammed flopped it onto the sidewalk to see if it was of suitable size for my dinner. Then he picked up a rusted monkey wrench.

"We must never forget," he said, raising the tool in the air, "that Iraq has enemies everywhere."

"Persians." Thuuunk.

"Syrians." Thwaaap.

"Zionists." Thluuub.

He gutted the bludgeoned fish with a few deft strokes

and propped it over a wooden fire. "No one," he said, wiping blood on his apron, "makes love to Iraq."

No one loves to visit Iraq either—certainly not three times in one summer, as I did in 1988. Baghdad was for me the most depressing of Middle East cities, though it had once seemed the most romantic. The name conjured images of a fantasy Arabia, a land of harems and slave dens, of Sinbad the Sailor and Ali Baba. It was the sort of place I imagined traveling to aboard a magic carpet.

The actual journey resembled walking through the gate of a maximum-security prison. Iraq Air officials in Cairo told me to report four hours preflight for security, and I needed every minute. Guards frisked passengers from toe to turban while X-raying their bags to the point of radioactivity. Then the soldiers lined us up on the burning tarmac to identify our luggage while they shook us down yet again before we boarded the aircraft.

Every personal effect was regarded as a potential weapon. One passenger had a small bottle of cologne, and the guard uncorked the perfume and passed it beneath the man's nose, presumably to see if it was chloroform or some other substance that could be used to disable the crew. The guard asked for my camera, aimed it at me and clicked, checking, I guess, for a gun inside the lens. Then he plucked the penny-sized battery from the camera's light meter and pocketed it; the Duracell could somehow be used to detonate bombs.

"You are lucky," said the Egyptian in line behind me. "Last time I flew, you could not carry on anything, not a book, not a pen, not even a diaper for the baby. It was a very boring ride."

At the airport in Baghdad it was my typewriter that aroused suspicion. Iraq requires the licensing of typewriters so security forces can take an imprint of the keys to trace anti-government literature. Behind the customs desk rose a ziggurat of other forbidden imports: videotapes, audio cassettes, binoculars—any instrument for gathering or disseminating information. Even foreign blood evoked xenophobia. The first sign welcoming travelers at immigration stated that anyone who failed to report for an AIDS test would be imprisoned. There was a certain irony to the sign, as few Westerners visited the country. Iraq didn't issue tourist visas. Never had.

The second sign—and the third and the fourth and the fifth—showed the jowly, mustachioed face of the Iraqi president, Saddam Hussein. Big Brother was watching from portraits on every wall surrounding the baggage claim. He was watching from a leviathan billboard outside the airport—Saddam International Airport. He was even watching from the dial of the wristwatch worn by an official sent to the airport, to watch me as well. "Saddam is like Superman," the official said, showing how the watch hands ticked across the leader's cheeks and brow.

The man pointed me to the back of a government sedan. As soon as I climbed in, windows eased up, locks clicked shut. We nosed onto a four-lane highway toward the city, past a huge sports stadium, past huge modern mosques, past huge billboards of Saddam, illuminated in the night.

My escort worked for the Information Ministry, which, by definition, made him a poor source of information.

"Is this near the presidential palace?" I asked as we passed a heavily guarded compound.

"Not far," he said.

"And where is the Foreign Ministry?"

"Also nearby."

Searching for neutral topics, I commented on the weather. Yes, he said, it is very hot. How hot he could not say. The weather in Baghdad was classified information, "for security."

We pulled up on the street in front of the hotel. Concrete pylons blocked the driveway. Pylons blocked the entrance to every hotel and government building we'd passed: security against car bombers. As the locks clicked up, I asked my escort if I needed to check in at the ministry the following day.

"It has been arranged," he said.

In the hotel room, Big Brother gazed out from the television screen as a chorus of voices sang in the background:

> *"We will challenge them if they cross the border, oh Saddam.*
> *The victory is for you, oh Saddam.*
> *With our blood and with our soul*
> *We sacrifice ourselves for you, oh Saddam."*

In Iraq, paranoia comes with the territory. The arid Mesopotamian plain has been overrun repeatedly by foreign armies: Greeks, Assyrians, Persians, Mongols, Turks, and now Persians again. It was this last incursion that I'd come to report on. Or rather, it was the war's recent turn in Iraq's favor that had prompted Baghdad to grant my months-old request for a visa.

Not that Iraq acknowledged that the war had ever tilted the other way, though it had for five or so years. The morning's *Baghdad Observer*, a slim and Orwellian paper, devoted the upper half of its front page to a picture of the president, as it did every day, apropos of nothing. Alongside the picture, War Communiqué No. 3221 announced that Iraqi troops had "liberated 13 strategic mountain peaks at the northern sector" and inflicted "thousands of enemy casualties." The enemy's original taking of the now-liberated peaks had never been reported. In eight years of war, no Iraqi defeats and no Iraqi casualties were ever reported.

At the Ministry of Information, Mr. Mahn, director of protocol for the foreign press, sat behind his desk with a red flyswatter in one hand and my requested "program" in the other. The fat, flyswatting official reminded me at first of Sydney Greenstreet in the movie *Casablanca*. Except that Mr. Mahn looked even more like Saddam. It was an unspoken rule that officials not only draped their walls with Saddam portraits and wore a Saddam watch, but also mimicked the president's squarish haircut and thick, well-manicured mustache. Unfortunately for Mr. Mahn, Saddam had recently decided to lose weight, and officials across Baghdad were now on what was known as the "Saddam diet." Officials' target weights were published, and those who failed to lose the proper weight lost their jobs instead. By my third visit to Iraq, Mr. Mahn had shed fifty pounds.

I'd been warned of the difficulty of seeing Iraqi officials and had listed every person I could think of on my program, beginning with Saddam Hussein. Mr. Mahn took out a red pen and crossed out the president's name. "His Excellency, of course, is too busy to see you," he said. Saddam's face was everywhere, but the man himself was elusive; he'd held one press conference for the Western press in ten years.

"This is no," Mr. Mahn said, crossing out the next official I'd requested.

"This is also no." He continued down the list, alternating strokes of the red pen with slaps of the red flyswatter.

"This is no." Thwap.

"Never mind.

"No.

"Still no. Thwap.

"Never mind."

After five minutes, Mr. Mahn had squashed a dozen bugs and reduced my epic-length list to three or four requests. One of them was to "see current fighting on the southern battlefront."

"This maybe you can see," Mr. Mahn said. "On video." He stuffed the list in his breast pocket. "Now you can go back to the hotel and wait. We will see what we can do with your program."

Wandering back to the hotel, shielding my eyes against the blinding sun, I seemed to be touring a city-wide portrait gallery devoted to a single subject. The traditional Islamic ban on representation of the human form had been overcome in Baghdad, in a very big way. Saddam's face perched on the dashboards of taxis, on the walls of every shop and every office, on clock faces, on ashtrays, on calendars, on billboards at every major intersection—often four pictures to an intersection. Some of the portraits covered entire building fronts. And to ensure that your eye didn't ignore the pictures from sheer repetition, Saddam appeared in innumerable guises: in miltary fatigues festooned with medals, in bedouin garb atop a charging steed, in pilgrim's robes praying at Mecca, in a double-breasted suit and aviator sunglasses, looking cool and sophisticated. The idea seemed to be that Saddam was all things to all people: omniscient, all-powerful and inevitable. Like God.

"There are thirty-two million Iraqis," went a popular Western joke in Baghdad. "Sixteen million people and sixteen million pictures of Saddam."

Iraqis didn't tell that particular joke. Article 225 of Iraq's penal code states rather baldly that anyone who criticizes the president, his party or the government, "for the purpose of raising public opinion against authority," will be put to death.

Technically, Iraqis required government permission to chat with foreigners. Those who did so regularly were likely to be questioned by the regime's five security forces, which spied not only on the people but on each other. The first man I approached on the street, to ask the time, held up his arm as if warding off demons and scurried away. More often, pedestrians or shopkeepers responded to my approaches by stating politely that their English, or my Arabic, was not so good.

"People just don't talk to you much, particularly about politics," complained a United Nations worker named Thomas Kamps, who had worked in Iraq for three years. "They know that's the fast lane to the electrodes and the dungeon."

Expatriates in Baghdad made a grim hobby of collecting police-state horror stories. One diplomat's wife had spent much of her two years in Baghdad pushing infants in strollers. She said not a single Iraqi had stopped on the street to smile at her babies or utter so much as a "koochie-koochie-koo." "They're scared even to be seen talking to infants," she said.

A Turkish diplomat attended the unveiling of a new wing at the arts center—Saddam Arts Center. Each time the opening speaker mentioned the president's name there was a twenty-second pause for the audience to applaud. "The speaker mentioned Saddam a lot, and his speech ended up taking an hour and forty-five minutes," he said, yawning in his office the following day.

A Japanese diplomat lost his way one night in the neighborhood of the massive presidential palace. Soldiers opened fire on his car, as they did at any vehicle motoring slowly by, or making a suspicious U-turn in the vicinity of Saddam's residence. "The policy is 'Shoot first and don't ask questions later,' " explained the diplomat, who escaped unharmed. He said two Westerners had been killed at the same spot several years before.

There were genies inside every telephone and telex. A United Nations worker from Ethiopia told of phoning a colleague in New York and switching, midsentence, from English to his native Amharic. A voice quickly cut in, instructing him to "please continue in a language we can understand."

The state forbade direct calls overseas and limited operator-assisted calls to three minutes. Western publications were often seized at the airport, as were short-wave radios. Censorship of the domestic media was total. And ordinary Iraqis were barred from traveling abroad, even to Mecca. Baghdad was airtight, hermetically sealed against the outside world.

At a stall in the city's cramped bazaar, under cover of commerce, I struck up a conversation with a youth named Tariq, who sold Smurf T-shirts and Adidas sweatsuits. "Born in the USA" blared from a nearby boom box, drowning out the tap and clink from the centuries-old copper market, where men crafted giant urns, plates, ashtrays and wall hangings with Saddam's face adorning the center.

"I not understand you Americans," Tariq said genially. "You make good clothes and music. You have California girls. But you start this war on us to help Israel. Why you do this?"

I tried to explain that most Westerners believed Iraq had started the war. Tariq looked at me blankly. Big Brother was watching from life-sized photos on two of the stall's three walls.

Tariq's neighbor, who owned the boom box, wandered over and began jabbing his finger at me. "He says you can have your Bruce music, you can have it all back," Tariq translated. "Now that we win the war, we not need to beg America for anything anymore."

Back at the hotel, I tried to telex New York, to give an editor a contact number. The telex machine was mysteriously broken. Three hours later, I returned to the desk to find other telexes sent, but not mine. "Machine still broken," the operator said. When I complained, a French manager appeared and took me into a back office. The telex operators, he said apologetically, all worked for security and were under strict orders to vet journalists' telexes with the Ministry of Information. It was the weekend and no censors were available.

I used the hotel's Xerox machine. The staff made copies of my copies, "for security." Hotel staff watched me carefully each time I went in and out. I tried to call New York. There were no open lines. In three visits to Iraq, there was never an open line. Apart from the stilted reports of the *Baghdad Observer*—and faint crackles of the BBC World Service—I received no news at all of the outside world.

This isolation unsettled me much more than the distance I'd felt in a country such as Yemen, cut off from the world by a Third World phone system and by the genuine remoteness of the place. Here there were touch-tone phones, five-star hotels and bland modern buildings of steel and glass. But I might as well have been on Pluto. America could vanish in a mushroom cloud and I'd still be sitting there watching Saddam on television as a chorus sang, "The people love you, oh Saddam, and you love the people."

Not all people loved Saddam, of course, and I eventually located a few Iraqis brave enough to speak out. An office worker whom I will call Saleh chatted politely over tea until his colleagues filed out for lunch. Then he turned up a radio and leaned across his desk, speaking in an almost inaudible whisper.

"My phone is tapped, this office is bugged, and for all I know my grandmother is wired for sound," he said. "But sometimes a man must speak his mind. Saddam Hussein, he is the worst dictator ever in the history of man."

Saleh said this with the grim but giddy urgency of a parachutist leaping from an airplane. "I could be shot," he added, smiling wanly, "for what I've just told you."

Saleh's job required him to write reports, and he'd applied several times for an Arabic typewriter. Each request had been denied, so he'd reapplied for a machine with English characters. He'd been waiting a year. "What am I going to do with an English typewriter?" he wondered, laughing. "Incite tourists to riot?"

Like most Iraqis, he'd stopped seeing anyone but his family and closest friends. "Who else can I trust? Can I even trust them?" And he limited himself to small acts of defiance that would have seemed petty in any other setting. While the walls of most Iraqi homes and offices dripped pictures of Saddam, Saleh displayed nothing more than a calendar adorned with the president's face. But he kept a carpet decorated with Saddam rolled up in the front closet of his home, just in case. "If there is a knock in the night, I can roll it out before answering the door," he said. "A man must be brave, but he must not be reckless."

A few days after my arrival, I was dozing through the afternoon heat when the phone rang. It was Mr. Mahn at the Information Ministry. "We have called this and this and that," he said wearily, adding that item number 16 on my program had been arranged: an interview with his superior, the Minister of Information and Culture. I had listed the minister as an expendable, to pad out the program, but I could hardly afford to turn him down.

As the first point of contact for the foreign press, Information Ministry officials are often slick, Western-educated bureaucrats, adept at chatting amiably with journalists and offering innocuous statements on almost any topic. They are the governmental equivalent of corporate flacks.

But in Iraq, public relations wasn't very well developed. Arriving on the top floor of the Information Ministry, I wondered for a moment if I'd been sent to the wrong department. The elevator door swished open and I found myself staring down the barrel of a submachine gun. The guard holding it studied me carefully, then led me along a carpeted corridor to an enormous sitting room with a suitably enormous portrait of Saddam. The guard gestured toward a pair of couches, then, when I sat down, he said that I'd taken the minister's seat. It was indistinguishable from the other couch, except that its back was flush with the wall, providing a clear view of the corridor and elevator door.

Another man appeared, clad much like the guard in olive-drab fatigues with a pistol strapped to his waist. He had the stiff bearing and watchful gaze of a secret service agent. He was the Honorable Minister of Information and Culture, Latif Jasim.

Jasim spoke no English, nor did he go in for the usual Arab pleasantries. He also didn't reveal much about himself. Curious about his qualifications as the highest cultural officer in the land, I asked Jasim about his career before Saddam and the Baathist party seized power in 1968.

"I was a party member," he said.

"At university?" I asked.

"Not necessarily."

We moved on to matters of state, and his answers seemed crafted from the pages of the *Baghdad Observer*.

On Iraqi support for the Palestinians: "Israel is an alien body in this region. Science is advancing all the time, and Israel should expect that one day rocks will turn into other things."

On the law decreeing death for those who insulted the president: "We are not in the United States. Your head of state changes every four years. Here we cannot accept a leader's being insulted."

On the ubiquitous portraits of Saddam: "The president

has nothing to do whatsoever with the portraits. It is a natural and spontaneous thing from the people."

The interview lasted half an hour, during which Jasim managed not even the hint of a smile. He was the antithesis of slick, the last person most Arab governments would wheel out to present a warm and unthreatening image to the Western press.

As the man with the submachine gun saw me to the elevator, I wondered why Jasim took such precautions; after all, there were armed guards downstairs, and concrete pylons blocking the driveway. As usual, the only explanation I received was from a diplomat.

"It's always best to have your own private bodyguard," he said. "Iraqi leaders don't have a history of dying peacefully in bed."

The history of modern Iraq reads like *Macbeth*, only bloodier. Since 1920, there have been twenty-three coups, not counting the scores of attempted revolts, such as the one Saddam joined in 1959. Then aged twenty-two, he stood on a street corner and emptied his pistol at the car of a military strongman, Abd al-Karim Qasim, who had himself seized power only a year before in a bloody coup that killed Iraq's royal family. Qasim, who was wounded, later boasted that he had survived twenty-nine attempts on his life. His luck ran out a short time later and he was executed following a coup that briefly brought Saddam's Baathist allies to power.

Sixteen years, two coups, and many purges later, Saddam muscled his way into the presidency. He celebrated the event by sentencing twenty-two of his closest conspirators to death on trumped-up charges of treason. Saddam served as a trigger man on the firing squad. Ever since, Amnesty International's annual reports on Iraq have read like transcripts from the Spanish Inquisition: prisoners fed slow-acting poison, children tortured into ratting on their parents, teenagers returned dead to their families with fingernails extracted and eyes gouged out. Top generals kept going down in mysterious helicopter crashes, and Saddam has even

liquidated members of his own family. The Minister of
Information could hardly be blamed for watching his back.

Between interviews, I wandered the streets of Baghdad,
which for lack of a better word could be called "sightseeing."
It wasn't easy to play tourist in Iraq. There was, first of all,
the matter of maps. There weren't any, and hadn't been
since early in the war. Like the weather report, maps were
banned because they could aid the Iranians in aiming their
missiles at the Iraqi capital. Maps could also, of course, aid
dissidents in plotting assassinations or coups

Broad areas of the city were sealed off, including the
presidential palace, which flanked a long stretch of the wide
and muddy Tigris. You could catch a glimpse of the complex
from the eighteenth-floor bar of the Sheraton, but you
couldn't photograph it: "For Security Reasons," a sign
announced, "It Is Forbidden to Take Photos in This Area."
It was also forbidden to photograph animals, which might
make the country seem backward. Even photographing
Baghdad's premier tourist attraction, a striking memorial to
the war dead, could be hazardous. One Japanese visitor had
attempted it at night and alarmed the guards with the flash
on his camera. They responded with a burst of machine-gun
fire, missing the Japanese man but riddling his car with bullet holes.

I went, without camera, to see the war memorial, which
is shaped like a huge broken egg and called the Monument
of Saddam's Qadissiyah Martyrs. The name says something
about the Iraqi mind-set—and about the long memories fuel-
ing conflict across the Middle East. Qadissiyah was the seventh-century battle at which Mohammed's general, Khalid
ibn Walid—nicknamed "Sword of Islam"—drove the ele-
phant-riding Persians out of Mesopotamia. Saddam's constant invocation of Qadissiyah was a way of reminding Iraqis
that their war with Iran was the culmination of a millennial
battle against Persian aggressors. Like Mohammed's horse-
men, they too would ultimately triumph.

On the Iranian side, Khomeini cast the conflict more

explicitly in religious terms. He named the repeated Iranian offensives after the Iraqi city of Kerbala, and spoke constantly of liberating both it and the neighboring city of Najaf. Iranians revere the two cities as the burial sites of seventh-century "martyrs"—Ali, Hassan and Hussein—whose deaths sparked the great schism in Islam between Sunni and Shiite. By invoking Kerbala, Khomeini was reminding Iranians that their cause was no less than a crusade against infidels.

The two leaders had one message in common: both advertised the conflict as a holy war, so those killed in battle were *shaheed*—martyrs—and entitled to a free pass to paradise. After eight years of war, Khomeini had reached Kerbala V, Saddam was busily erecting new monuments to Qadissi martyrs, and a million men had gone off to heaven, leaving the two leaders no closer to victory.

Beneath Baghdad's war memorial was a museum to Saddam's life, including a family tree tracing his ancestry to Mohammed, his birth certificate and his fifth-grade report card (he scored an 89 in history, his best subject). Not featured, though perhaps more revealing of his childhood milieu, is a pamphlet authored by his foster father, Khairalla Tulfah, titled: "Three Whom God Should Not Have Created: Persians, Jews and Flies." However, there was a photograph of the car Saddam filled with bullets while trying to kill Abd al-Karim Qasim in 1959. Saddam was wounded in the attack and reputedly dug the bullet from his own leg while escaping to Syria. A statue downtown marks the site where the shooting took place. Iraq was the first country I had ever visited that enshrined an assassination attempt as the most glorious event in the nation's history.

The rest of the capital seemed rather drab. As far back as the twelfth century, an Arab traveler lamented of Baghdad: "There is no beauty in her that arrests the eye, or summons the busy passerby to forget his business and gaze." The flat, sunbaked plain surrounding the city offered little to build with, except mud. Invaders had periodically leveled most of the great buildings that did once exist. And Iraq's vast oil wealth had finished the job, with swaths of the old city ripped down to make space for towering hotels and housing blocks.

To his credit, Saddam also spent much of Iraq's wealth on improving the lives of ordinary people. The onetime Ottoman backwater was now among the more prosperous countries in Arabia, with villages electrified and schools and hospitals dotting the countryside. This modernization, though, was hard to see firsthand. Traveling outside Baghdad required official permission and an official escort. Two escorts, actually. Ministry of Information officials weren't permitted to travel alone with foreigners, as there would be no one to listen in on the conversation.

This arrangement seemed rather cumbersome, so I opted instead for a day trip I could take on my own, to Babylon. The ancient city lies sixty miles south of Baghdad along a dull road bordered by date palms, mud-brick villages and fifty-foot-high placards of Saddam. Just outside Babylon, I came upon the biggest portrait I'd yet seen. It showed the president receiving inscribed tablets from a skirted Babylonian king, beneath the words "From Nebuchadnezzar to Saddam Hussein."

Most of what was once Babylon has been pilfered by archaeologists or carted away to provide bricks for nearby towns. The Iraqis have rebuilt the ruins into a kind of fairytale castle with gaudy, blue-painted walls simulating the original glazed brick of the Ishtar Gate. A museum inside records some of Nebuchadnezzar's haughty words: "Let everything my hand has made be immortalized for eternity." Not to be outdone, his modern-day heir has inserted several bricks in the rebuilt Babylon, inscribed with the information that they were laid "in the era of the leader Saddam Hussein."

On the day I visited, in mid-June, the temperature was about 110 degrees. There were no other tourists, only a handful of bedouin hustlers lurking in slivers of shade cast by free- standing pillars. One of them grasped my sleeve and unfolded his fist to reveal a tiny cuneiform tablet and a statuette of a Babylonian king.

"Very ancient," he said. And very cheap, at only ten dollars.

Another man offered to guide me to the Tower of Babel, a short drive away. His car looked as though it had recently been unearthed in the excavations. We stalled beside a mound of dirt, about like your average landfill. "This is Babel Tower," he said, adding in a hushed voice, "You need something old? You need a King Hammurabi?"

Depressed, and depleted by the heat, I drove back to Baghdad through the onetime Fertile Crescent, between the Tigris and Euphrates, as a voice on the radio wailed:

"You are the perfume of Iraq, oh Saddam,
The water of the two rivers, oh Saddam.
The sword and the shield, oh Saddam."

That night I went to visit Mohammed the fishmonger at his restaurant by the Tigris. He was clubbing and gutting fish while the radio reported another advance by Iraqi troops. The war was fast approaching its end, with the borders back to where they had been when Saddam first invaded Iran in 1980.

"Our enemies should not forget," Mohammed said, in a husky imitation of Rambo, appearing that week in Iraqi cinemas, "how we kicked Khomeini's butt."

The restaurant was empty except for four men riveted to a small television set, watching Iraq play soccer in the Arab Cup finals against Syria. Damascus had supported Iran throughout the eight-year Gulf war, exacerbating a long-standing feud between Saddam and the Syrian dictator, Hafez al-Assad. Their murderous rivalry was now being played out on the soccer field.

"This game is almost as important as beating the Persians," Mohammed said.

At halftime, with the scored tied at zero, Mohammed suggested we slip across the street for a beer. Though straitlaced in most respects, Iraq is remarkably unbuttoned when it comes to drink and entertainment. Mohammed's restaurant sat beside Abu Nawas Street, a neon-lit stretch of clubs and bars named for a medieval Arab poet who is famed for his erotic verse.

At one time, hundreds of Filipina and Thai "bargirls" plied their trade on Abu Nawas Street, but Iraqi women, some of them war widows, had recently inherited the trade. "The local talent," Mohammed warned, "is not so good."

We entered the first club just as two doormen carried out a white-robed Kuwaiti, feet first, smelling of whiskey and perfume. The Kuwaitis, barred from drinking at home, were among Abu Nawas Street's best customers and were renowned for being cheap drunks.

Inside, the scene was reminiscent of the New Arizona in Cairo, with men huddled around whiskey bottles as three musicians played an atonal tune on tambourine, drum and violin. Mohammed picked out a rear booth upholstered with fake red velvet and cigarette ash. It was so dark that I couldn't see Mohammed's face. We were barely seated before a woman squeezed in beside me, whispering in my ear. "Pretty boy want to fickey fickey? Madame good, very good."

Mohammed leaned across the pitch-black booth and lit a match an inch from the woman's nose, revealing a haggard, heavily made-up face and the shoulders of a longshoreman. "By Allah!" he cried, shooing her away.

Mohammed had chosen the dark to attract the bargirls, who collected fifty dollars for a beer and a brief cuddle. As a Westerner, I served as bait. No sooner had the first woman departed than another muscled in, clutching me in a playful hammerlock.

Mohammed lit a second match. "Good grief!" he groaned. "What species is this?"

He yelled at the bartender to bring him "good girls, not so ugly," and the procession continued, though the quality remained the same. In half an hour, Mohammed had exhausted his matches and the supply of women in the bar.

A dancer in a sequin dress took the stage and began a vague sort of gyration that was billed as "Oriental dance."

After five minutes of dancing, the woman began singing, and the acoustics were so bad that I couldn't catch a word.

"What's she singing?" I asked Mohammed.

He shrugged. " 'We love you, Saddam,' something like this." He scanned the bar for partners. The woman began dancing again, and perfumed, drunk Kuwaitis stood up to shake with her. One tumbled in a giggling heap and had to be carried off the stage by his friends.

Mohammed sank deeper into the gloom. "I not have girlfriend in three years," he moaned. "Who knows. Maybe when the war ends these Iraqi women get married and the Filipinas come back." Draining his beer, he suggested we move on to a club called the Ali Baba.

As we stepped outside, the Arabian night exploded with machine-gun fire. Bright-red tracers streaked across the Tigris from antiaircraft guns positioned on the opposite bank. All Baghdad was celebrating. A guard by the door gave us the news. Iraq had outdueled Syria in overtime, two to one.

Mohammed smiled. "Iraq," he said, "has kicked another butt."

8

THE IRAQ-IRAN FRONT
Bodies

*To what base uses we may return, Horatio! Why may
not imagination trace the noble dust of Alexander, till
he find it stopping a bung-hole?* —HAMLET

The telephone shook me awake
at six in the morning and a voice at the other end declared,
"There has been another great victory."

Half asleep, I wondered for a moment if I'd left the
radio on. "Come to the airport immediately," continued the
voice, which I groggily recognized from my visits to the
Ministry of Information. "Today you will go to the southern
front."

There were several dozen reporters already gathered at
the airport, an international hodgepodge of Turks, Russians,
Chinese, French, Americans and locally based Arabs.

"Where is your water?" asked one of the Iraqis, a veteran of trips to the front. I told him that I'd assumed water
would be provided. "Are you kidding?" He cradled two
water bottles as though they were vintage Moët. "And
food—in a few hours, you will only dream of it."

Information was also scarce. Even in victory, the Iraqis
rarely disclosed strategic details or even the precise location
of the battlefield. "Bodies, that's all you get," said an American cameraman. A few months before, the Iraqis had driven
him for six hours through the desert, then stopped at a flat

plain covered with Iranian corpses. "This Iraqi guy ran ahead of us shouting, 'Here! Here! More murdered Persians!' We filmed for an hour, then they drove us back to Baghdad. I never even found out where we'd been."

Our trip was following a similar formula. During a long, unexplained delay at the airport, we inquired about the "great victory" we were being taken to see. One of our escorts responded by turning on a television, to show us a "victory tape." It was stock footage of bombs bursting and rockets flaring, with Saddam's face superimposed and a Wagnerian chorus singing in the background:

"The victory is for you, oh Saddam.
With our blood and with our soul
We sacrifice ourselves for you, oh Saddam."

Exactly how many Iraqi souls had been sacrificed in the eight-year war remained a mystery. Two hundred thousand dead was the most common estimate, a staggering toll in a nation of only sixteen million people. Certain streets of Baghdad looked the way I imagined Berlin or Paris did in the 1920s. Young amputees gathered at the Babel Cinema, leaning their stumps on crutches as they studied posters for Bruce Lee films. Veterans rolled through the souk in wheelchairs, shopping piled on their plastic legs. Driving back from Babylon, I'd passed taxis with flag-draped coffins strapped to the roof. This was how bodies were ferried home from the front. At one point casualties were so high that the Iraqis stored corpses in freezers, releasing a few at a time to avoid panicking the public by flooding the capital with coffin-laden cabs.

To bolster morale, the Iraqis also tried to carry on as though the war hadn't disrupted everyday life. "The flight time to Basra is fifty minutes," the pilot announced as we settled into the Iraq Air 737, "and our cruising altitude will be twenty-seven thousand feet." Every passenger on board was a reporter or Iraqi official. No commercial planes had flown to Basra for years.

The veneer of normality evaporated as soon as we landed at Basra, Iraq's second city, near the convergence of the Tigris and Euphrates. Green camouflage covered the terminal, and military aircraft crowded the runway. The Iraqis issued us helmets and loaded us into helicopters that swooped low over the desert to avoid detection by Iranian radar.

Wars have a way of finding inhospitable terrain. The plain east and north of Basra, the scene of most of the war's fighting, is a treeless expanse of grit and marsh, torched by searing winds. Winter was the season for slaughter. In summer, when the temperature hovers at 120 degrees, small arms became too hot to handle and tank drivers risked being cooked in their metal canisters.

Closer to the front, the landscape had been completely made over for the convenience of killing. Barrels of long-range artillery bristled out of the earth, pointing the way to Iran. Bulldozers pummeled the plain into ridges and trenches that swelled, like waves of dirt, one after another for miles. From the helicopter, the Iraqi lines resembled sand-castle fortifications that some ugly gray tide had washed over. The only scenery was a billboard showing Saddam in a pith helmet and carrying a gun, as if ready to go "over the top" and into the Iranian trenches.

The helicopters set down, and we piled into buses, then into jeeps, then hurtled toward the front. At ground level, clutching the death seat of an army jeep, the war suddenly became real. Cannons drummed the desert, each thu-*thump* throbbing through the sand and rattling the jeep's thin floor. Columns of smoke rose from the distant horizon. The driver, a vacant-eyed Iraqi soldier, stared out through a tiny space in the windshield; the rest of the glass was smeared with mud so a flash of glare wouldn't lure the Iranian artillery.

Incoming shells had pockmarked the road. Every hundred yards or so, the driver slammed the brake to the floor, swerved around a blackened crater, then hit the accelerator again, reaching eighty in time to dodge the next crevasse. Tomorrow I may die, he said with his driving; today I may as well risk it all streaking down this fractured strip of tar.

He dropped two wheels onto the shoulder to pass a mangled jeep, splayed on the road like a run-over cat. There was a mechanical whirr as the photographers behind me loaded their cameras with film.

"Bodies, *mon ami*," a French photographer said to the driver. "We must have bodies."

The American beside him chimed in nonchalantly, "What we really need is a blown-out bunker with Iranians hanging out of it and Iraqis standing on top." He checked his light meter with a quick scan of the desert. "You know, victor and vanquished in the same shot."

The victors had told us nothing of the battle, except that it had taken place at a borderland of sand and marsh known as Majnoon. *Majnoon* is Arabic for "crazy," a prewar name referring to the region's gushing oil wells. The Iranians had captured Majnoon in 1984, and now, apparently, the Iraqis had crawled out of their trenches in a rare summer assault to "liberate" the territory.

We reached the foremost Iraqi line, a tangle of trenches and bunkers topped by leaking sandbags. In front of the trenches, barbed wire and spiked metal tank traps had been laid out as a welcoming mat for oncoming Iranians. Whatever shrubs had once sprouted here had been gassed, shattered or uprooted. There was no shade from the blazing sun and nowhere to hide outside the trenches. It looked like Flanders field, without the mud.

A bridge lay over the trench, and we drove across it, into what had been, until a few hours before, a no-man's-land between the two armies. It was now a smoldering junkyard of burned rubber and blasted metal. Flat land mines lay strewn across the dust like runaway hubcaps. At points, it looked as though a giant lawn mower had run across the plain, chewing up and spitting out jagged bits of jeep, rifle, boot, helmet, canteen and bloodied uniform. The driver turned on his windshield wipers to see through the swirling smoke and dust. And in the backseat, the photographers cleaned their lenses, resuming their grisly refrain.

"This is all very scenic," the American said, "but where are the goddam bodies?"

The jeep clawed through a cut in the ramparts and deposited us just inside the captured Iranian line. The Iraqis had cleared their dead from the field, but the Iranians lay where they'd fallen. A lone gunner sprawled straight back from his forward post, a splotch of red blossoming across his chest and staining the sand. His eyes and mouth were open in an expression of bemusement, as though someone had just shouted "Bang, bang, you're dead!" and he'd soon leap to his feet and start playing soldier again.

A short distance away, the scene wasn't so ambiguous. One stretch of trench was a corridor of splattered flesh, bodies overlapping one another, cut down together in a torrent of gunfire. Some of the bodies were beginning to bloat, giving off a horrible stench, as if from an outhouse stuffed with rotting meat. Limbs twisted in improbable, almost yogic contortions. One man had died clutching a gash in his groin, entrails oozing onto his thigh. Another's wounds were hidden; he seemed to be dozing comfortably with his head on the stomach of a friend, eyes closed and face tilted toward the midday sun.

Our Iraqi escorts had chosen their spot well. This bit of battlefield lay on a narrow isthmus of sand between expanses of marsh; there hadn't been much room for the Iranians to maneuver, and it was impossible to walk ten feet without coming upon more bodies. Bodies scattered amid loaves of bread, cans of Kraft cheese and an upturned teakettle, as though the predawn assault had caught the Iranians at breakfast; bodies flung like discarded clothing onto the tops of bunkers or halfway into the marsh; bodies curled up in foxholes; bodies that didn't look like bodies, just pieces fanning out from a bloody core where the shell or grenade had hit.

A Turkish journalist on his fifth visit to the front flipped open his notebook and lectured on the art of reporting war.

"First thing, always study the corpses," he said, nudging his toe against the crushed skull of an Iranian teenager.

"Are they fresh? Bullets in front or back?" He inspected the blood dribbling from the corpse's nose. "I think it is fresh. If the body is black and burst-open, then maybe it is old."

He scribbled in his notebook. Bullets in front. Bodies fresh.

"Number two. Are there signs of gas?" He plucked a mask from the dust and opened a frayed U.S. Army manual, a relic of the days when America supplied the shah's army. The manual showed G.I. Joe with buzz cut and fatigues, demonstrating how to wear the mask. "The Iranians expected gas," the Turk continued, "but bullets were enough." He slapped his notebook shut. "With corpses you must study these things."

Letters and journals fluttered across the field, and I collected a few for a Farsi-speaking colleague to translate. Mostly, they recorded the tedium of trench warfare. "At 15:00 the enemy has added two rows of barbed wire in front of his position," read a log filled with similar entries. One soldier had passed the time doing Farsi crosswords and doodling pigs. Another filled his log with crude sketches of a woman with luxuriant curls cascading down her shoulders; an un-Islamic daydream in a country of heavily veiled females. In the margin he'd scribbled what seemed to be verses to the girl he'd left behind. "I have seen your picture and puffed your perfume and wish I could be with you always enjoying your beauty and your beautiful smell."

In a letter from Tehran to a young soldier name Jalil, each family member contributed a thought, with a sister composing a poem and a brother adding the final words. "I hope that this war is going to finish in favor of truth," he wrote. "Then all the youngsters will once again come back to the warmth of their families. And you too." The letter lay beside the body of a teenager who might well have been Jalil, face up on the sand, his close-cropped hair and patchy beard matted with blood. Flies crawled in his one open eye.

Many of the corpses were those of men my own age, killed in the final days of a pointless war. But I found it hard to feel any connection. What I did feel was a mad

compulsion to stare. Look how fragile the flesh is! How easily a skull collapses! The whole scene wasn't so much night-
marish as numbing. What a piece of work is man! Putrid
flesh and crushed bones; lunchmeat for maggots, mold for
the loam.

I wasn't given long to wax Shakespearean. Soon after
we arrived, Iraqi bulldozers and trucks moved in to dig fresh
trenches and turn the Iranian guns around. There was no
room to maneuver, and no sentiment spared for enemy dead.
One huge vehicle and then another rolled over the bodies.
The corpses lurched up and jerked their arms under the
weight of the wheels, as if in a final protest, before collapsing
in an even spread of brains, bones, organs. A truck bogged
for a moment and then churned on, leaving tread marks on
the pancake of flesh.

As soon as the convoy passed, a group of Iraqi soldiers
crowded atop the gore, firing guns in the air and flashing
victory signs for the cameras.

"Mister, picture! Mister, picture!"

The photographers jostled for position. They had what
they'd come for: victor and vanquished in the same shot.

"Shadow!" the American yelled at the Frenchman. "Get
your goddam shadow off the goddam corpse!"

Away from the tumult, two Iraqi soldiers slumped
against a bunker, sharing a cigarette. They looked exhausted
but elated, suffused with the high of battlefield survivors.
Their eyes glowed, their chapped lips curved into glazed,
involuntary smiles. "We attacked for six, maybe eight
hours," said one of the men, whose name was Mahmoud.
"Then the Persians just got up and ran away." He nodded
toward the corpses. Present company excluded.

Beside Mahmoud, a gray-haired man named Naim
nursed a wound in his hand. His olive-drab uniform was
mottled with blood, and each crease of his face was a pocket
of grime. As he spoke, he spit dirt from between his teeth.
"I am tired, but I am not so scared of the enemy as I was,"
he said, shaking his head in disbelief. "They don't fight like
Iranians anymore."

Naim peered inside a pillbox, checking for corpses, then crawled halfway in to shield himself from the sun. "I do not like to see so much blood," he said. "But when the bodies are Iranian, I do not mind so much." He tipped his helmet over his eyes and didn't even stir at the celebratory bursts of gunfire unleashed for the photographers a few feet away.

By the standards of the eight-year war, this corner of the Majnoon battlefield was unremarkable. When the Iraqi advances stalled early in the war, the Iranians had counterattacked with "human waves" of young soldiers—many of them children—armed by the ayatollah with plastic keys to heaven's gate. In battle after battle, they clambered over their own dead and into the Iraqi trenches. Outnumbering the Iraqis three to one, the Iranians appeared headed for victory. But gradually the war bogged down in a Somme-like deadlock, a dreary exchange of the same few miles of desert ground. At Christmas of 1986, in one of many attacks that the Iranians termed their "final offensive," the Iraqis mowed down wave after wave of Iranians until the tide stalled two miles short of Basra. The slaughter was so stunning that it entered Iraqi war lore as "the Great Harvest."

In Baghdad, I later met an Iraqi who had survived the grim reaping near Basra. His name was Ali and he'd been driving a tank when an Iranian opened the hatch and tossed in a grenade. The explosive blew off part of Ali's skull and killed the other three men in his tank. Ali was shot in the hip as he struggled from the tank. He survived, he said, by "playing dead" until the Iranian assault petered out.

"It was January the twenty-second and I see this with my own eyes," he said, as though the intervening two years hadn't happened. "There were so many bodies I could not touch the ground." He crawled across the carpet of corpses until he reached the tank of a friend. "I banged and banged on the hatch, shouting, 'Hatem, it is me! Hatem, it is Ali!' " Finally Hatem let him in.

Ali spent six months in hospital and emerged limping but healthy. Once a star soccer player, he couldn't run anymore, but he'd taken up body-building instead. He rolled up his sleeve to show off bulging biceps. And he seemed proud of the soft spot in his head where a piece of his skull was missing.

But after boasting of his recovery, Ali had a confession. "I have dreams, whole weeks of dreams," he said. "I am in the tank, I look up, I see a hand, I see the grenade falling." Usually, that was when he woke up. But sometimes the nightmare continued until he found himself pounding on the hatch of Hatem's tank. In the dream, Hatem didn't let him in.

He paused, sweating, then dismissed the nightmare with a wave of his hand. "I should not complain," he said, limping off into the night. "I am alive. I am so lucky."

The Great Harvest had cooled Iranians' kamikaze fervor. So had Iraq's use of poison gas. A few days after Majnoon, a United Nations team inspected the dead and wounded on the Iranian side of the border battlefield we had visited. They found that preceding the early-morning assault, the Iraqis had lobbed gas-filled shells on the Iranian rear. The poisons included a crude form of mustard gas known as yperite, named for the World War I battle at Ypres where it was first deployed by the Germans.

The first symptoms consist of "a burning in the eyes," the UN report stated. "The burning is followed by blurred vision, vomiting and blisters that ooze an amber-colored fluid. Then the gas blackens and ulcerates the body's moist crevices: armpits, buttocks, groin."

The report included an inspection of a nineteen-year-old named Ali. "The skin all over the body is dark and cracking," it said. "Armpits black, with lesions resembling second-degree burns; groin is black, with areas where the skin has peeled. Wheezing can be heard in both lungs." Most such victims later died.

We traveled back from Majnoon through the gathering dusk as the spoils of battle were carted to the Iraqi rear. The

profligate ruin not just of men but of matériel seemed suddenly astonishing. The road was clogged with bent steam
shovels, burned bulldozers, overturned tractors and twisted
claws of machines I couldn't identify. A picture of Ali, the
seventh-century Shiite martyr, was emblazoned on the front
of captured Iranian tanks. The tank's Iraqi driver poked his
head from the turret, his face wrapped Palestinian-style in a
checkered keffiya, to keep out the dust.

As the traffic stalled, the Turkish reporter turned on his
radio and picked up War Communiqué 3230, announcing the
"liberation of Majnoon" in "a large and lightning offensive
supervised personally by President Saddam Hussein." According to the communiqué, the operation was part of a larger
assault known as Tawakalna-al-Allah, On God We Rely.
The news ended, and a chorus of voices began the ubiquitous refrain.

> "We will challenge them if they cross the border, oh Saddam.
> "The victory is for you, oh Saddam . . ."

That was the most we were ever to learn of the battle. As
night fell, we stopped five miles behind the Iraqi lines for a
military briefing, "brief" being the operative word.

"It was quite an easy engagement," said the Iraqi commander, who wore a Saddam-style haircut and thick mustache. "We attacked and the Iranians withdrew."

"How many dead?" asked the Turk.

"Many," the officer said. "Gentlemen, please. Let us
have tea." It was the first refreshment we'd had in sixteen
hours, except for a few swigs from soldiers' canteens.

When the tea was done we visited a wire cage where
several hundred Iranian prisoners huddled beneath blinding
floodlights. Earler in the war, Iranians had remained defiant
even in captivity, chanting "Khomeini!" and biting their
Iraqi guards. But at war's end, with estimates of the Iranian
dead ranging as high as a million, their spirit had drained

away, leaving a broken and silent rabble of teenagers and old men.

As we entered the cage, Iraqi guards brandished submachine guns and ordered the prisoners to sit down. It was a gratuitous gesture. Most of the men were already curled on the concrete, asleep or writhing from gruesome wounds. A shirtless youth rested his head on a sneaker, eyes wide with terror, hands clutching bloody swathes of cotton piled on his crotch. A friend tried to calm him by bringing a cigarette to his lips. One gray-haired man with a wound in his throat kept getting up and trying to say something to a guard, pointing feverishly at his trachea. His voice was almost inaudible, and the Iraqi, who evidently spoke no Farsi, kept ordering the man back to the ground.

As I wandered through the cage, one young soldier grabbed my sleeve and looked pleadingly at me with the dark, almond-shaped eyes of a prince in a Persian miniature. "From where you are?" he asked.

"America."

"Ever you go Iran?"

"Someday, I hope."

He asked for my notebook and scribbled his name in a mix of Arabic and Roman script. Then he added his birthdate according to the Islamic calendar: 1387. He was twenty-two and had been at the front for three years.

I wasn't sure what he meant by the gesture. But as the Iraqis herded us out of the cage, another prisoner called out in English. I turned to record a last-minute Iranian comment on the war. He gave me his name, then added in a weary voice: "Please, I have brother. He is principal of high school in Tehran. Please tell him you have seen me here."

It was midnight when we gathered for the two-hour drive back to Basra. Artillery still pounded in the distance, a gunpowder heartbeat. An Iraqi flare lofted into the sky to illuminate the enemy position; another concussion of shellfire shuddered through the sand. Then flares began whooshing and popping every which way across the desert. Machine-gun fire erupted all around us as soldiers emptied their automatic weapons into the air. The Iraqis were celebrating their victory.

I stood there, slack-jawed, marveling at how much the display looked like July Fourth fireworks. Then the Turk grabbed my arm and dragged me into a bunker.

"Third lesson of war reporting," he said. "All that lead has to land somewhere. Let us make sure it is not on our heads."

9

THE JORDAN RIVER
I Came for the Waters

River is deep and the river is wide.
Milk and honey on the other side.
—Southern black spiritual

Khalaf Ghoblan, his face framed by a black-checked keffiya, stood gazing across the Jordan River. Bare limestone hills climbed the West Bank above a thin band of green snaking along the valley's floor. Shielding his eyes against the setting sun, the eighty-seven-year-old bedouin pointed to the spot where his clan had once camped in long sheepskin tents by the river.

"There was a wooden bridge just there," he said, gesturing at the near bank, obscured by reeds. Israeli and Jordanian sentries now straddled the river bend, staring at each other through binoculars. "It cost half a Turkish penny to cross."

Ghoblan chuckled, a raspy, old man's laugh. To dodge the toll, he often swam across instead. "Half a penny was a lot in those days." The river was mightier then, and crowded with boats. Black Africans slaves, imported by the Turks, poled downstream on rafts filled with sheep. Russian Orthodox pilgrims canoed the other way, headed to a site near Jericho, revered as the site of Jesus' baptism.

When the young Ghoblan reached the other bank, he would buy cotton shirts from Jewish seamstresses, among the first of the Zionist settlers. To keep the clothes dry, he paid the half-penny toll on the return trip to his home in what is now Jordan. "I felt the Jews were fellow Semites and the river was ours to share," he said.

Then came the 1948 Arab-Israeli war, after which a stretch of the river became a tense border between Jordan and the new state of Israel. Still, Ghoblan recalled occasional instances of neighborly contact. When kibbutz-owned cows strayed through the shallow water, Jordanian farmers returned them and received chocolate as a reward.

But after the Six-Day War in 1967, the only thing Arab and Jew exchanged across the river was gunfire. Bridges closed. Barbed wire and minefields sprouted on both banks. And anyone who tried, like Michael of spiritual song, to row his boat ashore risked being shot by border guards. "I cry for the old times," Ghoblan said, turning his back on the river. "War is the only language Jews understand."

We wandered back to his house, a two-story stucco villa which had replaced the tent in which he was raised. He served me coffee flavored with cardamom, then ducked into his bedroom and returned carrying an enormous Turkish musket. "I used to shoot at the Jews many times in the wars," he said. With shaky fingers, he lifted the flintlock to his shoulder and aimed it across the river. "Thanks God," he said, "I never hit anyone."

I arrived at the Jordan River in November 1987, five weeks before the start of the Palestinian intifada. Like most journalists, I had no inkling that the tranquil, balmy autumn was the end of an era in Middle East affairs. Many Israelis still blithely supposed the Palestinian problem would somehow melt away. And Arabs returned the insult by pretending that the Jewish state simply didn't exist.

Astonishing effort went into sustaining this fiction. At a government office in Abu Dhabi, I'd studied a map of the Middle East with the name "Israel" carefully blacked out with magic marker. Officially, the word itself was unmentionable; on the news, Israel was "occupied Palestine," or the "Zionist entity." Western journalists in Cairo acceded to the taboo, confiding in hushed tones that they were off to visit "Dixie." The code name dated from the days when Middle East correspondents were based in Beirut and a trip to Israel had meant heading south of the border, to Dixie. It was considered offensive to Arab ears—and therefore ill-advised professionally—to utter the unmentionable word, even in Egypt.

I traveled to Dixie by land, through Jordan, a country that was the most Western of Arab states, yet the most insistent in blotting out the country occupying its entire western border. On the television news, the weather report skipped from the Jordanian cities of Aqaba and Salt to a mysterious locale called "the Western Heights," which included Jerusalem. One morning, I read in the *International Herald Tribune* that an Israeli tennis player had reached the finals of a major tournament. The Jordanian sports report that night included only the result of the women's matches.

In Amman, I shared a taxi with a Palestinian couple headed to the Allenby Bridge, a tightly controlled crossing between Jordan and the occupied West Bank. Israel didn't exist there either. Jordanian border guards checked the passports of incoming travelers and turned back anyone with an Israel stamp. There was no other country the traveler could have just come from. But appearances had to be maintained. Journalists and other frequent border-crossers carried two passports, or asked on entering Israel that their documents be spared the offending imprint.

It was the Jordan River I intended to write about. Unfortunately, like most travelers before me, I was woefully misinformed about the waters I had come to view.

"When I was a boy I somehow got the impression that the river Jordan was four thousand miles long and thirty-five miles wide," Mark Twain wrote in *The Innocents Abroad*. In fact, he soon discovered, "It is not any wider than Broadway in New York."

A century later, having been diverted for irrigation and poisoned by fertilizer, the Jordan wasn't any wider than Wall Street. As the border bus bumped across the wood-slatted floor of the Allenby Bridge, I aimed my camera out the window. A murky trickle came into view, but I didn't have time to focus before the River Jordan was gone. The Allenby Bridge is fifteen yards long.

A sandbagged pillbox loomed ahead, and a soldier stepped out holding a submachine gun loosely in one hand. In the seat beside me, the Palestinian couple visibly tensed. The soldier peered into our bus, said, "*Shalom*," and waved us through.

Before crossing the Jordan, I hadn't worried much about how being Jewish would affect my work in Israel. I felt I'd managed to report on Arab countries with journalistic "objectivity" and didn't see why reporting on Israel should be any different.

This high-minded professionalism lasted about as long as it took me to walk from the bus to the immigration hall. A blue-and-white Star of David fluttered above the building, stirring some inchoate allegiance bred of endless dull Sundays in Hebrew school. The little Jewish state, circled by hostile Arabs, like a pioneer wagon train, draining swamps and dancing the hora.

Inside the immigration hall, Israeli soldiers stood behind tables, going through bags and asking questions. I approached a soldier with thick glasses and a tiny yarmulke pinned atop red kinky hair. The big bad Zionist looked like a pimply classmate whose name I could no longer recall. I half expected him to ask if I wanted to sneak out back to bet my allowance on a few rounds of *dreydl*.

Instead, he flipped through my passport, studying the Arabic stamps on every page. After several months in the Middle East, my passport resembled a pocket Koran.

"Horwitz?" His eyes swam behind Coke-bottle lenses. "Do you have any special connection to the Jewish community in America?"

"No. Except that I'm Jewish."

He handed back my passport and smiled. "Welcome to Israel. I hope you will have a good time." He hadn't even bothered to unzip my bags.

I stepped outside and gazed at the stark hills of the Promised Land. Arid gullies and ridges rose on all sides, enclosed by barbed wire and dotted with signs saying "Danger! Mines!" Taxis were parked nearby, their Palestinian drivers prostrate on the ground, reciting midday prayers. The hill behind them was emblazoned with an enormous Star of David, facing Mecca.

I'd agreed to share a taxi to Jerusalem with the Palestinian couple from Amman. It was forty-five minutes before they emerged from the immigration hall. The husband's face was purple and his wife was crying softly. While I'd been reliving Hebrew school with the redheaded soldier, they'd been having their suitcases emptied, their shoes X-rayed and their orifices probed for weapons and "anti-Israel" material, a category including everything from PLO keyrings to copies of *The Merchant of Venice*.

The couple, resident in Jordan for twenty years, had come across the river to attend a funeral. "I was born here in Jericho and now I must be naked for a Jew so I can see my cousin buried," the man said, straightening his black suit. "I feel like a dog."

I nodded gravely. I was to spend a lot to time nodding gravely as bile poured from both Palestinians and Israelis. It was easier than explaining that I thought they were both right, or both wrong. I wasn't sure which.

The first thing you notice, coming to Israel from the Arab world, is that you have left the most courteous region of the globe and entered the rudest. The difference is so profound that you're left wondering when the mutation in Semitic blood occurred, as though God parted the Red Sea and said: "Okay, you rude ones, keep wandering toward the Promised Land. The rest of you can stay here and rot in the desert, saying 'welcome, most welcome' and drowning each other in tea until the end of time."

In Egypt it is considered abrupt to begin any conversation without at least half of the following:

Good morning.

Good morning to you.

Good morning of light.

Good morning of roses.

Good morning of jasmines (and so on, through the rest of the garden).

And how are you?

Fine, and you?

Fine also, thanks be to God.

Thanks to God.

Welcome, most welcome.

Welcome to you.

(Chorus)

The same tedious singsong is reprised upon departure, with a minimum of two cups of tea or coffee served in between. A lot of this hospitality is false, of course, particularly when it comes from Arab officials; the sipping and small talk help conceal the fact that the bureaucrat you're interviewing hasn't imparted one comment of even trivial significance. In Cairo, I often tore home from government offices, pumped up on Turkish coffee, to type up my notes and rush them into print. Only to find, flipping through my notebook, that all I had to write was "Thanks be to God" and "Would you like some sugar with your coffee?"

It came as a rude shock, then, to pick up the phone my first day in Jerusalem and have the following conversation with an Israeli secretary.

ME: *Shalom.* This is Tony Horwitz. I'm a reporter—

SHE: *Ma?* (What?)

ME: I'm an American reporter and I'd like to speak to Mr. Levi.

SHE: So who wants him?

ME: I told you. Tony Horwitz. I'm a—

SHE: *Ma?*

ME: Horwitz! H-O-R—
SHE: Not here. (Click)

Taxi trips in Israel also elevate the blood pressure, though
reckless driving is the least stressful part of the ride. Rather
than disable their meters, in the Egyptian fashion, many
Israeli cabbies prefer to hide their meters in the glove com-
partment. Discovering this midway through my first ride, I
politely asked the driver to turn the meter on. Then I asked
him again. On third request, he grudgingly flipped open the
glove box and turned the switch. Then, when we reached
the hotel, he tacked ten shekels (about five dollars) onto the
fare for the half-mile we'd traveled off the meter. I protested.
He yelled. I yelled. We almost came to blows.

   "Cus ummak!" he screamed, finally giving in. *Cus ummak*
is the one Arabic phrase known to every Israeli cabbie. It
means "your mother's cunt."

   There were compensating pleasures, of course. I went
to a Woody Allen movie and ate borscht. I gawked like a
fifteen-year-old at women in short skirts and sleeveless
blouses, something I hadn't seen for months. And I even
found it refreshing to join the Israeli fray: butting into lines,
shoving to be the first off buses, shouting *"Cus ummak!"* at
cabdrivers—behavior which would have got me knifed or
deported in Arabia. But after two or three days, after losing
more shoving matches than I'd won, I found myself drifting
toward the Arab quarter to exchange a dozen or so pleasantries over three or four cups of sugary tea.

   "How are you?"
   "Fine, and you?"
   "Very well, thanks to God."

   The second striking thing about Israel, arriving from the
Arab world, is how much the two cultures have in common.
Hebrew and Arabic are closer to each other than to any
third tongue. The Arabic greeting *salaam aleikum* ("peace be
upon you") is *shalom aleikum* in Hebrew, though it's not a
phrase often spoken between Arab and Jew. Many other

Arabic words I'd learned were identical in Hebrew: *beit* (house), *yom* (day), *lila* (evening).

Roughly half of all Israelis are first- or second-generation émigrés from the Muslim world, particularly Morocco and Iraq, and their olive skin, dark hair and strong features often make these "Sephardic" Jews indistinguishable from Arabs. Religious fanaticism has also bred a certain kinship. Bowing their beaver hats and sidelocks at the Wailing Wall, the ultra-Orthodox Chasidim reminded me of nothing so much as the bearded, skullcapped fundamentalists in Cairo, bowing toward Mecca. Both share an attachment to bygone days: one pines for the spiritual purity of the Polish shtetl, the other for the desert asceticism of Mohammed. Both see God's hand in everything they do, and godlessness in everything done by anyone else. Orthodox wives, hidden beneath kerchiefs and trailed by herds of children, seemed, at first sight, a mirror image of the veiled, housebound wives of Arabia.

Ask almost any Israeli over forty to tell you his or her life story and you'll hear a tragic tale beginning with the Holocaust and continuing through the 1948 war, the 1967 war, the 1973 war and so on. Ask any Palestinian to tell you his or her life story and you'll hear a tragic tale beginning with the 1948 war and the diaspora that followed (known as *Al-Nakba*—the Disaster), then continuing through the 1967 war, the 1973 war and the occupation of their land that followed from these conflicts. I later met Palestinians as far away as Tunis and Baghdad who had never laid eyes on their homeland, but who still kept the keys to homes in Haifa or Jaffa that their parents had fled in 1948.

Palestinians also tend to be well educated, entrepreneurial and distrusted by other Arabs, who stereotype them as cliquish, grasping, arrogant and suspect in their allegiance to whatever country they've settled in. Palestinians, it seemed obvious, were the Jews of the Arab World.

The next thing you notice, once you've tallied all these similarities, is that Palestinians and Israelis are alike in ignoring the kinship completely. Ask people if they see parallels between the two populations and they will most likely answer with a resounding Hebrew *ma*? (what?) or an Arabic *mish mumkin*! (impossible!).

Deciding to leave this tangle of contradictions for another day, another story, I rented a car to finish my reporting on the Jordan River. Driving out of Jerusalem, I offered a ride to a Palestinian hitchhiker. He seemed surprised I'd picked him up and relieved to discover I was American, not Israeli. As we passed the Damascus Gate, I commented on the beauty of the ancient walled city. He glanced out the window; his eyes latched onto a blue-and-white pennant fluttering in the breeze. "This flag, it is very ugly." Soon after, we passed through the edge of the Jewish quarter. Young children scampered across a small playground. "Look at all these babies," he said, his face wrinkling in disgust. We wound down the hills toward the Jordan, and I turned on the radio. He asked if I'd mind lowering the volume. "Hebrew, I cannot stand the sound of it."

I let him out in Jericho and headed north along the river, through a desolation of army camps and unsown fields labeled "restricted security zone." This stretch of the occupied territory seemed largely unoccupied, except by hitchhiking soldiers. The first one I picked up was a twenty-year-old woman named Orna, who had just finished her army training at a sentry post near the Dead Sea. It had been her job to stare through binoculars at Jordan and write down everything she saw, as warning against terrorist attacks. "For six months, all I ever entered in the book was donkeys," she said.

I laughed for the first time in several days. Relaxing, I glanced across at Orna. She had my coloring, my mouth, my nose. Her grandparents could have come from the shtetl next door to mine. For a moment I felt the same familial glow I'd experienced with the redheaded soldier at the Allenby Bridge. As the road dipped, revealing the deep rift surrounding the Jordan River, I slowed down to take in the view.

"Nice, huh?"

Orna looked at me strangely. "So what's to see?" She was staring the other way, at a Palestinian village beside the road. Then, without prompting, she added: "If the Arabs want a state they can have it—on the other side of the Jordan River." She was suddenly irritable. "Always we feel guilt problems. Why? America moved out all the Indians. So what if we do the same?"

We drove to the next army camp in silence. Orna climbed out and two other hitchhikers climbed aboard. In front sat a soldier named Nati, returning north to "walk the line" in Lebanon. He wasn't looking forward to resuming the dangerous night patrols.

"If you see an Arab you shoot," he said, shifting the submachine gun between his legs. "If you sleep, you die. I almost make a shit in my pants many times."

The other passenger, Yitzhak, was from a kibbutz near Jericho. He gave me a leaflet about the kibbutz printed in halting English. It said: "See the greening of the desert, experience unique way of life! Time warp back with us 2000 years!"

"It is something like a joke, this paper," he said, staring disconsolately at the riverside fields, hemmed in by sentry posts and security fences. "We can make the desert bloom, but not minefields. If the Arabs want it back, they can have it."

And so the drive went, all the way through the Jordan Valley; a fanatic, a liberal, a cynic, a fanatic again. If I had two hitchhikers at the same time, they were almost sure to disagree. If I had one, he was sure to disagree with me. It was exhausting, and after a few hours I accelerated past the long lines of hitchhikers. Why should I feel guilt problems?

Late in the afternoon I pulled in at a kibbutz called Kfar Ruppin, the closest Israeli settlement to the Jordan River. It seemed like the logical place to gather a counterpoint to the bedouin, Khalaf Ghoblan, whom I'd interviewed on the Jordanian side of the river. A gardener named Micha Hellman put down his trowel and offered to show me around. He was a handsome, square-jawed kibbutznik my own age, with clear blue eyes and blue work clothes that stank of manure. Like Ghoblan, he'd spent his whole life by the river, and he toured the bank with a proprietorial air. "I know the history of every stone in this place," he said of the fifty-year-old kibbutz. "I either put it there myself or I know who did."

Hellman showed me the underground bunker where he slept as a child. After the 1967 war, Palestinian commandos roamed the opposite bank and often shelled Kfar Ruppin, killing several people. Hellman and the other children at riverside kibbutzim slept below-ground for three years, becoming known in Israel as "shelter kids."

"In the morning we boys would come out and collect missile tails," he said. Then the missiles were traded, like baseball cards. "One-twenty-one-millimeter shells were the best. The made nice candle holders." Sometimes the incoming shells turned up shards of Byzantine pottery and Roman coins as well.

To defend against terrorists, the Israelis mined the river's bank. In 1970, they added an electrified fence and a graded strip of sand, which soldiers checked daily for footprints. Though the border was now peaceful, cows at Kfar Ruppin occasionally stepped on unexploded mines and blew themselves up.

Hellman walked me to the fence and pointed through the wire at a small patch of muddy Jordan, just visible between tall reeds. "Kids grow up here now without ever putting a toe in the water," he said.

Jordanian farmers picked oranges in a grove just on the other side of the river. Hellman said they sometimes shouted at their Israeli neighbors, but because he didn't know Arabic he couldn't understand what they said. Technically, Israel and Jordan were still at war. Even telephoning across the narrow divide was impossible.

At sunset we sat on a bluff overlooking the river valley. A Jordanian village was clearly visible on the other bank, and the evening call to prayer wafted across in the twilight. "I have sat here almost every day of my life, watching them do the same work as us, wake up with us, go to sleep with us," Hellman said. "And I do not even know their names. I do not even know the name of their village." He went silent for a moment, then turned and asked, "Do you think neighbors anywhere else in the world live like this?"

I rolled along the Israeli side of the river for two more days before returning to Jerusalem through the occupied West Bank. At the Palestinian village of Marj al-Naja I pulled over to balance my story with one more Arab voice. The village was as run-down and unprosperous as the kibbutzim to the north were lush and fertile. A hunched farmer named Mohamed Abu-Helal was carrying his eggplants in from the field and stopped to exchange pleasantries. He invited me for a cup of tea at his home, a windowless one-room hovel that he shared with his wife and six children. It was so cramped that the family rolled out mattresses each night, then rolled them back up to make living space in the morning.

Mohamed's English was poor, so one of his boys ran off to find the village schoolteacher to translate. I sat there awkwardly, swatting flies, and looking around the cramped room. I couldn't help wondering about the couple's sex life. Did they have none? Did the children just lie there in the dark and listen?

The boy returned with a twenty-five-year-old named Ahmed who had bitterness oozing from his pores. He introduced himself by saying that he'd spent several months in an Israeli prison for painting pro-PLO slogans.

Taking out my notebook, I asked Mohamed about his life by the river, and he launched into a rambling monologue. I picked up a few words; it was mostly about sheep and goats and oranges. I turned to Ahmed for a complete translation.

"He says for you that Palestine was once a paradise, but now the Jews make us live like donkeys." This was all Ahmed said.

I asked Mohamed whether he had family on the river's

east bank and how often he saw them. Again, the farmer's answer was amiable and long-winded, and he often pointed to one of his boys with pride. I turned to Ahmed.

"He says for you, the West Bank and Jordan used to be one big village. Now the river is one wall in a big Palestinian prison."

After half an hour I abandoned the interview. I'd learned that the government subsidized kibbutz water but not that of Palestinian settlements; there was no electricity in Marj al-Naja and one toilet for the school's one hundred fifty students. The land was so poor that villagers worked as day laborers in neighboring Jewish fields. But I had learned very little about Mohammed's view of life by the river.

Ahmed walked me to my car. "Listen to what he says for you," Ahmed said, jabbing a finger at my notebook. He was bothered that I hadn't taken down every syllable of his tirade against the Israeli occupation. "He says for you, there will be bloodshed unless the Zionists leave our land."

I reached Jerusalem at sunset and sat in a café by the Damascus Gate, sipping Turkish coffee and watching the stones of the old city glow pink and orange in the fading autumn light. Greek Orthodox monks scurried past in their long brown robes. At sunset, a siren's blast announced the Jewish Sabbath, mingling with the Muslim call to prayer from the city's minarets. It was, for the moment at least, a peaceful and harmonious vision.

I tapped out my article, giving it a hopeful spin. There was the young Jordanian farmer who had told me, "You must say hello to your neighbor, whether you like him or not." There was the Israeli artist who had begun sculpting the word "PEACE," in Arabic, on a bluff facing Jordan. As a counterpoint, I included the story of Mohammed Abu-Helal, the poor Palestinian farmer, though I treaded cautiously on the bits Ahmed had claimed "he says for you." Overall, it seemed to me that residents of both banks were weary of conflict and eager to get on with their lives, in peace.

Three weeks later, the occupied territories exploded in violence. The *intifada* had begun. An editor returned my Jordan River feature, which hadn't yet run, and suggested I consider a rewrite. When I returned to Jerusalem, along with hundreds of other journalists, the cobbled alleys of the old city echoed with the high-pitched pop of rubber bullets. In the West Bank town of Ramallah, I watched an Israeli patrol beat an old woman until she crumpled to the ground. Five minutes after driving into the Gaza Strip, a chunk of concrete crunched through the window of my rented car. And I realized too late that I should have been listening to what fiery-eyed Ahmed had been saying for me.

LIBYA
The Colonel's Big Con

Woman is a female and man is a male.
—MUAMMAR QADDAFI,
The Green Book

The summons came, like so many others, on a bad phone line in the middle of the night. America had shot down two Libyan warplanes over the Mediterranean earlier that day, and after dialing twenty times, a colleague in Cairo finally got through to Tripoli.

"Please," the Libyan official shouted through the static, "tell all journalists, come." Then the line went dead.

"That's it?" Geraldine asked when a correspondent called us to share the news. " 'Please, all journalists, come'?"

"That's it." There was a flight to Italy in the morning, he said, and a connection to Libya in the afternoon. "If we're lucky, we'll all get stranded in Rome."

Tales of journalistic woe in Libya were legendary. Not-so-secret police shadowed your every step. There were no decent phones. No one to talk to. And worst of all, no booze. "You feel depressed all the time, and followed in your depression," said a Yugoslav reporter named Bosko. "Libya is the Romania of the Middle East."

Libya was also one of those Middle Eastern countries—Iran and Saudi Arabia were two others—that routinely ignored journalists' visa requests for months, then granted entry with a few hours' warning, to everyone. But even by these minimalist standards, the invitation to Libya seemed thin.

The Italian agent issuing my ticket to Tripoli was skeptical. "American journalist?" he asked, checking my passport in Rome. "Horwitz? No visa?" He chuckled, shaking his head. *"Buona fortuna.* I wish you much luck."

Twenty reporters were already at the airport bar, taking on liquids in preparation for the thirsty days ahead. The Middle East press corps, at least at the time of my tour, had its share of old-school hard drinkers.

"In a few hours you'll be dreaming of this," declared one veteran Englishman, holding aloft a glass of white wine. The only booze available in Libya, he added, was bathtub gin called "flash."

"First you get drunk, then you go blind." He chuckled, refilling his glass. "Then the Libyans give you eighty lashes."

The Jerusalem-based press corps was rather more sober, searching bags and pockets for stray shekels, El Al stickers and forgotten laundry receipts written in Hebrew. Libya wasn't the sort of place where you wanted to arrive carrying any evidence of contact with the Zionist entity.

Not that an American passport was anything to crow about. Qaddafi liked to call the United States "Enemy Number One of Humanity," and he had once advised young soldiers to "drink the blood" of Zionists and Americans. Now, to make the relationship even worse, the United States was claiming that a factory in Rabta, south of Tripoli, was about to produce poison gas; there was even talk of an American air strike on the plant. The Libyans were apparently letting us in to present their side—that the Rabta plant made medicines.

"Aspirin, extra-strength," quipped a half-drunk reporter. "And deodorant."

"Spray-on," a companion chimed in. "The kind you wear a gas mask while using."

I made the naive suggestion that if the Libyans were really producing mustard gas, they'd be crazy to let us in to document the fact. An Australian across the table looked at me incredulously.

"Mate," he said, splashing more wine in my glass, "this is Libya. Logic doesn't apply."

Waiting in line to board the Libya Air plane, I gravitated toward the one passenger who wasn't wearing rumpled khakis and the besotted grin of a foreign correspondent. He was slight and balding, clad in tight jeans with a black leather belt and fierce tattoos on both hands. He looked like a cross between the local handyman and a Hell's Angel. His carry-on—eight cartons of duty-free cigarettes—marked him as a regular traveler to Libya.

"Can't get decent fags in Libya," he explained with a North England burr. "Can't get decent anything in Libya. Got forty-seven kilos of canned food in me check-through."

Jim Stead said he worked as a diver on an oil installation near Tripoli. He had been there eight years because he liked the "green stuff," the money. "Not much else to like about the place," he said. As the plane lifted off over the Mediterranean, he chatted amiably about the oil business, about his week's R and R in Italy, and about his former profession: killing people.

"Mercenary for eight years, I was," Stead said flatly. "Cyprus, Belgian Congo, few other bad spots." He laughed. "See the world, kill people."

He showed me his right hand, tattooed with a skull and crossbones and the words "Death or Glory." He called it a "mercenary's badge." His left hand bore another tattoo, of a samurai with a sword through his head. "Can't remember what that one means," he said. "Too pissed on gin the night I got it."

There were other badges of his trade: a bullet wound in his left arm, another in his right leg, and a bayonet scar on his shoulder. "Didn't get the bloke who gave me that scratch," he said, shaking his head the way a fisherman does when recalling the big one that got away. But plenty of others hadn't escaped.

"For my money, a crossbow's best, 'least for assassinations," he went on. "For one, it's quiet. Don't hear it, d'you?" He smiled, winking slightly. "Main thing, though, you can shoot through glass. A bullet, now glass deflects bullets. You can aim for the head and get a shoulder instead. But an arrow cuts clean through glass. Take a head shot, get a head shot."

I nodded. Take a head shot, get a head shot. And what kind of gun did he prefer?

"Different jobs demand different guns," Stead said. "Now an AK-47, it's got better range than your M-16. A Uzi is good for a tight job, if you've got to take out a bunch. But for a single target, well, can't beat a Kalashnikov."

I nodded again, trying to remember every word; I didn't want to clam him up by taking out a notebook. How about knives?

"Speaking for myself, don't like knife jobs," he said. "Too close. Now there's some blokes, born killers, now they might be an ace with a knife. But I'm more of a crack machine gunner."

He paused as a steward came down the aisle with soft drinks. "Thing is," he said thoughtfully, sipping orange soda, "no matter what the weapon, you got to have the right personality, know what I mean? You got to be inhuman. You can't start thinking about the politics, about what you're doing, or what they're going to do to you. That's when you get careless."

I asked him if he ever thought of getting back into the business. He shook his head. "You'd want seven hundred quid a week for it now. But the demand's gone. No one gives a monkey anymore about doing the killing themselves."

Stewards came down the aisle again, this time with landing cards, which were printed only in Arabic. Qaddafi regarded European languages as a corrupt influence on his pure Arab state and had banned their use on official forms, street signs, even soda bottles. The landing card included the usual questions: name, nationality, date of birth, religion. Up until now, I'd never seen any reason to conceal my religion. But I'd never flown into the world's most fanatically anti-Zionist country, without a visa, to a capital where the U.S. embassy had been sacked and American diplomats withdrawn some years before. Writing in "Jew" seemed a recipe for expulsion, or at the very least, a way to attract unwelcome attention.

"What do you reckon?" Geraldine asked, staring at the question as well. "Buddhist? Infidel?"

I put down "Quaker," having attended a Friends school for eight years. Who could kick out a Quaker? I didn't let Stead see. Somehow I didn't imagine he'd have much use for Quakers.

Stead scribbled down his address at a camp outside Tripoli and invited us to come out and "get pissed" on the weekend. "Me and me mates brew one hundred and eighty liters of beer every week," he said. "And we drink it all." He was the friendliest mercenary I'd ever met.

We arrived at Tripoli's airport to be greeted with discouraging news. The first planeload of journalists had been issued visas and allowed in. But the second, arriving several hours before ours, had been sent straight back to Rome. We sat in a corner of the terminal, waiting for what we assumed was to be the same fate.

The airport was unadorned, except for the bewildering messages scrawled on he walls. The prohibition of English apparently didn't extend to the pronouncements of Colonel Qaddafi. Not that this made them any easier to understand.

PEOPLES ARE ONLY HARMONIOUS WITH
THEIR OWN ARTS AND HERITAGES.

DEMOCRACY MEANS POPULAR RULE, NOT
POPULAR EXPRESSION.

IN NEED, DEMOCRACY IS LATENT

The slogans were the first clue to the wackiness of Libya—or rather, the Socialist People's Libyan Arab Great Jamahiriya.

Jamahiriya was a word coined by Qaddafi, meaning, roughly, "republic of the masses." He had added the "Great" after the U.S. bombing of Tripoli in 1986, an event which, in the inverted logic of Libyan propaganda, constituted a glorious victory.

The second sign of mental disorder was the comment of the official who appeared with our passports. He had stamped each one with a seven-day visa. I asked him why the plane before ours had been turned away.

"*Zachma*," he said, which means "crowded." This failed, of course, to explain why the fifty reporters on board our flight had been allowed in. But I was learning to go with the Libyan flow. Logicians need not apply.

A bus carried us through the dark empty avenues of Tripoli and deposited us at El-Kabir, the Grand Hotel, on Revolution Street. At the Rome airport, a rumor had swept the press corps that credit cards and dollars were unacceptable to the Libyans and that we should change all our money into Italian lire instead. Several had, at unfavorable airport rates, boarding the plane with lira-stuffed satchels. At the Grand Hotel we were quickly informed that lire were worthless; only dollars were accepted, and the hotel wanted us to pay the bill for our one-week visit in advance, at a rate of $125 a night.

"Fucking typical," groaned a TV reporter, who ended up lending out all his money. TV reporters always travel with thousands of dollars in cash, like drug dealers. This makes them easy prey for strapped print journalists.

One hundred and twenty-five dollars at El-Kabir bought a not-very-grand room with a television blurrily broadcasting a reading of Qaddafi's *Green Book*, a Sahara-like compendium of the colonel's thoughts. Qaddafi had consigned communism to the dustheap of history, along with capitalism, as a failed ideology superseded by his own "Third International Theory." But with typical contrariness, the colonel borrowed freely from Marxist and Maoist symbolism. He had authored his own *Green Book*—green being the color of Islam—and launched his own Cultural Revolution, to purge Libya of

non-Islamic influence. Tripoli, like Moscow, has at its center
a revolutionary square—Green Square, not Red. Officially,
the state had wilted away; the masses ruled directly through
organs such as the General Secretariat of the General People's Congress for Information. Even Libya's embassies had
been taken over by the masses and renamed People's
Bureaus. In a nation of only 3.5 million citizens, many of
them still seminomadic, it seemed incredible that there were
enough souls to staff all the People's Committees, People's
Congresses and People's Secretariats.

At midnight the word went out that we were to gather in
the lobby at eight in the morning for "the program." In
controlled situations such as this, Arab information minis-
tries always had a "program." And like every other, this one
was to begin with a bus pulling up at the hotel early in the
morning—presumably to take us to the Rabta plant.

    "Any minute it comes," one of our escorts said, at eight
o'clock.

    "It is coming now, any minute," he said at nine.

    By ten, having ingested the hotel's entire supply of nico-
tine and coffee, the press corps was becoming mutinous.
Pack journalism is never pretty, but it is never so ugly as
when the pack has nothing to feed on. Starved for facts,
reporters inevitably begin devouring themselves.

    Floodlights illuminated a corner of the hotel lobby, and
the pack surged forward to see what was happening. It was
a bored television crew, reporting nothing. "Phil," the pro-
ducer yelled to his cameraman, "give me a 'reporters in the
lobby' shot." Drifting away, the pack spotted a solitary journalist speaking to an Arab-looking man—and barged in once
again.

    "Do you think they're making gas at Rabta?" someone
shouted.

    The man looked bewildered. "Lunch begin at one
o'clock," he said. He was a waiter at the hotel.

    When someone did score a shred of information—a
veiled comment by one of our escorts, or a ninth-hand rumor

picked up from another journalist—the pack circled again, pens poised, taking down details that were now tenth-hand.

"How do I source that one?"

"Dunno. 'Observers said'?"

"Informed Western sources?"

"Informed Western sources, I like that." The reporter chuckled, composing the lead for his story. "Informed Western sources in Tripoli said today that they knew absolutely zip about a poison gas plant in Rabta. . . ."

I passed the time reading that day's English translation of *Jamahiriya News* (*JANA*), Libya's official organ of information. *JANA* pumped out the pulpiest propaganda fiction I'd yet seen in the Middle East, which was saying a lot.

"MORE CONDEMNATIONS AND DENUNCIATIONS OF U.S. AGGRESSION, THREATS AND PROVOCATIONS CONTINUE THE WORLD OVER!" screamed the lead headline. "The world over" included "prominent political figures and organizations" such as:

> The Chairman of the National Congress in the Canary Islands!
> The Secretary General of the Workers' Union of Malta!
> President Didier Ratsiraka of Madagascar!"
> Muslim Authors Organization in Tanzania!

General Noriega of Panama sent a cable of support, as did Abu Mousa, a breakaway PLO leader, who praised Libya's "revolution against all attempts to harm the nationalist stance rejecting Imperialist-Zionist-Reactionary plots!"

Reading *JANA* was a bit like scanning supermarket tabloids. I imagined the *JANA* "journalists" with certain interchangeable epithets already keyed into their computers, each ending in exclamation points: "IMPERIALIST CRIMINAL!" "ARROGANT SUPERPOWER!" "COLONIAL STOOGE!" All they had to do was reshuffle the insults, punch in a source—from a list of obscure revolutionary movements—and print the story in the biggest typeface available.

THE SECRETARY GENERAL OF THE VAN-
GUARDS OF PEOPLE'S LIBERATION WAR DE-
CLARED THAT AMERICA WANTS JAMAHIRIYA TO
BE A PUPPET TOOL SUBJECTED TO ITS DOMINA-
TION AND CONTROL!

Unfortunately, *JANA* could be read in the time it takes to
down a single cup of Turkish coffee. I waited anxiously for
Geraldine. Having been in these situations before, we had
agreed to pool our resources, with one of us staking out the
lobby while the other wandered off to interview diplomats
or people on the street. As the morning wore on, with no
sign of a trip to Rabta, I decided I'd use my shift outside
the hotel to visit Jim Stead, the fellow we'd met on the
airplane. If nothing else, I might manage a *JANA*-style "Profile of a Mercenary."

Geraldine returned with bad news. She had run into an
Englishman who happened to work with Jim Stead. "Jim
Stead," the man told her, "is the biggest bullshit artist who
ever breathed."

At midday, when the pack seemed ready to run amok
through Tripoli, two buses pulled up in front of the hotel.
"We are going out of the city," one of the Ministry of Information officials announced, and the horde of gullible journalists clambered aboard.

We were, indeed, headed out of the city, past cinder-
block apartments and onto a highway south. The two government escorts on our bus claimed they had no idea where
we were headed, though they assured us we'd be there "in
one hour." Reporters with maps followed the bus's progress,
calling out every few minutes: "South" (the direction of
Rabta). "East." "South." "East." "East." "Still East."

"What the fuck?"

"They're taking us to see Qaddafi."

"They're taking us to another plant."

And most optimistically, "They're taking us to the
airport!"

In fifteen minutes we were out of the city and into a pleasant landscape of rolling hills, blanketed with olive and palm. The view surprised me; I'd somehow expected all of Libya to be a huge hot sandbox with towns resembling some drab suburb of Warsaw. The beauty of the scenery, however, couldn't distract from the fact that we were now headed northeast, in the opposite direction from Rabta. One of our escorts came down the aisle to break the news. "You are very lucky because we take you today to someplace very special." He paused dramatically. "We go to Leptis Magna."

"Leprous what?"

"Leptis Magna," he repeated. "Finest Roman ruin in North Africa. You like?"

A collective groan reverberated down the aisle. We were going fifty miles the wrong way, to sight-see. Gazing disconsolately out the window, the reporter beside me spotted a flock of sheep grazing on the roadside. "Look!" he shouted. "Another group of journalists!"

And the chorus went up across the bus— "Baa,baa,baa"—as the pack rolled on through the countryside to the finest Roman ruin in Africa.

On day two, "the program" began just as it had on day one, with an official circulating through the lobby, telling reporters to be out front at eight sharp for the bus. At ten o'clock, when the program seemed set for another long intermission, I left Geraldine to keep watch for the buses and wandered out for a walk through Tripoli. Gathering street "color" was, for me, always the best part of Middle East reporting. It was also the easiest. Except in Iraq, I rarely walked five minutes in any Arab country without being approached by students, shopkeepers or passersby who wanted to practice their English, offer me tea, peddle blackmarket goods, or just study me in the same way that I was studying them. No matter how difficult it might be to extract official information in an Arab country, it was usually easy to take the pulse of the place.

In Tripoli, though, there was no pulse to take; walking

through the city was like holding a finger to a mummy's wrist. It was Saturday morning, the beginning of the Arab week and usually the busiest day, yet there was almost no one at all on the streets.

The few people I did encounter weren't Libyan. As in other oil-rich and underskilled countries, Libya imported laborers, mostly Palestinians, Sudanese, Lebanese and other migratory serfs. I pitied them for washing up here.

"It is always like this, my friend," said a Lebanese engineer named Hakim, hanging out at an empty intersection. "It is like cemetery." Hakim had come a week before from Beirut, in search of work, and was waiting for a man who had promised him a job. Hakim had been waiting there every morning, for three days running, and the man still hadn't appeared. "Maybe he is dead," Hakim said.

I asked him where everyone was.

"You know, the peoples of Libya are very busy. People's Committees. People's Bureaus. People's Prisons." He chuckled at his own joke. "Really, this is all bullshit. Mostly the peoples do nothing."

Hakim did the same. Tripoli wasn't a happening sort of town for a single young Lebanese in tight blue jeans and Ray-Bans. There were no bars or nightclubs in Tripoli. There were two tattered movie theaters, offering a Bruce Lee film and a B-grade Indian flick. "I see them nine times," Hakim confessed. And in a metropolis of one million people, there was nothing at all going down on the streets, day or night.

"It is crazy, I know, but I miss Lebanon," Hakim said, smiling wanly. "In Beirut, always there is action."

Tripoli could never be mistaken for a capital swimming in the international mainstream. There was no American or British embassy, but there were missions for Nicaragua, North Korea, and Cuba, as well as a run-down building labeled "The International Secretariat for Solidarity with the Arab People and Their Central Cause Palestine." Intrigued, I looked for an entrance, but couldn't find one. There were tattered posters showing black men in green berets, clutching submachine guns, or bloodied women of indeterminate ethnicity, waving clenched fists. A short list of the insurgencies to which Qaddafi lent his support included the IRA, Basque separatists, Kanak rebels in New Guinea, radical Aborigines in Australia, Tamil Tigers, Abu Nidal's Fatah Revolutionary Council, and assorted rebel cells in Sudan, Chad, Niger, Mali and Senegal. If Tripoli was anything to judge by, the victory of all these liberation movements would make for a very dull globe.

I went to the souk, the liveliest quarter of any Arab city and the easiest in which to make chat. Here, at least, there were Libyans: women with henna painted on their faces and baskets balanced on their heads, and men clad in Qaddafi-style ensembles of woolen cloaks and caps. Narrow alleys wound between whitewashed homes and workshops where men with tiny hammers beat brass into urns and platters. There was even the requisite fortress, perched by the Mediterranean, a reminder of the days when America had sent battleships to the shores of Tripoli to put down the pirates of what was then the Barbary Coast.

But the market was oddly unspirited, a kind of wax-museum casbah. All the elements were there—except for the hustle, the stink of saffron and sweat, and the untidy business of buying and selling wares. Everyone seemed unnaturally subdued, as though reserving whatever energy he or she possessed for the stage-managed, fist-waving frenzies I'd seen on television.

One reason for the quiet was the lack of things to buy and sell. Qaddafi dolloped up generous servings of Semtex explosives to his revolutionary allies. But to his own people, "Brother Leader" offered little except sacks of Cuban sugar and cans of Bulgarian cooking oil.

Qaddafi's mercurial edicts also discouraged whatever entrepreneurial spirit might once have existed in Libya. The year before, in a characteristic burst of ideological insanity, he'd decreed that it would henceforth be illegal to employ any one but family members, as the wage system was exploitive. PARTNERS NOT WAGE EARNERS! was one of his favorite slogans. Shopkeepers were barred from selling "decadent" goods that they hadn't produced with their own hands. Bakers were about the only ones left with wares to sell. There was also talk of abolishing currency and restoring the barter system. Not surprisingly, private commerce in Libya shut down overnight.

All these decrees had since been rescinded or forgotten, in the Libyan fashion, but there remained a tentative air to the souk, as though merchants expected a People's Committee to sweep through at any moment with some new and even more bizarre regulation.

"When I read about Americans complaining that their economy is too regulated, I have to laugh," said Ali Eshbini, sipping tea at his empty metal shop. He planned to shut down as soon as he'd sold his remaining goods: three sheets of dented aluminum siding.

Eshbini proved to be the only merchant I could engage in conversation. At each shop, I'd pick something up, ask its price, then exhaust my limited stock of overblown Arab pleasantries: about the fineness of the day and the fineness of Libya, praise Allah. And at each shop the merchant would nod politely, or offer a meager half-smile, and return to his tea, or to rearranging the meager merchandise on his shelves. In two hours of walking, I encountered not one "Where you from?"; not a single "Is you English man?"; not even a "Welcome, my friend. For you I make special deal." I had anticipated suspicion, even rabid hostility, toward Enemy Number One, but all I got was stony, uninterested silence.

Fear was undoubtedly a factor, though the security presence in Tripoli was as muted as its populace. There was none of the police-state apparatus that I'd come to accept as part of the scenery in Arab capitals, like palm trees and minarets. No soldiers poking submachine guns through car windows; no guards slumped over AK-47s in front of government buildings; no trucks full of soldiers straddling main intersections and coup routes. In fact, apart from a few policemen directing nonexistent traffic, there were no guns or soldiers at all. Qaddafi had either killed, exiled or imprisoned every dissident in sight, or else the population was too somnambulant to require any vigilance.

Glorification of Brother Leader was also restrained. There were entire bookstores devoted to Qaddafi's *Green Book*, and to the "commentaries" that had grown like Talmud around the original text. But the Leader's face wasn't plastered on every wall and billboard, as was the custom in other one-man regimes. The one exception was Green Square, a vast spread of asphalt covered in cracking green paint, overlooked by a painting of the colonel in dark glasses and military uniform. The portrait was big but not towering, nothing to compare with the ubiquitous pictures of Saddam Hussein in Baghdad. As in Iraq, Big Brother was watching, but there really wasn't much to keep an eye on. Apart from two Polish engineers' wives with Polaroids, and a beggar from Ghana—all of whom I interviewed, in desperation—there was no one at all in the square.

I returned to the hotel with about a paragraph of "color," wondering what in the world I could write. Suddenly several cars screeched to a halt and a phalanx of brawny men in green fatigues jumped out. One tall head of black curls poked up from the huddle. It was the colonel himself. I rushed up against the bodyguards and was swept with them through the door and into the hotel lobby.

Qaddafi's visit was unannounced and caught the pack lounging about the lobby, still waiting for the program to begin. Within seconds, two hundred journalists leaped to their feet, discarded lit cigarettes and swarmed around the colonel in a riot of floodlights, microphones and shouted questions.

"When will we go to Rabta?"

"Are you making gas?"

"Colonel, what can you say about Italian-Libyan relations?"

Ignoring the tumult, Qaddafi promenaded from one end of the lobby to the other, chin raised high, eyes trained on the middle distance, like a prince on a tour of his realm. He was, as always, sartorially resplendent, in a togalike cloak slung across a braided vest and tartan sweater, with a red woolen cap perched atop his coal-black curls. Designer dictator.

The pack surged behind him, desperate to get within camera and microphone range. TV men hoisted each other on their shoulders, radio men thrust microphones between bodies, print journalists positioned their pads against the backs of the people in front of them. At one point the crush was so great that I felt myself lifted off my feet. And as soon as the pack had positioned itself, however uncomfortably, Qaddafi wheeled around and ambled off the other way, with his bodyguards running interference in a rough scrum of thrust elbows and raised knees.

Finally, when the crowd became so dense that Qaddafi couldn't move, one of his retainers addressed the pack.

"He would like to drink some coffee, that is all," the man said, as the Leader gazed distractedly at the crowd. "He did not think you were here."

The colonel, apparently, just happened to be passing the El-Kabir and thought he'd pop in for a quiet cup of coffee. Only to find two hundred reporters who had been waiting frantically for thirty-two hours for something to justify their plane bill, their hotel bill, their planned layovers in Rome on the return trip. Qaddafi, for all his madness, knew how to get the media's attention.

He meandered several feet more, paused in front of a portrait of himself and wearily consented to answer a few questions, though only in Arabic. This was logical. Ninety-nine percent of the assembled journalists spoke English, as did Qaddafi himself, having gone to Britain as a young officer for military training. Perhaps two percent of the pack spoke decent Arabic, though even they struggled with Libyan accents, considered the most difficult in the Arab world. And just to ensure that even this small group wouldn't understand a word, Qaddafi spoke in an almost inaudible whisper.

I had witnessed Qaddafi's perversity once before, at an Arab summit in Algiers. Flanked by female bodyguards, he'd worn a single white glove, like Michael Jackson, to avoid tainting his flesh when greeting Morocco's King Hassan, who had once shaken hands with the Zionist Shimon Peres. Standing before five hundred journalists, Qaddafi had insisted on taking all the group's questions before answering any of them. After listening to each, and taking careful notes on a pad of paper, he proceeded to deliver a rambling, almost incoherent speech in Arabic that had nothing to do with any of the questions.

This time, at least, I had a front-row view, having clung close to the bodyguards. From a distance, Qaddafi matched his imperial TV presence: chiseled features, fixed gaze and upturned chin. Close up, under the glare of TV lights, he was shrunken and strange. The dashing twenty-eight-year-old who had seized power twenty years before and terrorized the West ever since seemed now a dissipated and unimpressive figure, pushing fifty. Skin hung in folds from his creased and oddly bloated face. Sweat gathered on his upper lip. His dark brown eyes seemed blank and his voice was toneless, as though Brother Leader, like the People he commanded, was in a vague sort of lithium stupor.

Perhaps he had mouthed the same words so many times that they were putting him to sleep.

"Libya is facing official terrorism from the United States. . . . America is full of terrorists, and Israel, too. . . . Libya will continue to fight for the liberation of Palestine from the river to the sea. . . America is the imperialist aggressor, and we are just a little nation, seeking peace. . . ."

Qaddafi's vocabulary was the same as *JANA*'s, consisting of interchangeable slogans and insults, to be recited over and over like verses from the Koran, as if the repetition might somehow make them true.

Qaddafi spoke for perhaps twenty minutes and then he was gone, hustled out the door and into a small white Peugeot, which he drove himself, without passengers. When an aide came too close as Qaddafi climbed into the car, the colonel scowled and slapped the man across the face. Then, without blinking, he broke into a broad and engaging smile for the crowd that had gathered, miraculously, all along the corniche, chanting *"Down down U.S.A!"*

As I watched him drive off, waving gaily through his open window, I tried to imagine any other Middle East leader—any American or European leader, for that matter—driving himself through the streets of a capital city, in a modest sedan, with virtually no security. It was either another bit of Qaddafi stagecraft or a clear sign that the man was much more secure in his power than the West liked to think.

"Qaddafi, he is my love," said one woman bystander, whom I'd run up to interview, desperate for an animated, English-speaking Libyan. She clutched her heart as she spoke.

"And what do you think of Reagan?" I asked.

She laughed, pantomiming automatic weapon fire. "What you call this? Machine gun? I say machine-gun Reagan. He is crazy man. Not like Qaddafi."

In the twenty minutes Qaddafi spent at El-Kabir, the pack had laid waste to the lobby, upending plants and ashtrays and leaving a trail of broken glass and furniture across the floor. A French woman had been taken to the hospital with trample wounds. It was one of those scenes that make you proud to be a member of the fourth estate.

Bruised but happy, the pack was now fighting to get in line for the telex machines.

Copy, copy, we've got copy! Don't know what it is yet, but Allah be praised, we've got a story to send!

At four in the afternoon, when the lobby was deserted for the first time in two days, three buses pulled up in front of the hotel and handlers jumped out to shepherd us aboard.

"The program goes now to Rabta," one of the men declared. His tone was clipped and officious, as though we were right on schedule, although thirty-two hours had passed since the original announcement that journalists were to gather in the lobby. The pack scoured maps to make sure there wasn't some other Rabta off in the desert—the site of a Saracen fortress, say, or the birthplace of an obscure ninth-century sheik—and reluctantly boarded the buses.

We drove southwest through a semiarid plain and toward a chain of low-lying hills. We passed radar and sur-face-to-air missile emplacements, and continued on toward a bright glow emanating from what looked like the gray outline of a factory complex. The pack stirred from its propaganda-induced slumber.

Rabta! The light at the end of the program!

None of us had any way of confirming that this was actually Rabta. All we knew about the plant was what we'd been fed by diplomats and U.S. intelligence: that satellite photos of Rabta matched aerial pictures of poison-gas plants in Iraq; that there had been suspicious shipments of chemi-cals not normally used for pharmaceuticals; and that inter-cepted phone calls had caught panicky Libyans quizzing German chemists about how to handle a toxic spill at the plant. The whiff of mustard gas seemed incontrovertible.

"American media, why so cynical?" asked a handler who sat across the aisle from me, listening in on the journal-ists' patter. He was an amiable young man named Abdullah who said he worked for "the Center for Resistance Against Zionism, Imperialism and Reactionary Plots."

I told him that the Libyans hadn't offered much evi-dence to counter the U.S. allegations. In response, Abdullah unfurled a copy of that day's *Jamahiriya News* and read a statement by the Syrian Health Minister upon his visit to Rabta. He hailed Rabta as a great contribution to Arab medi-cine, and his opinion was echoed by the Libyan demonstra-tors camped out by the plant. The paper reported:

"It is one of the factories decided to establish by the basic People's Congresses to make available medicines! They have declared their readiness to defend this civilized monu-ment at any cost!"

Abdullah stopped reading and said, "You see, it is all American fabrication, these lies about poison gas."

I explained that by the standards of the American press, the Syrian Health Minister hardly qualified as an objective source.

"What means 'source'?"

"Source of information. You know, some person or document you can rely on for the truth."

"But Qaddafi has spoken. So has our Syrian brother. Why you need more source?"

I hadn't thought it possible that anyone actually believed what was said by *JANA*, or by Qaddafi, or by Libya's fellow outlaws. But it gradually dawned on me that this earnest twenty-five-year-old from the Center for Resistance Against Zionism, Imperialism and Reactionary Plots was absolutely sincere. And why shouldn't he be? After all, he'd been five when Qaddafi seized power. His entire sentient life had been set to a chorus of Qaddafi's thoughts, beginning with recitals of *The Green Book* in grade school and continuing with nightly readings on the radio and televison

"Libya's voice is heard by three hundred million blacks living in America!" he went on, continuing his reading from *JANA*. "Eighty million Red Indians hear our voice! Pariahs everywhere hear our voice!"

"Abdullah," I interrupted, "there are about thirty-five million blacks in America and maybe a million Indians. No more. I swear it."

He paused for a moment, letting the statement sink in. "This is possible," he said, "because you have killed all the rest."

Not all Libyans were quite so committed. In fact, many among the several thousand demonstrators who greeted us near Rabta appeared to have arrived on buses an hour before. Bored and cold, they mustered a desultory "Down! Down! U.S.A.!" as soon as the TV cameras turned their way, then went quiet the instant the cameras shut off. It was the sort of gathering known in the trade as "rent-a-crowd."

While the cameras rolled, I tried to lose myself in the mob and meander off for a closer look at the plant looming a mile or so up the road. I had made it two hundred yards when Abdullah appeared, anxious and out of breath.

"Please!" he yelled, tugging at my elbow. "Back to the bus!"

"But I just want to chat with some people."

"This is not in the program," he said.

Back on the bus, we drove straight toward the gate of what looked like a huge industrial park. A few feet short of the gate, the bus swerved left and parked beside a low building where yet another stage-managed rally was in progress, this time involving a crowd of young boys shaking their fists and shouting, in Arabic, "Fuck America! Fuck Reagan!"

The day was now almost gone and in another ten minutes it would be too dark to take photographs. Ignoring the demonstrators, the TV crews rushed toward the fence abutting the industrial park and began assembling their tripods and lights. Photographers and journalists followed. Hundreds of eyes and camera lenses were quickly trained on a horizontal building several hundred yards away, the closest of perhaps a dozen structures in the factory complex. The building was windowless and gray, resembling an enormous warehouse or airport hangar, and ringed with construction cranes. In the waning light, it was impossible to tell anything more about the place.

Floodlights and microphones went on and the network reporters, jostling for position, prepared for their unrehearsed stand-ups. Three, two, one . . .

"The factory here behind me in the Libyan desert . . ."

"A controversial plant that the U.S. alleges . . ."

"Chemical weapons that could be used against Israel . . ."

Cameras rolled, shutters clicked, pens scrawled. In a few hours this sprawling gray structure would flash onto television screens across America, and onto the front pages of dozens of newspapers, described in sinister tones as possibly the largest poison-gas plant in the world.

I spotted Abdullah standing to one side of the pack, taking it all in with a sour expression. The American media, perpetrating another Zionist-Imperialist-Reactionary Plot.

"The pharmaceuticals plant," I asked him, pointing at the gray building, "so this is it?"

He shrugged and said, "As you wish."

We were given a few more minutes before the handlers herded us through the crowd of juvenile demonstrators and into a cafeteria, apparently designed for workers at the plant. Pepsi, doughnuts and tangerines had been laid out for our benefit. I had been on enough official tours to know that food was a bad sign, indicating that the program was headed for maximum stall.

Sure enough, a man stood up at the front clutching a twenty-page statement and wearing a glazed expression. His words, tedious enough to begin with, were translated from Arabic to English and then to French, to waste as much time as possible.

"We welcome you to the peaceful village of Rabta," he said tonelessly, studying his notes. "We welcome you as pharmaceutical personnel and as administrators of the new medical facility."

"Who is this clown?"

"We welcome you to this peaceful village," he droned on, ignoring the jeers, "that has been under threat from American arrogance. Arabs have always been leaders in medicine and pharmacology—"

"Bloody hell. Give me some aspirin!"

"—and this plant is another achievement for the realization of the future of Arab children. Libya, that bastion of peace and guidance, and *The Green Book*, the final solution for human justice—"

"Phil, give me a reporters-in-the-cafeteria shot."

"—as stated by the Leader of the El Fatah Revolution, Colonel Muammar el-Qaddafi."

The speech lasted forty minutes, by which time the cafeteria looked worse than the El-Kabir lobby after Qaddafi's surprise appearance: cigarettes stubbed in doughnuts, tangerine peels carpeting the floor, reporters slumped across tables, snoring. The director of the peaceful people's pharmaceutical plant at Rabta folded up his notes and melted away, failing to answer a single question.

"And now," Abdullah said, "we go to see the plant."

Outside, the sky was black and the bus windows were already fogging up from the cold. We drove through the gate of the plant, or what looked like the gate of the plant; it was impossible to tell. Factory buildings loomed on either side. Factory buildings, or maybe parking garages, I couldn't be sure. At one point, the buses paused before a large, well-lit tent. Through the open flap we glimpsed a dense crowd of men waving fists and chanting. It seemed that this was the next stop on our program, but after a brief consultation among the handlers the buses kept rolling through the night.

I asked Abdullah where we were going.

"We go now to sub-branch of plant."

We drove for another ten minutes. Abdullah corrected himself. "We go now to old Rabta, then to see plant." After another ten minutes he updated our plans yet again. "I think maybe there is change in the program."

Ten minutes later, as we turned on to what felt like the smooth asphalt of a major highway, Abdullah announced, "We go back to Tripoli. There is no point in visiting the plant in the dark."

The pack was too weary and too inured to Libyan stunts to muster much indignation. Still, the chutzpah of our handlers was impressive. In most Arab countries, if a government wants to conceal something, it simply keeps journalists out, or smothers them in silence. Faced with the same situation, the Libyans opted for the Big Lie—pharmaceuticals, not poison gas—and the Big Con—a two-day bus ride to nowhere. Adding insult to injury, *JANA* would no doubt use our nonvisit as fodder for another bonfire of lies.

TEN THOUSAND JOURNALISTS VISIT PEACEFUL
  VILLAGE OF RABTA!
REAFFIRM THAT THE ABOVE PLANT IS A MEDI-
  CINES FACTORY!

MASSES MOBILIZE AGAINST AMERICAN ARRO-
GANCE AND FABRICATIONS!

Domestically, the charade at Rabta would no doubt bolster
the regime. But for an international audience, the phony
tour was calamitous. By the time we'd reached the hotel,
the pack had penned a hundred variations on the same
theme; namely, that the Libyans had hurt their own case by
producing nothing but fibs and evasions. The only "fact"
gleaned from the entire program was the sight of radar and
surface-to-air missiles at Rabta, hardly the sort of scenery
surrounding the average medicine factory. It wouldn't take
much reading between the lines for the Western public to
surmise that Libya was guilty as charged.

But the Libyans had one last trick up their sleeves. The
pack had just begun tapping telexes and shouting down
crackly telephone lines when all communications in the hotel
went dead. Then an announcement came over the loudspeaker. "All journalists are kindly requested to bring their
bags to the buses by ten p.m."

"My friend," an English journalist explained, "you've
just been PNG'ed from Libya." PNG is journalese for "per-
sona non grata," a polite way of saying we were kicked out
of the country. The Englishman shook his head. "I haven't
filed a bloody word. And my smalls are still at the laundry."

The hotel staff had a surprise of its own. Though we'd
paid for a week's accommodation, in dollars, and thus far
spent only forty-eight hours in the hotel, the desk announced
that we'd be refunded for only four nights, in Libyan dinars.
The Libyan dinar is perhaps the world's most worthless currency, even in Libya. We'd been lied to, sent on a two-day
wild-goose chase, kicked out of the country—and now
fleeced as well. Perhaps this is why we'd been allowed in to
start with, to inject some hard currency into the Libyan
economy.

As a long line of journalists protested over their bills, I
wandered over to Abdullah to get one last comment from
Libyan officialdom.

"Why are we being expelled?"

"Expelled? No one is being expelled." He looked genuinely hurt. "Mr. Tony, the program is over."

True to form, the buses didn't appear for another ten hours. The various People's Committees responsible for the foreign press weren't well coordinated. Either that or they wanted more dollars. Whatever the reason, and there probably wasn't one, the pack was granted an overnight reprieve, which gave reporters time to haggle over their bills, recover underwear from the laundry and make restaurant reservations in Rome.

Although there was only one scheduled flight to Rome, on Alitalia, we were assured at El-Kabir that there would be flights waiting at the airport, "to take you anywhere." This was true, after a fashion: there were the usually scheduled and half-empty flights to Bulgaria, Burkina Faso, Bangladesh and other nations friendly to the Socialist People's Great Arab Jamahiriya. But like the buses, the promised planes to Europe never appeared. And a Libyan Air ticket was about as convertible as a Libyan dinar; Alitalia didn't want to touch it.

I was standing in a long line, hoping to convince Alitalia to change its mind, when I felt something brush against my hip. As I turned around, a young man sprinted off through the terminal. The airport was crowded, and I caught him in a clumsy tackle near the door. My wallet was still in his hand.

Wrestling on the floor of a Middle East airport is a quick way to attract attention. I looked up to find myself surrounded by submachine guns. The soldier escorted us to a small room, bare except for a portrait of Qaddafi. Then an official appeared whom I recognized as one of the handlers who had shepherded the pack for the past two days. I explained what had happened. The pickpocket said nothing. Then two soldiers grasped him by each elbow and he began screaming at the top of his lungs. He was thin and sallow-faced; his cheeks were covered in tears and his eyes seemed to bug out of his head. Then he disappeared into an adjoining room, and the official offered me a cup of tea.

"Really, it's no big deal," I said, regretting that I hadn't let the young man run out of the airport. After all, the hotel had robbed me almost clean already. "I just want to get on the plane."

One of the guards returned with the pickpocket's passport. "You see, this man is Algerian, not Libyan," the official said, showing me the document. "This does not happen in Libya." There were loud thuds from the adjoining room. Then screams.

"This does not happen in Libya," the official said again.

"Fine. I believe you. Now please, let's just forget the whole thing. I don't want anyone hurt on my account."

The official took me by the arm and opened the door to the other room. The Algerian was curled on the floor, clutching his head and weeping. One of the guards kicked him in the gut. "You see," the official said, pulling the door shut, "we do not allow such things to happen in Libya."

For two days, I'd regarded Libya as a cartoonish regime, hardly deserving the demon status it had assumed in American imagination. But this small instance of brutality made all its other supposed crimes a little more believable.

"What flight are you on?" the official asked. He didn't want me hanging around. I showed him my Libya Air ticket and explained that the only flight to Rome was on Alitalia. He took me by the arm again, led me to the front of the line at Alitalia and talked briefly with the man behind the counter.

"There was a mistake, but it has been corrected," the official said, handing me two boarding passes. He hustled Geraldine and me past a hundred other journalists and straight through security and immigration.

"Remember, this does not happen in Libya," he said one last time, then added with a half-smile, "And please, tell all journalists, come to Tripoli again."

II

KHARTOUM
This Is the Way the World Ends

When Allah made the Sudan, Allah laughed.
—SUDANESE PROVERB

The man behind the desk at the Sahara Hotel stared at me in disbelief.

"You want to what?" he asked.

"Walk. You know, stretch my legs."

"Where?"

"Outside."

"But why?"

"To see Khartoum."

"There is nothing to see. And it is dark."

There was nothing to see inside, either. The power had blacked out soon after my arrival, and the hotel's only other guest, a Welsh water engineer, sat in the lobby reading a month-old London *Times* by candlelight. When I persisted, the man behind the desk gave in with an exasperated shrug. "If the power returns, I will give you our kerosene lamp so you will not fall in the holes," he said.

The Welshman laughed. "Give 'im a bloody blowtorch. That way he can keep the beggars away, too."

An hour later, the power was still down, so I ventured into the dark with the Welshman's cigarette lighter instead. A leper squatted on a scrap of cardboard blocking the hotel's door. As I stepped over him, he reached out and grasped my thigh.

"*Floos,*" he said, offering the Arabic word for money. He tilted his head toward the dimly lit door so I could see his face. His eyes were covered by a milky film and his nose was a shrunken button. I clinked a coin in his metal cup and stepped into the street. He rattled the cup, and small boys enveloped me in the dark, shouting "*Floos! Floos!*" Their black skin was masked by fine white dust, like eerie trick-or-treaters. "*Floos! Floos! Floos!*" I scattered more coins and hurried off into the gloom.

The night was so black that I paused every few paces to flick on the lighter and peer ahead. The street, which adjoined Khartoum's central square, was edged with heaps of flyblown rubbish, or bundled beggars, it was hard to tell which. A few people still stirred in the night, rearranging meager blankets of newspaper and sackcloth. An old woman crouched to defecate by the curb. Each time I flicked the Bic, a soldier would approach from a doorway or sentry box to ask for a cigarette. Coup attempts were common in Khartoum, and I wondered how the soldiers distinguished enemy from friend in the dark.

I was retracing my route to the Sahara Hotel when a figure stepped forward, announcing himself with the flicker of a match. He had coal-black skin and a wide, toothless grin.

"Is you English man?" he asked. I nodded. He held up a large sack tied at one end with black cord. "I am Ali. Everything you want, I have." He looked suggestively at the bag. "Gin, beer, bongo."

"Bongo?"

"Is Sudanese hashish." He lit another match and prodded the sack. It twitched. "Also I have python skin," he said. "Life or dead. You choose."

The match died and I ran ten paces down the street before tripping over something in the road. I flicked the lighter. It was a downed power line, strung a foot or so above the ground. Just beyond it was one of the holes the hotelkeeper had warned about, deep enough to swallow a bicyclist.

A hand reached out and helped me to my feet. It was Ali

again, rattling his bag of gin, weed and reptile skin. "Python, life or dead," he said. "Your choose."

I had come to Khartoum on impulse, with only the sketchiest of story ideas. For the free-lancer, Sudan offered distinct advantages. The local currency had tumbled six hundred percent in the previous year, making Sudan the cheapest country in the Arab world. And it remained relatively unexplored: one of those blighted spots only visited by aid workers, nuns, natural disasters and representatives of the International Monetary Fund.

"You can't believe Khartoum is a capital," said John Kifner, a *New York Times* correspondent and one of the few reporters in Cairo who'd actually visited the place. "I mean, the place is total dreck. Literally. The streets are paved with shit."

American diplomats in Khartoum received a twenty-five percent pay boost, as a hardship bonus. Even Egyptians regarded their southern neighbor with distaste. Sudan was filthy and poor, they observed without irony, and the Sudanese were lazy. This from a country where a government survey once concluded that the average Egyptian worked twenty-six minutes a day. A country that made Cairo look industrious and orderly by comparison was something I had to see for myself.

On the plane from Cairo, I riffled through official literature whose vagueness rivaled the qat-addled prose of Yemen. The name Khartoum was derived from an Arabic word meaning "elephant's tusk" or "sunflower seed," though the reason for either moniker wasn't explained. According to the *Sudan Tourism Guide*, "Currency exchange rates are, from time to time, announced by the Bank of Sudan." Taxi rates were set "according to an official tariff announced from time to time." From time to time, a new government also announced itself, usually over the radio waves, at odd hours, with an accompanying score of gunfire. Civil war raged in the south, as it had, from time to time, for twenty-one years. "Yet the people," the tourism guide assured me, "are peace-loving and friendly."

Upon landing in Khartoum, it seemed miraculous that anything got done from time to time, or at all. The city was paralyzed; first by temperatures that crossed 100 degrees a few hours after sunrise, and then by choking dust storms, called *haboobs*, which gusted in from the desert, mingling sand with what was already an airborne compost heap of grit, shit, rotted fruit, rotted flesh, sweat and bongo breath. Traffic jams began at dawn as cars queued for scarce gas rations. They continued through the morning as commuters crawled toward the city center along three- and four-lane avenues reduced to one-lane ducts by craters, broken stop-lights and drooping power lines. By the time most travelers reached downtown, the brief workday was almost done. Then the traffic fanned out of the city again, until three in the afternoon, at which point the city went completely dead, stricken by heat that was now beyond the endurance of even the ever-patient Sudanese. Then night fell, the power failed, and another day in Khartoum ended, exactly like the one before.

Reporting in any ordinary sense of the word was futile. The telephone system was so bad that many phones in Khartoum hadn't rung for years. Most appointments had to be made in person, and reached on foot. After two days of hiking through the heat and dust, never knowing if the person I sought would even be in, my three-week visa seemed suddenly but a grain of sand in the vast, wretched wasteland of Sudan.

"Give it a rest, mate," an English-accented voice called out from the darkened hotel lobby. I was waiting for the telex lines to open so I could let an American editor know that I had nothing to report. The English voice called out again, "No one gives a stuff about this country, anyway."

The man's name was Geoff Bulley and he worked at a refugee camp called Kilometer 26, which denoted the dis-tance from the nearest highway. He'd traveled several days to Khartoum, in hopes of buying medicine, posting a few letters and picking up money wired from England. On the day he arrived, pharmacists went on strike in Khartoum, as did bank workers, bus drivers, postal workers, doctors, engineers and university staff.

"I'm going back to the bush with the same shopping list I brought here," Bulley said. His only successful purchase was a pint of bootleg Ethiopian gin. "In most African cities, you can bribe your way through the chaos, even run someone down if you've got the money," he said. "Here, it's so far gone that you can't find anyone to pay."

Bulley invited me onto the balcony to share the gin, and we sat long into the evening, watching darkness descend twice: first as the sun set, and then, inevitably, as the power collapsed for the night. Slowly, as the darkness and gin took hold, I began to discern the outline of a story in Khartoum's rubbled skyline. I would write a profile of the world's most blighted city. Missed appointments, broken phones and blinding haboobs would simply become part of the story.

Bulley approved of the idea. "Now that we've well and truly fucked the Third World," he said, languorously sipping gin, "it is the white man's burden to sit back and watch it fall apart."

It had long been the white man's burden to keep Sudan's "fuzzy-wuzzies" in abject submission. The history of Khartoum was nasty and short. Before 1820, the windswept plain at the confluence of the Blue and White Niles was uninhabited, except by passing camels. Then the Ottomans and Egyptians, and later the British, chose this malarial spit of riverbank as the ideal site for a garrison. Samuel Baker, an early English governor in the Sudan, knew better. "A more miserable, filthy and unhealthy place," he wrote, "can hardly be imagined."

Khartoum quickly distinguished itself as the leading slave market in Africa. By some estimates, half the city's inhabitants in the 1850's were slaves, destined for Arabia or Turkey. The Sudanese eventually revolted, under a messianic figure known as the Mahdi, and laid siege to a small

British force under the command of Charles George Gordon. "It is a useless place and we could not govern it," Gordon wrote from Khartoum in 1884. "The Sudan could be made to pay its expenses, but it would need a dictator, and I would not take the post if offered to me."

It wasn't. Instead, Gordon's severed head was offered to the Mahdi, then stuck atop a pole on the banks of the Nile. Thirteen years later, Sudanese dervishes charged out of Khartoum, clad in chain mail, to meet British Gatling guns in the battle of Omdurman. The British lost twenty-eight men; the Sudanese ten thousand. Winston Churchill, who took part in the battle, called it "the most signal triumph ever gained by the arms of science over barbarians." A war correspondent of the day wasn't so impressed: "It was not a battle but an execution." The British hurled the Mahdi's head into the Nile and settled in for sixty more years of dominion.

Now, after three decades of independence, Khartoum was a sprawling junkyard of British imperialism. The graves of eighteen-year-old Cameron Highlanders and 1st Grenadiers felled by Dervish spears—or more often by malaria—lay in a weed-infested cemetery at the edge of town. George Gordon's own gunboat rotted on the city's riverbank, unmarked and unremembered, near where the slate-gray waters of the Blue Nile meet the dull dishwater brown of the White Nile. Five miles upstream, naked boys fished from the half-sunk hulls of rusted British paddle-wheelers. Khartoum's broad avenues had been laid out at the turn of the century in the shape of a Union Jack, with the streets forming three superimposed crosses. Now the city plan was a tangled, potholed smudge. Trapped in the perpetually stalled traffic, it was impossible to avoid feeling, as George Gordon had, that the only important question in Khartoum was how to "get out of it in honor and in the cheapest way . . . it is simply a question of *getting out of it* with decency."

At Sudan's Natural History Museum, the Living Collection was mostly dead.

"This pond for rare Nile fish," the guard said, pointing toward a pool of brackish water where several rare species floated belly-up on the surface. "Pipes rusted," he continued. "Rust no good for fish."

We moved on to the reptile collection.

"This rare desert snake," he said. I searched the unmarked pen for signs of snake before picking out a half-decomposed python, well camouflaged by the dead weeds and thorns filling its cage. "No rabbits," the guard explained again. "No food not good for snake."

We moved on past dead turtles, dead birds and a som-nambulant crocodile to the one mobile creature in the entire collection: an uncaged baboon, foraging through heaps of jagged metal and discarded jawbones. A small boy stood throwing stones at the creature's red, swollen buttocks.

"This called dog-faced monkey," the guard said, shaking his head. "He be dead soon also."

I tipped the guard a few pounds and went inside to look at the collection of stuffed animals. There were dioramas of cheetahs and gazelles, most of them mislabeled. A stuffed aardvark had fallen over, taking a mock acacia tree with it. I found Fathi al-Rabaa, the museum's curator, in a dusty office beside a bank of seven phones. They, too, were dead. "This one rang last year," he said, pointing at the nearest phone. "It was a wrong number."

I asked him about the museum's collection and if there were plans for improvement. He shook his head.

"It is better now than it was," he said. "The floods last year washed away many of the animals. It is better to drown than to starve."

The museum suffered from the same problem as every other institution in Sudan. Its budget had remained stable for the past five years. Unfortunately, the Sudanese pound hadn't, nor had inflation; the museum's meager allotment was now worth five percent of what it had been five years before. Al-Rabaa had tried to raise money abroad to buy new animals and feed the surviving ones. But with the phones, telexes and mail routinely out of service, it was hard to know if any of his missives had made it, or if they'd been answered.

"I am still hopeful," he said, sitting there, waiting for one of the phones to ring again. "In Khartoum one must learn to be patient."

Later that day, I wandered across town to the office of *Sudanese Business*. I'd picked up a copy of the "economic and business weekly" at a newsstand. The motto proclaimed on its pages—"to promote individual initiative, drive and excellence and entrepreneurship"—struck me as insanely quixotic.

The editor, Ali Abdalla Ali, agreed.

"It was a stupid idea, really," he said, wiping a brow stained with ink and sweat. "We posed ourselves the question 'Is there a meaningful private sector in Sudan, and what are its prospects?'" After six months, he thought he'd found the answer. "Sudan has no stability, no private initiative, no hard currency and not a single clear policy. The prospects for business are nil."

I asked him what he would advise foreign investors. Ali laughed, the deep hearty laugh of the Sudanese. "I'd have to tell them, 'Please, go away.'"

He borrowed my pen and began listing, with grim relish, a few of Sudan's key economic indicators. By the time he was done, he'd filled an entire page with what read like a bankruptcy filing.

1. A foreign debt of $14 billion, on which Sudan paid nothing and which now accounted for a third of all overdue payments to the International Monetary Fund.
2. Inflation rate of 100 percent a year.
3. Factories running at 5 percent of capacity.
4. Imports running at three times exports.
5. A per capita income of $279, lowest in the Arab world.
6. Chronic shortages of bread, fuel and water—and a black market in everything, even stamps.
7. A brain drain so severe that most Sudanese with education and skills quickly fled overseas.

"Those without skills stay to run the government," Ali said, adding without shame that Sudan was "the worst basket case" in Africa, perhaps in the world. "I do not know. I have heard Burma and Bangladesh are maybe this bad."

I asked him about the prospects for his publication.

"Advertising is very poor, sales are worse," he said. "So I think we will expand to twice a week."

I looked at him quizzically.

"All of Sudan is in debt. I have some catching up to do." He gave me an inscrutable smile, and an inky handshake, and returned to work on the previous week's issue, which hadn't yet made it to the streets.

The out-migration of skilled Sudanese was matched by an inward flood of liberal-minded Westerners. Sudan, after all, was a vast laboratory of human misery, offering everything a researcher or philanthropist might need: war, famine, flood, plague and pestilence. "It's like living in the Bible," said a wide-eyed American aid worker, who was recovering from malaria when I met her in the lobby of the Acropole Hotel.

The Acropole was the strangest and most entertaining hotel in the Middle East. Run by a Sudanese family of Greek extraction, it was a way station for all the aid workers, missionaries and free-lance Good Samaritans who passed through Khartoum between visits to the black hole of Calcutta or the famine-stricken fields of Ethiopia. During a single afternoon in the hotel's lobby, I met a Canadian tree surgeon just in from Malawi; a one-armed Eritrean working for the rebel movement that had been fighting the government of Ethiopia, next door, for twenty-five years; an English missionary in a woolen cardigan who was navigating through the 100-degree heat in search of a street urchin to adopt ("The Lord told me to"); a Swiss intern who was sleeping off some fever he'd contracted in the south of the country ("There are diseases here I have never seen, except in medical textbooks"); and a Dutch "meat consultant" who asked me to hold up putrefying slabs of beef so he could photograph them to shock his colleagues back home ("In Holland we would not feed such meat to pigs").

I also met journalists drawn like me to the Acropole's cheap rooms, its colorful clientele, and most of all its owners, who spoke a dozen or so languages and could fix everything from a permit to take photographs (without which your camera would be seized) to a bogus record of inoculations (without which it was impossible to land in any country after visiting the disease-ridden Sudan). The Acropole even offered an occasional video, flashed against a screen on the hotel's rooftop, with the blacked-out skyline of Khartoum providing a more than adequate backdrop.

Through the Acropole it was also possible, from time to time, to make appointments. The hotel was one of the few addresses in Khartoum where overseas mail actually arrived. Savvy Sudanese used it as a substitute postal address, and also as an alternative to the futile phone system, leaving notes for each other as to the time of business meetings or dinner parties. One day I left a message in the box of a prominent social scientist and two days later he left a message in mine, suggesting I visit him at his office at the University of Omdurman the following morning. There was a pleasing subterfuge to the system, as though we were all part of some clever underground, passing notes to each other despite Sudan's best efforts to foil communication.

Unfortunately, scheduling a rendezvous was much simpler than keeping one. Omdurman lay just across the river from Khartoum, within plain view of the traffic gridlocked on the Nile bridge from dawn to dusk. Abandoning my cab, I covered the last two miles on foot, arriving at the university bathed in dust and sweat.

"I'm so sorry I'm late," I blathered to the secretary. My appointment had been scheduled for nine o'clock and it was now eleven-thirty.

Late? For what?" she asked. The professor hadn't yet arrived. She suggested I stroll around the campus and return in an hour or so. "If he is not here by then, it means he gave up on the traffic and went home for the day."

The campus was a shabby collection of unpainted buildings circling a dusty courtyard. Notices were plastered to the walls announcing that classes had been suspended for the day because of the bus strike, the postal strike and the strike by university staff. But because there was no way to circulate the news, many students had shown up anyway.

"It is no matter," explained a young woman named Sowsa. "Even when the university is open many professors do not make it." The students had learned to educate themselves, and Sowsa invited me to join a small group pulling up chairs in a circle at the edge of the courtyard.

Typically in Muslim countries, students are segregated by sex and universities have become bastions of fundamentalism. But here, the sexes sat comfortably together. The women wore loose scarves that covered just enough hair to qualify as Islamic. While the men wore long white robes and absurdly tall turbans wound from four yards of white Sudanese cotton, the women wrapped themselves in brightly colored sarongs that clung to their tall, slim figures. Swathed in purple and orange and striding through the dust with the loose-limbed grace of newborn fawns, the women lent an ethereal splendor to what was, in every other detail, a hideously blighted landscape.

The students in the courtyard had gathered for an impromptu poetry seminar, and they took turns reciting Arabic verse. Sowsa whispered their meaning to me in English, though many of the poems seemed to lose something in translation. "This one is about monkey magic," she said. "This one is about a camel party."

The themes of other poems were obvious enough, and rather surprising. One student recited a ditty mocking the government's incompetence, and his audience responded with peals of laughter. Sowsa recited a poem about the brutality of the civil war, causing several students to weep. Then she turned to me and asked if I could offer a verse in English. My tiny repertoire of limericks didn't seem appropriate. So I recited the only other poem I knew by heart: Shelley's "Ozymandias."

For most of the students, the high-blown language was incomprehensible, even if images of "decay" and "colossal wreck" were all too familiar. But they clapped politely and insisted that I recite the sonnet a second and third time. When I finished, Sowsa laid her long fingers on my arm and gazed at me with wet, mocha-colored eyes.

"Tony, this is a sad and beautiful poem," she said softly. "Is it the first one you have written?"

I found Professor Abdul Rahman Abu Zayd massaging his worry beads behind a dune of dusty papers. Unaware of the bus strike, he'd waited for an hour that morning at the stop by his house, then hitched a ride to the center of Khartoum. From there he'd caught a taxi which was stuck in traffic for so long that the ride cost him sixty Sudanese pounds, almost equal to his weekly salary.

"This country is a total mess and the government is a total failure," he said, before I'd asked a single question. "It is just every man for himself, living by his own wits."

Like every other person I'd met in the Sudan, the professor was strikingly candid; there was none of the studied indirection or straight-out lying to which I'd become accustomed in the Arab world. I was beginning to like the Sudanese very much.

"Isn't anyone afraid of speaking out?" I asked.

"Afraid? Of what?" He chuckled. "The government is on strike like everyone else. Who will come to arrest me?"

The openness, in fact, went deeper than that. Sudan, almost alone among Arab countries, was committed to a degree of democracy and free speech. In between coups, there were polls that resembled popular elections and the newspapers were free to lambast the government, which they usually did.

"The problem," Abu Zayd said, "is that democracy doesn't work so well in a country such as this. You must agree on a few things to have civilized debate. Here, we agree on nothing."

Sudan's population was divided among 500 tribes, 115

languages, and 60 political parties. Like other Arab and African nations, its borders had been drawn for the convenience of European colonialists; the country didn't make much sense as a modern state. "You can't decree national identity," Abu Zayd said.

Our chat was interrupted by a power failure, which plunged the windowless office into darkness. Abu Zayd shrugged. Even with power, he said, his appliances were useless. He had a photocopy machine but no paper. The typewriters were missing keys. And the university hadn't been able to purchase new textbooks in five years, for lack of funds.

"It is hard to call this a developing country," he said, searching his desk for candles, "because most of the movement is the other way."

I asked Abu Zayd how much longer people could manage in these conditions before rebelling—or before losing what little freedom they had left.

"Six months, maybe three, who knows? Whatever the day, I don't want to be around when it happens."

As it turned out, Abu Zayd was overly optimistic. Six weeks later, tanks rumbled through the streets of Khartoum and an army colonel crackled onto the airwaves to announce yet another change of government, Sudan's thirtieth in thirty-three years.

Myra Potts had a lilting Welsh accent, a gimpy arthritic leg and the most ghastly occupation of anyone I'd ever met.

"I go three times a week to the lepers' colony outside town," she said, sipping mango juice on the bougainvillea-splashed balcony of a private British club, "and dress the old people's stumps."

She worked without pay, to pass the time while her engineer husband saw out his stint in Khartoum. "Of course, we can't give the lepers back what they've lost," she said. "When a finger or toe's gone, it's gone." She paused as a servant deposited a tray of fish and chips on our table. "But at least we can keep them from getting gangrene."

I declined the offer of lunch but accepted an invitation to go on rounds with her the following day. This was, after all, what I'd chosen to report: the worst that the world's worst city could deliver. It was also hard to shirk the offer when Myra's twelve-year-old daughter, Elizabeth, pleaded to go as well. "One must show some pluck if one is to learn about the world," the young girl said, devouring her fish. So joined by Myra, Elizabeth and her eleven-year-old brother, Thomas, I found myself in the back of a four-wheel-drive, bouncing out of Khartoum and into a wretched refugee camp called Miyo. The settlement's residents were among the million refugees camped out in the capital: on the streets, in abandoned cars or in miserable shanty towns like this.

"Children, I hope you're taking this all in," Myra said, as tall black women, their breasts no more than milkless folds of skin, held shriveled infants aloft in the morning sun, pleading for piasters. "I expect five-page essays from each of you tomorrow."

"Mother!"

"Thomas, don't be a twit about this. Stiff upper lip."

The lepers numbered about one hundred and lived at the edge of Miyo in straw-and-scrap-metal huts chinked with cow dung. They'd been there twenty years and had even nominated a "sheik" to make representations to aid agencies and the government. "Not that it helps much," Myra said. "The state doesn't want to know about them." Whenever a leper went to the hospital, two others had to go along as porters, because orderlies refused to handle them.

We parked in a narrow, unpaved alley, beside a dead goat. Men and women instantly began swarming around the jeep, thrusting their limbs through open windows. One man grasped at my arm with what remained of his hand: a shapeless paw, scaly and almost reptilian to the touch, with five raw ulcers revealing where his fingers had been. On Thomas's side, the window was closed, and a man pressed his face to the glass; his nostrils were two tiny holes sunk deep into cheekbones so wasted that his eyes drooped level with his shrunken nose. A woman, noseless, toothless, poked her head through Myra's window and tried to speak. A high-pitched "uh" sound was all she mustered. "Leprosy's got her larynx," Myra said matter-of-factly.

The lepers stood in a disorderly queue as Myra introduced them, one at a time. When each one's name was called, he or she held out a limb for a welcoming shake. Unsure what the etiquette was in such situations, I opted for a sort of soul-brother elbow grip, and Thomas and Elizabeth followed my lead.

"Tony, you play nurse and I'll play doctor," Myra said, pressing a wad of gauze into my hand and shoving a stool in my direction. We had stooped inside a makeshift clinic of mud, and the lepers crowded in behind us for treatment. Thomas and Elizabeth stood against one wall, swatting flies.

"Ladies first," Myra said gaily, and though the lepers understood not a word of English, they were evidently accustomed to the routine. A woman who looked to be at least a hundred hobbled forward and offered her bare foot. According to Myra, the woman's actual age was forty-two. One toe remained, bent at an improbable angle, and crooked nails still protruded from the nubby flesh where the other four toes had been. Her other foot was square and scaly, like an elephant's hoof.

"Oh dear," Myra said, plopping both the woman's feet onto my lap and digging into her "bag of tricks." She pulled out scissors and cut off dead skin, then poked a gloved finger into an abscess near the woman's heel. Her finger disappeared.

"Still got that flippin' hole, don't you?" she said to the woman, who didn't even flinch. "Got no nerves left, I guess. But dearie, clunking around will just make it worse."

As Myra cleaned and dressed wounds, she lectured absentmindedly on leprosy's grim course through the flesh. Contrary to popular notion, extremities don't just drop off like leaves from trees. Rather, the bones and tendons shrink and the skin recedes around them. Circulation weakens so that lepers usually can't even blush. Then the nerve ends go, the lepers lose all feeling, and each time they pick up a burning pot, or walk on wasted toes, another body part crumbles away.

"Eyes are a big problem," Myra continued, inspecting a woman's reddened irises. As the bridge of the nose collapses, the eyes sag so low that the lids no longer close, even in sleep. This leads to infections, and many of the lepers are not only crippled but blind as well.

Ironically, leprosy is one of the world's least contagious diseases, requiring years of constant skin contact to catch. And by the time it has reached the stage of eroding extremities—the point at which lepers have traditionally been packed off to colonies—the disease has usually burned itself out.

For a time I managed to take this all in with scientific detachment, nodding dully as Myra probed gashes, stuffed gauze in gaping ulcers and studied infected toes, declaring, "No need to bother with this one. It'll be gone on its own by next week."

But as the morning wore on, and the women gave way to the men, the heat and stench of putrid flesh began to close in. After visiting the Iran-Iraq front, I'd thought nothing could faze me. But a corpse, however disfigured, is past its pain; it is possible to distance yourself just a bit. It is quite another matter to confront humans whose flesh is still being ravaged almost as you watch. I found myself inadvertently wiggling my toes and scrunching my nose, a subconscious check to make sure everything was still attached.

"Here's a real beauty," Myra said, thrusting an oozing stump directly in my face. The man looked as though he'd caught his hand in a combine, then left it to heal with the shredded bones and skin still clinging to his wrist. "Gangrene, I 'spect," Myra said, depositing the man's arm in my hand.

I felt a sudden urge to flee from the hut, past the heaps of trash and mangy goats and into the clear desert air. The way was blocked by the next man in line, sitting cross-legged, picking with blunt fingers at a loose bit of scabrous, fly-ridden skin. The air was breathless, the walls began to swirl. And the problems of the world seemed suddenly too big for me to take in.

"All done," Myra said, clapping her hands. We'd been there two hours. The woman was a saint. As she gathered her gauze and scissors, I rushed into the alley and stepped straight into a fetid pool of open sewage. Two male lepers, squatting against the wall, broke out laughing, clapping their stumps together. The American is standing in shit! Their mirth was contagious and I stood there for a moment, knee-deep in gunk, gulping the foul air and chuckling along with them. It was the least I could do, lighten a leper's day.

Back at the Acropole, after a long and miserably cold shower, I found myself standing in line for the telex beside a lanky American. The kinship was instantaneous. Clutching a notebook of cramped, illegible notes, he wore dusty khakis and the anxious expression of someone who'd spent too many hours like this, queued up to send messages on a broken telex with little hope of ever getting an answer.

"Journalist?" I asked.

"Uh-huh."

"Free-lance?

"Second-stringer, sometimes third."

We exchanged names and inflated press credentials. Scott was just out of college, bumming around Africa until his free-lance earnings and intestines gave out. The journalism was really only a way of paying for the travel. Most of the time, he entered countries on tourist visas, then filed stories on the sly to cover his costs. It was an ingenious and improbable ruse—a tourist visa to the Sudan?—and I was happy to meet someone whose modus operandi was as half-baked as mine.

"Got a story to file?" he asked.

"Not really."

"Me neither. Let's blow it off and go catch some Khartoum nightlife."

Khartoum nightlife was a contradiction in terms—or so I'd assumed. There was an eleven-o'clock curfew, laxly

enforced, but worrisome nonetheless; a trigger-happy teenager with an AK-47 can be dangerous, particularly when
he's awakened from deep slumber, in a city where coup plots
are constantly rumored and not infrequently carried out.
There was also the sad fact that six years before, in a fit of
Islamic pique, Sudanese officials had hurled the city's entire
liquor supply into the Nile and announced the imposition of
Islamic law: flogging for drinkers, severed right hands for
thieves, hanging followed by crucifixion for particularly hei-
nous crimes. Islamic law had been suspended some time
before my visit, but the sentencings continued and there
were still four hundred people on Amputation Row.

"They've got moonshine here that moves like a butterfly
and stings like a bee," Scott said, mimicking Muhammad
Ali.

"Mmmm. Particularly after eighty lashes."

"That's for Sudanese," Scott said. "We only get forty.
Anyway, the worst they're likely to do is take all our money
and deport us."

I was intrigued, and depressed by the alternative: my
sixth consecutive night in the darkened hotel lobby, waiting
for the telex to kick on. So we headed off into the night.

Scott's contact was a jack-of-all-trades named Monem:
sometime money changer, sometime black marketeer and all
times standing in front of the Acropole, waiting for Westerners to hustle. "You need driver's license, I can fix that, too,"
he said as we rode a taxi to the edge of town. I wondered
what use I could possibly have for a Sudanense driver's
license, except as a novelty item.

We climbed out in the middle of nowhere, a half-mile
hike from our actual destination. "The taxi driver, maybe he
is informer," Monem explained. He led us through streets
of brick dust and garbage and into a narrow alley running
behind what looked like an abandoned tenement. "Maria,"
he whispered into the dark. "It is Monem." A tall black
woman in a purple wrap came out of the building and
motioned us wearily to the bar—a tree stump, an overturned
crate, and a blown-out truck tire. Then she ducked inside,

emerging a moment later with a plastic detergent bottle and a single filthy glass.

"*Araki* very good for digestion," Monem said, splashing clear liquid from the detergent bottle into the glass.

"I bet it is," Scott said. "Instant case of Mahdi's Revenge." He belted the *araki* down in a single gulp, then winced and flapped one arm, chickenlike. Monem filled the glass and handed it to me. It smelled, in equal parts, of rum and paint thinner. I took a tentative sip and felt the *araki* sear my chest.

"Great stuff," I gasped. "What's in it?"

Monem shrugged. "Dates, I think " He downed two glassfuls. Scott laughed. "Eye of newt, and toe of frog," he recited. "Wool of bat, and tongue of dog." He downed another glass. I took a sip. Monem downed two glasses. "Maria," he said, tapping the detergent bottle. "More *araki*."

During our second round, other drinkers wandered through the alley, almost invisible in the dark. One of them struck a match beneath his chin; it was Ali, he of the python skins. In Khartoum, low-life was a small, closed circle. "Life or dead, your choose," I muttered. Scott giggled and the others smiled politely. Two strange white men laughing at strange, white men's jokes.

With each glass of *araki*, Monem's English deteriorated and so did his mood. "Sudan no good," he moaned. "Government no good. Money no good. Just bongo and *araki*. And for this, they send you to jail. Or worse." He rose unsteadily to his feet and lurched inside to see if Maria would let him spend the night. Through the open door there was the dim glow of candlelight and five or six children huddled asleep on the floor. Monem returned a moment later, looking even more depressed.

"She tell me I am no more good than a dog," he said. We wandered back out into the street, past families sleeping on mats of cardboard in the open air. We paused to urinate against a wall.

"In Sudan there is only drink, piss and—what you call this?" Monem asked, making a vomiting motion.

"Puke," I said.

"Byook."

"Puke," Scott corrected.

"Buke." Monem smiled and made the motion again. "Okay, Mr. Tony and Mr. Scott. You write in your papers that Monem, he buke on Sudan."

There were no taxis on the main road back into town, so we stood waiting for cars with which to hitch a ride. After twenty minutes or so a rusted sedan pulled over to let us in. I climbed in front, beside an immaculately clad man in a starched white robe and a tall white turban.

"I can only take you as far as the prison," he said, in perfect, clipped English.

The prison? Had he picked up the *araki* on my breath?

"It is just a few miles from here," the man continued. "I work the night shift as warden."

"Oh." There was an awkward pause. "And how is it, working at the prison?"

"Not so good now that Sharia is no longer enforced as it should be," he said. "Sharia" was the Arabic word for Islamic law. "A man who drinks deserves the whip," he added, "and a man who steals deserves the sword."

I resisted the urge to glance over my shoulder to check Monem's expression. Buking, I suspected.

"What were you doing back where I picked you up?" the warden asked. "It is a very bad part of town, you know."

"Really?"

Scott snorted, inhaling a giggle. Then he blew his nose to keep from cracking up.

"Do you mind if we get out at the corner just ahead?" I asked the driver. "I think we'll walk it from here."

He seemed surprised. We were still some miles from the city center. But he pulled over and dropped us off in the dark. Monem watched carefully until the car's lights disappeared in the distance, as if he expected the warden to return with a hooded swordsman in tow. "This Sharia is very bad," he said, urinating in the dust, rather shakily. "I not want to give my right hand for Allah."

After a half hour's wait, we managed to flag down another car, crammed with five men and reeking of bongo. As soon as we'd piled in, the driver took off in a cloud of dust, narrowly missing a huge cement block lying in the middle of the road. The driver laughed, gunned the engine, almost ran over a dog and burned rubber down the empty road into town.

"Africa, I love it," Scott sighed, relaxing in my lap. In the morning he was off for Tigre Province in Ethiopia, to tag along with a band of mountain guerrillas. "Tonight we drink, for tomorrow we may die," he said, clasping my hand as I climbed out at the Acropole. He was staying aboard, just for the ride. The car roared off with the door still open, and I never saw Scott or Monem again.

12

SOUTHERN SUDAN
Six Dinka Deep

Khawaja (pl. khawajat) A Persian word meaning notables or merchants. In the Sudan it is used for white foreigners.

—BUKRA, INSHA'ALLAH:
A Look into Sudanese Culture

As it turned out, Scott had found one of the surer escape routes from Khartoum. It was easier and probably safer to trek over the Ethiopian border with Tigrean rebels than it was to travel across Sudan by road or air. In a country one-third the size of the continental United States, there were only 800 miles of paved highway; a drive to El Obeid, just 250 miles from Khartoum, could take three days. Flying was worse. Sudan Air, the state-owned domestic carrier, was a sort of cistern in which all the chaos of the nation collected. Planes routinely skipped stops, made unplanned layovers of several days, left without passengers—or, most commonly, didn't leave at all. Sudan Air's pilots celebrated my arrival in Khartoum by joining almost every other work force in the city and going out on strike. The job stoppage was redundant; Sudan Air's entire fleet was already grounded with maintenance problems.

The only alternative was hitching a ride on one of the

small Western-owned relief planes ferrying between Khartoum and the famine-stricken south. It took me ten minutes in the Acropole lobby to locate a flight and two days in dusty government offices to cajole and bribe a travel permit from Sudanese officials. The government didn't want journalists reporting on the civil war, which pitted the entire Sudanese army against a ragtag band of bongo-smoking Dinka rebels. The war wasn't much of a contest; the confederates were winning. The only effective weapon left to the government was scorching the rebels' turf by refusing to send food to the beleaguered south and by arming Arab tribes, who promptly raided Dinka cattle and took Dinka refugees as slaves.

"There's not much milk of human kindness on either side," said the UNICEF official who secured me a seat to Muglad, a town at the edge of the war zone.

From what little intelligence I could gather in Khartoum, southern Sudan hardly seemed worth fighting for. Most of it was swamp, and the rest, in the words of a nineteenth-century Englishman, was "god-forsaken, dry-sucked, fly-blown wilderness . . . a howling waste of weed, mosquitoes, flies and fever." Boarding the four-seat UNICEF cargo plane at dawn, I wrapped a mosquito net around enough bread, water and antibiotics to see me through a week in hell.

The passenger beside me, a beefy Germany reporter named Bart, came even better prepared: he'd packed industrial-strength sunblock and fifteen days' worth of German K-rations. "Some breakfast?" he asked, offering me a cracker smeared with canned schmaltz. I shook my head. "I have thought the Ruhr Valley was the worst place on earth, but now I know different," Bart continued, wiping grit from his gold-rimmed half-glasses. "Khartoum, it is like something from Kafka."

Across the aisle sat a Canadian mechanic who had spent the previous month in a Khartoum hospital bed, delirious with malaria. He had contracted the disease during his first week in Muglad and wasn't looking forward to returning south. "Did you know there are sixty-three species of mosquito in Sudan?" he said, quaffing chloroquine. "Down south, those bugs are real Dinkas. Big, black and hungry."

While he and Bart compared malaria tablets, I gazed out the window as the plane lifted off over the turgid brown waters of the White Nile. Within minutes the city vanished and we flew across a vast expanse of semidesert, dotted with mud-brick homes. It was a typical Arabian sandscape, arid and dull and conducive to deep, undreaming sleep. I drifted off soon after takeoff and awoke three hours later, over Africa. The plane swooped in low across flat savannah, over stout baobab trees and cone-shaped huts and patches of something I hadn't seen in months: grass. It was the end of the dry season, still scorched and tan, but after Khartoum, the fields of elephant grass looked verdant and soothing.

We bounced down a narrow strip of tar and straight up to a terminal the size of a dentist's waiting room. A dozen people stood crowded inside, hoping to hitch a ride on the flight back to Khartoum. One carried a spear; another a goat. When the pilot said he could take only four passengers, the others turned away without apparent disappointment and sprawled on the floor, a little more comfortable now that there were only eight sharing the tiny space. The next flight was due in forty-eight hours.

In Khartoum, the UNICEF office had told us it would radio relief workers in Muglad to come to the airport and look after us until we were ready to join the outgoing queue to Khartoum. But the message never got through. So we were ushered instead to a small packed-mud building, which turned out to be the Muglad police station. A scowling officer in green fatigues rifled through our packs, then asked for our wallets. He plucked out my photographic permit, which I'd spent a day and more dollars than I cared to recall prying loose from the Khartoum bureaucracy. He tore the permit in half. Then he took my camera.

"*Mish surra*," he said. No pictures.

He dove into my wallet again and fished out a letter from the Ministry of Information, which said I had permission to interview refugees in the camp outside Muglad. He stuck this in his pocket.

"*Mamnoor*," he said. Not allowed.

I assumed he would shortly pluck out all my remaining money and pocket that as well. But he had all he wanted and pointed us in the direction of Beit Khawajja, "White Man's House," which housed Western aid workers and served as a sort of hotel for Westerners passing through. As we left the police station, with vague assurances that my photographic gear would be returned on departure, a deputy sat knocking my Nikon against the edge of the desk. Finally, the lens cap popped off and he peered through the viewfinder with wondrous delight.

Muglad wasn't accustomed to Caucasian visitors. As we made our way through the village, teenagers crowded behind us screeching like birds—"*Khawajja! Khawajja! Khawajja!*"—and reaching out to touch our skin. A French aid worker later told me that when he'd first visited southern Sudan, fifteen years before, tribesmen were so confused by his color that they'd asked him, "Were you born underwater?" and "How did you lose your skin?"

Muglad's people were as exotic to me as I was to them. Lying just north of the traditional border between Arab and African Sudan, the community was a multi-hued stew, mingling bronze Muslim nomads with black African tribesmen who herded, and worshiped, cows. Tall Dinka men—fantastically tall men—swished past in white Arab robes, speaking pidgin Arabic interspersed with the tongue-clicks of their native language. Greeting each other in the street, they touched their hearts, then placed their right hands on one another's left shoulder, saying *sheebak* (Dinka for "hello") and *salaam aleikum* (Arabic for "peace be upon you").

In Muglad a hole was measured in man-lengths—a well, say, was "six men deep"—and the scale came with an ethnic proviso. Arab or Dinka? If Dinka, each man-length was at least six inches greater. The Dinka were also exceptionally lean, striding through the village with the stick-figure majesty of Giacometti sculptures.

As if to compensate for their inferior height, the Arab men—in this region, almost as black as the Dinka—wore absurdly tall turbans. At first glance their costume seemed to consist of matching bedsheets: one for the body and one piled loosely atop the head. Turbans revealed who was Arab and who not, as did the sharp, short daggers that Arabs carried in goatskin sheaths strapped across their upper arms.

The women were also distinguishable by their head coverings, with the Arabs in loose-fitting scarves and the Dinka bareheaded, except for bundles of firewood or jugs of water balanced deftly atop their cornrows. That the African women wore any clothes at all was a concession to Muslim norms. The Arab women wore nose rings and neck rings and tribal scarifications cut across their cheeks, just like the Dinka. Their gossamer robes, ending at the knee and elbow, would have been judged indecent in stricter regions of the Muslim world.

So entrancing were the people that at first the landscape barely registered. There was something odd about Muglad, something I couldn't place. We dropped our bags at Beit Khawajja, an unmarked mud-brick compound, and introduced ourselves to the three young *khawajjat* who lived there. They worked for an Irish aid group, Concern, which distributed food to refugees in and around Muglad. The year before, when little food had gotten through, 250,000 people had starved in southern Sudan.

A young man named Kevin invited us to tag along as he made his rounds through the village. "The Arabs resent the refugees getting so much free food," he said, smiling slightly. "So we try to keep them happy with a wee bit of graft." There were high-protein biscuits from Australia on sale in the market, alongside beans, oil and other food donated by European countries. There were also sacks of American sorghum, siphoned from supplies arriving at the airstrip. The merchants called it "Reagan sorghum"; news of the Bush presidency hadn't yet reached Muglad. The low-grade U.S. surplus, used as animal feed in America, didn't fool the Sudanese. They sold it at half the price of local grain.

Seated beside the sorghum sellers, women used mortars

and pestels to pummel the grain into a dense paste, which they used to make porridge or rolled flat to bake as bread. As we chatted with the women, something behind us suddenly exploded. Bart and I both dove to the ground.

The women laughed with wide, toothless cackles. "It's just the grist mill," Kevin said. "The generator is kicking on." The mill squatted beneath a strip of sheet metal across the way and consisted of several crude belts that turned two stones that ground the grain. The generator motor clanged loudly and belched black smoke into the cloudless, unpolluted air. A mob of villagers surrounded the mill, openmouthed and wide-eyed, gawking at a mechanism that ground an entire bag of sorghum in the time it took them to mash a single bowl by hand. And I realized then what was so strange about Muglad. Apart from this generator, there was no electricity. There were no power lines, no TV aerials, no cars or trucks. I felt for a moment as though I were standing in some English village at the cusp of the Industrial Revolution, on the day a mad and wonderful machine called the cotton gin came to town.

The few modern goods that had made it to Muglad were carefully recycled as soon as they had served their original purpose. One man fashioned sandals from withered truck tires. Another took apart cans of powdered milk and refashioned them as stout little coffee jugs, with the body of the can forming the pot and the leftover strips used for the spout, handle and strainer. The jugs then migrated down the street to the tea and coffee sellers: Arab women seated on straw mats beneath broad-limbed trees, cleaning tiny glasses with the folds of their robes and filling the cups with sweetened tea.

Kevin's destination was a mud-brick shopfront where a bent metal verandah provided a slim bit of shade. Beneath the verandah stood a short dark man with a huge turban and flowing white *galabiya*. He was barking orders at a small troop of listless workers. "This is Faki," Kevin said, smiling. "The Godfather of Muglad."

Faki delivered food for the aid groups, and he was

supervising sweaty workmen as they heaved bags of sorghum into battered trucks. When the loading was done, Faki yelled at the lead truck to depart. No one budged. Faki climbed down from the verandah and stalked over, apoplectic with rage. Several tribesmen stood studying a mangy dog dozing in the shade of the lead truck's front tire. One man tugged the cur's ear; another nudged its rear. Losing patience, Faki grabbed a tribesman's spear and sank it in the dust an inch from the animal's nose. The dog bolted and the trucks rumbled off past mud huts and baobab trees and into the parched savannah.

Spotting us, Faki wandered over and smiled broadly. "Faki is the only man in Muglad who can make the food move," Faki said. Straightening his foot-high turban and brushing dirt from his starched white robe, Faki resumed barking orders at a crowd of workers who, like the dog, were searching for shade from the blinding afternoon sun.

Faki Naway was a trader, truck owner and teamster boss, rolled into one. When aid workers first arrived in Muglad, they had needed someplace to store grain. By the following day, Faki had bought every warehouse in town and doubled the going rate. When relief workers went looking for trucks and truckers to carry the grain south, they ran into Faki again. The local militia, an irregular army of spear- and carbine-toting tribesmen, was the only force capable of securing safe passage through the war zone. Faki had the militia in his pocket. Anyone else who tried to move grain would find his truck convoy under attack by the same militia they'd failed to pay off.

"It's not a pretty business," Kevin said, "but you either do the job their way or you don't get it done at all."

Kevin had come to negotiate a new delivery contract. Faki waved us inside for tea, and three loafers were unceremoniously dumped from their chairs so we could sit. By Muglad standards, the office was high-tech. Faki had a dented filing cabinet, a UNICEF calendar from the previous year and an ancient wind-up phone with five Eveready batteries strapped to the back, to power the pulse through the

static. It had a range of fifty miles. Faki also had the only
personal car in town, a shiny Toyota pickup, minus the hood.
It was parked beside the office and three young men took turns
wiping it clean of dust each time the wind swept through
town.

Kevin and Faki made chat in Arabic, then got down to
business. There were endless obstacles to the contract Kevin
had offered. The rainy season was about to begin, turning
the roads into goat tracks. The guerrillas grew stronger every
day and had recently blown up one of Faki's trucks with a
land mine. Faki could do what Kevin asked, but only for a
sum double the one Kevin had offered.

Kevin balked, sipping at his tea and talking with Bart
and me instead, as though he'd lost interest in the contract.
Somehow, I hadn't imagined Western aid workers haggling
like tourists in a rug shop to get food delivered. Like any
good Arab merchant, Faki had a few theatrics of his own.
As we chatted, two sinister-looking men appeared on the
verandah. One, whom Kevin identified as the commander of
the local militia, wore a safari suit and sunglasses, and he
carried a sharp-pointed stick. The other, his lieutenant, had
a Kalashnikov slung over one shoulder of his jungle fatigues.
Nodding silently at Faki, the two men sat on the edge of
the verandah and stared off into space.

Kevin groaned, opened a small canvas sack and spilled
several thousand Sudanese pounds onto the floor. It was the
first installment of Faki's contract. "Good, very good," Faki
said, trying out his two words of English. Flashing a gold-
toothed grin, he stuffed the pounds into the breast pocket of
his robe, beside a Bic pen. "The white man was brought
here by Allah," he said.

That night, on Faki's invitation, I went to dinner at his home
at the edge of Muglad. Since I was barred from visiting the
refugee camp, I'd latched onto Faki as the next-best subject
for a story about Southern Sudan. I was writing, at the time,
for *The Wall Street Journal*, and Faki struck me as the sort of
ruthless entrepreneur with whom bond sharks and arbitrag-

ers might identify. Muglad's Mover and Shaker. Donald
Trump in turban and *galabiya*.

That evening I saw another side: Faki the village sheik
and chieftain. His home lay at the end of a long dirt road,
behind a high fence of sorghum stalks. I arrived to find a
dozen other guests sitting in the open yard, sipping water.
Faki's house was invisible, hidden behind trees in the twilight. One of the men explained that we were the first shift
to dine at Faki's table, with two other groups to follow. Faki
entertained every night, feeding family, neighbors, clients
and militiamen.

After half an hour our host appeared with a freshly
pressed *galabiya*, new plastic thongs and a small white skull-
cap in place of his turban. The skimpy headgear revealed
something I hadn't seen before: a "prayer bump" on Faki's
forehead, a sign of Muslim piety earned by years of kneeling
and pressing his forehead to the ground.

I told Faki that I was a journalist and that I wanted to
profile him for the businessmen who read my paper. The
notion flattered him. But as an interviewee he was rather
elusive.

"How old are you?" I asked through his nephew, who
served as translator.

"Something over thirty. It is not important." He looked
more like forty-something, and I told him so. He laughed.
"It is because my work makes me old." He pulled up his
robe to reveal a deep, ugly scar on his thigh. "A spear
wound, from fighting the guerrillas," he said. "The man who
did it went away looking much worse." He offered no further details.

I asked him about his career, and on this subject he was
more forthcoming. The son of a Muglad shopkeeper, he'd
begun as a humble trader and trucker, doing small jobs for
the army and local merchants. Then the aid groups came,
and they'd naturally turned to him. "Faki, is the only honest
man in Muglad," he said, speaking, as usual, in the third
person. Other truckers skimmed grain from the bags of sorghum, delivering their cargo half empty, or stuffed with dirt.

"Faki's bags always arrive full," he said. I knew from Kevin that this was so.

I asked him about his ties to the militia, and whether this helped his business.

"It is true, I have friends." He smiled. The gold incisors flashed again. Then he swept his arm across the courtyard and said, for the benefit of everyone, "What is a man without friends?" The others nodded obligingly and responded, almost in chorus, "Nothing, Faki, nothing."

Faki also wasn't reticient about the growth in his estate. The food deliveries had transformed him from a small-time trucker to a provincial tycoon who now possessed seven trucks, sixteen Dinka house servants, five hundred head of cattle, and three homes—one for each of his wives. "I change houses each night, for six nights, then sleep alone on the seventh," he said.

I asked him if he felt at all strange about becoming so rich from feeding starving refugees.

"Without Faki, many in the south would have nothing to eat." Then he spoke *forte voce* again, turning to the others. "Without Faki, many in Muglad would have nothing to eat!" When the laughter died down, he waved us to a large table at the center of the courtyard, adding, "My friends, it is time."

Tall Dinka servants emerged bearing large platters with multicolored woven lids. Somewhere in the dark a generator rumbled, and a dim light glowed in the courtyard. The second shift of dinner guests had already gathered, sitting silently in the shadows at the edge of the courtyard.

Faki stood at the head of the table, with six guests on either side, and took the top off each of the platters. One was filled with steaming chicken, another with goat, another with beef. There were also bowls of mashed, spiced peanuts and baskets of steaming bread for scooping up the food. Bart, who sat across from me, whispered through the steam: "My editors, they want I should write about a starving child, and here we eat so well!" After a few seconds the guilt passed, and as soon as Faki had thanked Allah for the food, we greedily dug in.

Faki himself sipped water, waiting for the night's final shift before taking food. Continuing our interview, he said he planned to turn his business over to his sons and go into export-import, based in Khartoum. He also hoped to acquire a fourth wife, a young nurse in Muglad who was not only beautiful but fluent in English and French as well. "This will help Faki to go international," he explained. The price tag for the takeover was steep. A fine wife in Muglad could cost up to thirty thousand Sudanese pounds or thirty head of cattle, whichever the bride's family preferred. The two sides were still negotiating.

"In the future, someday, Faki would like to go to New York," Faki said. "Look for another house, maybe some cattle."

Faki clapped his hands and the Dinka servants reappeared, clearing away the ravaged platters and setting down cakes and tea in their place. When this too had been consumed, Faki glanced meaningfully into the dark, where the next shift of diners waited. The guests at our table thanked him with handshakes and bows and slipped quietly into the night.

Faki held my hand for a moment and gestured at my notebook. He had one more thought for Wall Street. "Even if I never see New York," he said, "I can count my cattle and say, 'There is no man in Muglad like Faki.' "

Bart and I stumbled through the pitch-black night to Beit Khawajja, burping all the way. The aid workers were already asleep on cots in the open air, with a half-dozen Sudanese rolled up in sheets on the ground. Two cots remained empty, for us. I thought for a moment about the malaria-stricken Canadian I'd met on the flight from Khartoum, and tried to cover myself with my mosquito net. It was hot and uncomfortable, like lying inside a giant cobweb. So I threw it away and lay there in my underwear, on a narrow cot, feeling oddly content. My belly was full—indecently full—and I gazed up at a bright tapestry of stars, undisturbed by clouds or smog or urban glare.

Bart's mind drifted along a similar plane. "It is strange, no?" he asked with a chuckle, sitting on his cot. He was shining his flashlight into a gourd of water. A dubious silt of sand and twigs lay at the bottom. "Here I am, no toilet, no light, no beer." He drank down the water. "Tomorrow I probably die of malaria. And tonight I am such a happy man." We said our good nights and I fell asleep, waking once in the night and gazing dreamily at the brilliant sky, wondering why it was that no one had hit off the lights.

The following day, Kevin figured out how we could skirt the policeman's prohibition on visiting the refugees. He had business at the next town up the road, called Babanoosa, and doubted that the arm of Sudanese law stretched that far.

The road was a rutted track through acacia and thorn, and the twenty-mile journey took us over an hour. We arrived at a sleepy railroad junction of mud-brick Arab homes, bordered by a sprawling refugee camp. Ten thousand or so Dinka were huddled in hovels of sorghum stalk and mud, with ten latrines for the entire population. The stench was overwhelming. Kevin left me at the entrance to the camp and we agreed to rendezvous four hours later.

Two hundred new arrivals squatted beside a makeshift clinic, waiting for a single Sudanense doctor to inspect them. Most had reached the camp on foot after journeys of two weeks or more, arriving with nothing but the filthy rags on their backs and gourds of brackish water. Their bare feet were swollen and dusty and their bodies so emaciated that the women's chests were almost indistinguishable from the men's.

One boy had a thin string tied around his bloated belly, a Dinka folk cure for stomach pains. From a pile of free clothes he had plucked an undersized sweatshirt that read "Somebody Loves Me." Another boy had tea leaves stuffed in his ear, a Dinka remedy for infection. A teenager, stark naked, walked back and forth with a monkey tied to a string. It was his only belonging, and he offered it to passersby for thirty Sudanese pounds, or an equivalent quantity of food. There weren't any takers.

"We keep track of the dead by what the gravediggers have been paid," said an English-speaking Dinka nurse who worked at the clinic. In Muglad the previous wet season, the death rate had been thirty a day out of a population of three thousand.

The nurse offered to translate while I interviewed some of the refugees. He took me to a low grass hut, returning a moment later with a cane-carrying teenager named Lual Garang. Lual was seven feet tall and had to bend almost double as he came in through the hut's low doorway.

Lual was unsure of his age—nineteen, he said, maybe twenty—but he knew exactly how many hungry Dinka had fled his village three weeks before, and how many remained when they arrived in Babanoosa. "We began with one hundred and eighty and now we are only ninety-six," he said. "Arabs with guns took the rest as slaves."

Last spring an Arab tribe had arrived in the village armed with machine guns they'd been given by the government. They burned the Dinka grain stores and took most of their cattle. Lual sketched the scene in the dust with his cane, drawing quick messy lines to represent flames. The Dinka went hungry through the wet season and then had no seed with which to plant a new crop.

By spring they were eating grass and tree leaves to stay alive. Faced with starvation, the elderly and sick, joined by the women and children, headed north on foot while healthy adult males stayed behind to tend the few remaining cattle. Lual went along because he had a chest infection. "I am no use to anybody," he said, tapping his wasted rib cage.

The group was traversing an isolated stretch of scrub when Arab tribesmen charged up on camels and horses, brandishing carbines. The Dinka, armed only with spears and clubs and weak from hunger, were unable to defend themselves. The Arabs shot one man, then tied up the healthiest Dinka and disappeared with them back into the bush. "It was as easy for them as herding cows," Lual said. Stooped and ill, he was spared, and staggered north with ninety-five survivors. His mother and several others died along the way.

I asked Lual how long he planned to stay in the camp.

"Until I am well," he said, his voice weak and hoarse, almost a death rattle. "I want to go home and kill Arabs."

Lual limped out and other Dinka wandered in, with stories as awful as his. One woman told of friends who had sold their children into slavery in exchange for a few days' food, or a ride north in the back of a truck; it was either that or watch the children starve. The famine was so severe that the price for a healthy girl had fallen from thirty dollars to only five dollars. The girls either became concubines or were sent to the fields to shepherd cattle and cut thorns.

A middle-aged man named Andreea Atyek had come north to search for his three children, snatched two years before in an Arab raid. He had wanted to come earlier, he said, but felt he had to provide first for his remaining family members. "Two wives and eight children—this is more important than three stolen ones," he said, revealing the grim calculus of raising a family in southern Sudan. Despite his efforts, three of his children had starved.

As Andreea explained it, the loss of cattle was, for the Dinka, almost as tragic as the loss of children. The Dinka worshiped their cows, sang to the animals, even recited love poetry to them. A few calves were slaughtered each year for meat, but killing cattle was otherwise frowned on. Wealth was measured in cows, as were dowries. Cattle even served as blood money to compensate for crimes. A murder cost thirty-six head. In Dinka society, a man without cows was nothing.

As he got up to leave, Andreea unfolded a piece of paper he kept in the breast pocket of his tattered shirt. It was covered with crude sketches of giraffes and hippopotami, drawn by a seven-year-old daughter who had died on the long trip north.

"She would find it sad here," he said, sobbing. "It is a barren land, nothing like home. There are only rabbits and birds."

After two hours of interviews, crushed by heat and depression, I staggered out of the hut and lay down on the ground to shut my eyes for a moment. What sounded like drums began beating in the distance. I opened my eyes to find five little boys staring intently at my face. "*Khawajja! Khawajja! Khawajja!*" they cried, tugging at my hair.

Tracking the drumbeats, I wandered out of the clinic, through a crude marketplace where the Dinka sold Reagan sorghum they'd gathered in town. I'd seen them that morning, in Muglad, trailing the trucks full of grain, hoping for a little spillage. Kevin said the Dinka still ate as they did during times of plenty down south, feasting on their weekly ration until they were full, brewing the rest into homemade beer and waking up the next day with nothing.

I stopped to watch one woman pummeling the grain with a stick as big as herself. She thought I'd come to admire her earrings, and moved closer so I could have a look. They were crafted from old English halfpennies, bearing portraits of Edward VII. She spoke no English or Arabic, so I could only guess at their origin: a gift from a missionary, perhaps, or bit of charity from some English traveler who had passed through decades ago.

I walked toward the noise, which came from a crowd gathered beneath a desiccated baobab tree, the only shade outside the clinic. What I had taken for drums was actually the sound of several hundred hands clapping. The temperature was easily 110 degrees. Many of these people hadn't eaten in days. Yet at the center of the circle, six women were singing and dancing as the others cheered them on, shouting a refrain that came out as "ay-yi-yi."

I couldn't understand the words they sang, but I could understand their motions. Looking at the ground, the women stamped their feet and thrust out their withered breasts, raising bony arms behind their heads and pointing fingers at the sky. They were mimicking cattle. At home, they'd sung to their bulls and cows, named them, recited the names of their ancestors. Here, with nothing left of their former lives, they could only remember the cattle by dancing.

The dance was evocative and erotic in a sad sort of way. The women hadn't much left to shake, and their arms waved in the air like withered tree limbs. Emaciated breasts flopped from their shredded frocks. But the women kept dancing, uninhibited and ecstatic. I was the only male present and the only *khawajja*, but no one seemed to mind.

I watched for a while and then left them there, clapping and singing beneath the baobab tree. I walked back into Babanoosa to catch my ride. Veiled Arab women slipped in and out of doorways on the narrow streets, and Arab men in tall white turbans moved toward the mosque as the afternoon call to prayer wafted out across the scrub.

We made it back to Muglad in time for a sunset soccer game at a field adjoining the refugee camp. Normally, Kevin and one other aid worker played in the weekly contest, but they had work to do and asked Bart and me to go as substitutes. I was weary from the long day in Babanoosa and wearier still at the sight of the field: a two-hundred-yard expanse of thorn and scrub, with crooked sticks forming a goal at either end. The field was almost as wide as it was long and edged with sand and brambles. An underfed goat grazed at the hundred-yard line.

The teams, twenty to a side, were as irregular as the field. One squad was mostly Dinka, the other included members of a clan called Nuer. Tribal markings were the only way to tell the two groups apart. Dinka men have their six bottom teeth yanked out at the age of eight, and four lines cut across their foreheads at adolescence. The Nuers' faces are marked with six lines and small raised dots. This distinction would no doubt be obvious to an anthropologist. But in fading sunlight, on a playing ground the size of an Iowa cornfield, the players were indistinguishable to me.

When I suggested with pantomime that one team identify itself by disrobing from the waist up, in the American tradition of "shirts and skins," half of the players politely obliged and half didn't, irrespective of which squad they were on. Then a self-appointed referee, who had evidently never played soccer before, tossed a lumpy brown ball in the air and announced that the match had begun.

Tents emptied out and the refugees crowded along the sidelines, shouting and banging on sticks. Adults gathered behind one goal and children behind the other, though neither group seemed to be rooting for a particular team. The game, after all, was a complete novelty to most of them, as were Bart and I. No sooner had we lined up, on opposing sides, then a deafening roar began:

"*Khawajja! Khawajja! Khawajja!*"

Posted at left wing, the only player I could identify was a Dinka with red sneakers who appeared to be on my side. This was hard to confirm, as everyone crowded around the ball rather than playing in position. The referee stood passively by as the players delivered groin kicks and tackled each other in the thorns.

What the players lacked in finesse they made up for in stamina. After two or three sprints down the endless field, I was clutching my stomach and gasping for breath. My teammates, many of whom had recently limped into Muglad with swollen feet and bellies, raced up and down as effortlessly as gazelles across the savannah.

Given the size and condition of the field, scoring should have been impossible. Perhaps to compensate for this, both teams had passed over their seven-footers and chosen as goalies two youths who were, by Dinka standards, virtual dwarfs, no taller than I. As the goals were thirty yards wide and the posts lacked crossbeams, even wild kicks sailed past the goalies' arms or over their heads. After twenty minutes of play the score was 10 to 7.

The crowd showed no interest in the scoring, apparently unaware that this was the point of the game. Instead, they were riveted to the miscues, laughing loudly whenever players kicked and missed or let balls roll between their legs. After days spent waiting for rations of sorghum, the soccer game wasn't sport, it was comic relief. And it quickly became clear that Bart and I were the champion clowns, midget men with straight blond hair and pale skin, loping in slow motion behind the fleet, tall Dinka. Each time either of us touched the ball, the cry went up from the sidelines: "*Khawajja! Khawajja! Khwawjja!*"

Deafened by the noise, I dribbled through the thorns until my wind gave out, then looked for the red-sneakered youth—yelling, pointlessly, "Yo! Dinka in the red!"—and kicked the ball as hard as I could.

"*KHAWAJJA! KHAWAJJA! KHAWAJJA!*"

After an hour, the sun sank into the scrub in a blaze of purple and orange, with the score tied at 21. The referee called the game. The other side didn't hear, or didn't care, and rushed down the field, kicking the ball through the posts after our goalie had fled. The referee threw up his hands. The Nuer had won, 22 to 21. And the refugees wandered off through the dark to pick up firewood and cook their sorghum porridge as another band of refugees wandered in.

Two days later, five planes touched down at the Muglad airstrip and disgorged a U.S. congressional committee onto the tarmac. The group had chosen Muglad as the last stop on a one-day "fact-finding" tour of the famine-stricken south, accompanied by Sudanese officials, TV crews and several dozen reporters who'd been granted visas for the lighting visit. Reclaiming my camera from the police—miraculously intact—I rushed with several hundred locals to the airport. Tribesmen with spears stood majestically at the edge of the airstrip, waving banners that read: "We has the plegsure to welcome the govermor and delegation." I waited for them to break into a chorus of "*Khawajja!*" but they didn't, perhaps because the first congressman off the plane was Mickey Leland, a black Democrat from Texas. He showed his solidarity by walking along the line of welcomers, teaching them to high-five. His raised palm came up to the average tribesman's nipple.

Gary Ackerman, a New York Democrat, followed Leland's performance by attempting to lead the tribesmen in a sing-along about the five boroughs of Manhattan.

"New York, hello, how are you?"

The tribesmen looked at him blankly.

"I'm good," he persisted. "Me, too."

More blank stares.

"New York, hello, how are you?"

Aides scrambled behind the congressmen, making sure the TV cameras were well positioned and booking reporters for briefings later that day, back at the Khartoum Hilton.

"Gary's been real involved in this hunger thing since the start," confided one of Ackerman's aides. When I told her I'd spent four days in Muglad and a week before that in Khartoum, she hustled me over for some quick-fire fact-finding by her boss.

"Did you meet any slaves?" he asked. "Do they appreciate the American aid? Tell me about shopping in Khartoum. Is it junk?"

Before I could answer, he cut in—"Sorry, got to run"—and rushed off with the others for yet another photo op: tossing bags of U.S. sorghum from a relief plane onto the tarmac. "It's tough being out in the bush, eating dirt," Ackerman said, grimacing theatrically as he lifted a bag. Such missions could, in fact, be tough. A few months later, Mickey Leland died when his small plane crashed on a similar trip in Ethiopia.

The delegation was whisked to the nearby refugee camp to pose for the cameras again, kissing swollen-bellied babies and nodding meaningfully as mothers poured out their woes in untranslated Dinka. Then, having gathered all the facts it needed, the delegation rushed back to the airstrip for takeoff, with Bart and me in tow. The delegation's visit to Muglad had lasted forty minutes.

"Tragic, isn't it?" one of the aides said, settling in and unfurling a three-day-old *USA Today*. Within minutes, the grass-and-mud skyline of Muglad fell away and a warm haze of American chitchat embraced me. We talked about the food at the Hilton. About the first flight out of Khartoum. About preseason baseball. By the time we hit the clouds, Faki and the dancing Dinka and the mad soccer game had receded. Exhausted, I drifted off and wondered, half asleep, if it was all some strange dream I'd been having.

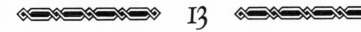

13

ARABIAN FLIGHTS
Sky-High over Islam

Trip Planning

1. *Don't assume the typical "It can't happen to me" attitude. The fact that you're traveling in a foreign country makes you a prime target for terrorism.*
2. *Don't wear cowboy boots, Hawaiian shirts, school or university sweatshirts, flashy buckles and the like. Try to "blend in" as much as possible.*
3. *Keep your hair style simple, not flashy. Terrorists may assume that men with very short hair are in the military. Wild hair styles—Mohawk cuts and so on—identify you as decadent to many terror groups.*
4. *To ensure your family's financial security in the event you become a terrorist victim, make sure that your will is up-to-date.*
> *—The Terrorism Survival Guide: 101 Travel Tips on How Not to Become a Victim*

Back in Khartoum, I began plotting my escape from Sudan. This was no easy feat. April was the start of the haboob season, when fierce desert winds Hoover up all the dust from the desert and deposit it on the capital, blotting out the sun and reducing visibility to nil. As there was no radar at Khartoum's airport, haboobs made takeoffs and landings risky. One runway for small planes was littered with the charred remains of crafts that hadn't made it.

Many Western airlines had abandoned Khartoum, forcing travelers to scramble for scarce seats aboard Sudan Air. Sudan Air's code in international flight guides is SD. As every Middle East traveler knows, this stands for "Sudden Death." A Sudan Air pilot once mistook the White Nile for the Khartoum runway and landed on the water instead. Shortly before my visit, a plane had been forced to return empty from London because British officials declared it too decrepit to carry passengers.

"No sensible person flies Sudan Air unless he absolutely must," warned a British engineer in Khartoum. "Of course, when you absolutely must, you can be sure the plane won't take off anyway."

It wasn't my first encounter with the fear and loathing of Middle East travel. Just getting to and from the Cairo airport could be treacherous; the black airport taxis sped with such kamikaze intent that Egyptians called them "flying coffins." Most trips also began with a choice between the world's ten most likely to be hijacked airlines. Added to this was the fact that the passenger log invariably listed 250 men in turbans and robes, named Ahmed, Mohammed or Ali, and one white American male with a surname best known for adorning boxes of a leading brand of matsoh. It wasn't hard to figure my chances if some terrorist decided to establish his negotiating position by dumping a body on the tarmac.

Fortunately, airlines have a stake in keeping you alive. Anyone who flies the Israeli carrier, El Al, is subjected to interrogation by a corps of fingernail-pullers in training, a kind of farm team for Mossad. If one bead of sweat appears during the questioning—which it inevitably does, standing in Cairo's un-air-conditioned terminal in mid-July—your dirty underwear, condoms and spare surgical truss will be turned out of your bag for the amusement of the two hundred people behind you. One night in Cairo, an overzealous El Al-nik picked through each item in my luggage, barking, repeatedly, "What's in this?" until he'd searched everything except a brown-bag snack. "What's in this?" he demanded, seizing a tangerine.

First World airports are antiseptic places, so uniform in lay-out and barometric pressure that the jet-lagged traveler may wonder if he has somehow landed at the same terminal from which he took off. This soothing convention rarely applies in the Middle East. It is at the airport—waiting hours for the faint stamp of Arabic calligraphy in your passport, changing hard currency into soft, being strip-searched for weapons and alcohol—that the character of the society out-side begins to reveal itself.

Cairo, a class-ridden city, had adjoining airports labeled "one" and "two" but known to taxi drivers as "old" and "new." Like all new structures in Cairo, terminal two is prematurely aged: baggage belts creak, public address sys-tems shriek with feedback, dust hangs in the air. Still, by Egyptian standards, it is a comfortable and orderly place. Air conditioners sometimes hum and planes have been known to depart on schedule. It is here that Western tourists and Per-sian Gulf sheiks board Swissair, Lufthansa and Saudia to take off over desert sands that begin a few feet from the end of the runway.

Terminal number one caters to a different clientele: Air Somalia, Sudan Air, Interflug—to name only a few—and terrorist risks such as El Al. The idea seems to be that if someone wants to plant a bomb, better they blow away ter-minal one than terminal two. At terminal one, there is no such thing as allocated seating, though overbooking is assured. Egyptair, an innovator in this regard, has a special class of ticket called "confirmed waiting list," which allows the airline to book twelve hundred people for the two hun-dred seats actually available. Long-suffering flyers of Egypt-air have dubbed the carrier "Insha'allah Air." *Insha'allah* means "if God wills it." According to a 1990 survey, Egyp-tian is second only to Aeroflot in the number of fatal acci-dents over the past twenty years.

Once you've cleared check-in and security, there is the

interminable wait for flights that rarely leave on time. For reasons that aren't entirely clear, flights between Middle East capitals almost always depart between midnight and six in the morning. So there you sit, in Khartoum or Baghdad or Tripoli, nursing a cup of three-hour-old coffee and listening anxiously for your flight to be called. As any security expert knows, the best way to foil would-be terrorists is to make frequent and arbitrary changes in procedure, such as changing the departure gate at least four times before takeoff. Although your fellow passengers—and competitors for over-sold seats—appear to be sound asleep, they actually possess a sixth sense that allows them to wake at a dead sprint for the departure gate. They also have the advantage of being native Arab speakers. As you try to dope out yet another static-clouded announcement (*wahed*, that's one, *tamenya*, that's eight, *sifr*, that's zero—that's my flight!), they're already off, leaving you at the wrong gate beside a blind old man and a veiled woman trying to change her baby's diaper.

In flight, the mayhem resumes. Most Middle East stewardesses make quick work of the safety demonstration, or dispense with it altogether. Given the condition of the "safety features," this is understandable. As the plane rattles down the runway, luggage compartments fly open, tables pop out and stuffed toy camels bounce down the aisle. The only thing that never jars loose is the oxygen mask, ripped out years ago for emergency use as a diaper or ripped out years ago when the cabin last depressurized somewhere over the desert.

Just before takeoff, the NO SMOKING sign flicks on, which is the signal for passengers on both sides of you to instantly light up. Ninety percent of Arab males smoke, always on airplanes and particularly during takeoff. Nicotine helps ease tension if you've never flown before, and particularly if you have. Alcohol, of course, is banned on many Arab airlines.

Luckily for sweaty-palmed fliers, the generally cloudless skies across the Middle East make for little turbulence—outside the aircraft. Inside, as soon as the red SEAT-BELT sign goes on, passengers begin lurching around the plane to light each other's cigarettes. Reading is difficult, sleep impossible, and the less said about the toilets the better.

The food at least isn't much worse than the plasticized fare provided by airlines elsewhere in the world. And meals help to pass the time on flights that are inordinately long, given the distances. As the crow flies, most Middle East capitals are an hour or two apart. But crows don't have to dodge radar, MiG fighters and surface-to-air missiles. Egyptian planes can't fly through Libyan airspace; Iraqi planes can't fly over Syrian airspace; and everyone avoids the dagger-shaped landmass adjoining the Mediterranean, also known as the "Zionist entity."

Arab airlines offer unusual in-flight activities. As my plane to Saudi Arabia taxied down the runway, the steward recited the Prophet Mohammed's travel prayer over the loudspeaker. There was also a "Mecca indicator" on the ceiling of the plane: a bobbing, compasslike needle that allowed passengers to know, even in the clouds, which way they should bow their heads in prayer. For reading matter, I had a choice of the *International Herald Tribune* and an English-language Saudi paper. The *Trib* had been so carefully scissored by Saudi censors that reading it was like unfurling a tangled ribbon. An article on Saudi Arabia was missing, as was an advertisement for Courvoisier. Another alcohol ad remained, though black ink concealed the liquor bottle, the two glasses and the scantily clad woman about to take a sip of the forbidden substance. At least the Saudis weren't sexist in their censorship: I later read a copy of *The Wall Street Journal* in which an ad using Da Vinci's nude drawing of man was also blacked-out.

The English-language Saudi paper was still in one piece, though there were curious omissions. I spent several minutes trying to figure out the following passage from a page-long Question and Answer on the Koran.

Q. Does Islam say anything about a wife who refuses to comply with her husband's wishes with regard to sexual fulfillment? (Name and address withheld)

A. Islam views this very seriously, because it constitutes an encouragement to seek fulfillment elsewhere which may lead to committing adultery. As for the second part of your question it is strongly recommended to remove pubic hair and armpit hair from time to time. There is no restriction on the frequency, but we are recommended to do it once in forty days.

With time, I learned like other correspondents to accept the perils of Middle East travel with grim good humor. During the long hours of waiting in terminal one in Cairo, I'd flip through my airline guide in search of carriers elsewhere in the world that sounded even more dubious than the one I was on. Bop Air. Muck Air. Suckling Airways. I never did fly the Lebanese carrier, which sensibly calls itself Middle East Airlines to avoid reminding passengers that its Beirut hub is every hijacker's airport of choice. I also managed to avoid the national carrier of Bangladesh, which once launched an advertising campaign featuring the comforting slogan "We're better than you think."

Sudan Air had no slogans, nor did it have a reliable schedule; passengers were simply told to arrive for flights at eight o'clock on the day of their supposed departure. On the day of mine, no Sudan Air planes were leaving Khartoum because of a weeks-old pilots' strike and a shortage of jet fuel. Luckily, I was one of the thousand or so people who managed to secure a "confirmed waiting list" ticket on Egyptair instead. The flight was scheduled to depart on the first day of Ramadan, the holy month during which Muslims fast from dawn to dusk and spend the hours between in a state of half-starved irritability. This made the atmosphere at the airport a little edgy. So edgy, in fact, that I arrived to find several thousand people standing in the 120-degree heat outside the terminal, waving confirmed waiting list tickets and struggling to get in. Soldiers stood pinned against the wall of the already overcrowded building, keeping the mob at bay with the butts of their submachine guns.

Fighting my way to the front, I waved a twenty-dollar bill at the nearest soldier and managed to slip inside. The cramped terminal was filled with travelers sleeping beside suitcases held together with string. They looked as though they'd been camped there for days. I went to the desk marked "Flight Information" and asked whether the plane to Cairo was leaving on schedule.

"It leaves soon," said one man.

"There is no flight to Cairo," said a second.

"*Bokra, insha'allah,*" said a third. Tomorrow, God willing.

The airport cafeteria was closed for Ramadan. So I settled on the floor beside a Sudanese student who translated each announcement for me, just in case a plane to Cairo was called. Five hours later, I was still waiting.

Finally, at sunset, as the haboob winds began to swirl, a message came over the loudspeaker announcing the flight to Cairo. Eight hundred people surged toward the gate, and the first two hundred of us scrambled aboard. As soon as the plane took off, the cabin erupted in cheers. Allah be praised! We're out of Sudan! Stewards came down the aisle with trays of food for passengers now mad with hunger. As the stewards reached the first row of seats, the plane lurched, then leveled out, then dipped toward the ground. The food vanished. There was a crackly announcement in Arabic. The passengers on either side of me buckled their seat belts and searched for nonexistent safety cards. A man across the aisle began to pray.

"What's going on?" I screamed at one of the stewards.

"It is nothing," he said, suddenly pale. "The Sudanese forgot to give us gas."

There was one other Westerner on board, a Dane who happened to be an amateur pilot. He was as pale as the steward. "The pilot is throttling back," he said as the plane seemed to slow. Then the roar of the plane dimmed slightly, becoming more of a hum. "One of the engines has died," the Dane said. We dropped several thousand feet and began tossing this way and that in what felt like a fledgling haboob.

"They say every cloud has a silver lining," the Dane said. "I think it is a stupid saying."

Ten minutes later, the pilot managed a wobbly landing at a desert strip just across the Egypt-Sudan border. Once again the cabin erupted with cheers. Allah be praised! We're out of Sudan! A fuel truck rumbled out from the hangar. This was the cue for everyone on board to light a cigarette, including the captain, who had emerged from the cockpit with a stunned expression on his face. Then suddenly we were evacuated from the plane and herded into a concrete pillbox at the edge of the runway.

"What is it?" I asked one of the crew.

"Exactly I do not know," he said. "Something technical."

An hour later, I asked again.

"It is nothing," he said. "Only something wrong with the wheels."

Two hours later, I inquired once more.

"It is something with the nose of the plane. Not serious."

I went back inside the pillbox, where the other passengers sat slumped on the concrete floor, meditating on bellies that had been empty since sunrise, sixteen hours before. I meditated on the mosquitoes feeding on my arms and legs and wondered if they were malarial. At two in the morning we were ushered back on board the plane.

"What was it?" I asked.

The crewman shrugged. "Exactly they do not know."

Reassured, I climbed back in my seat and chain-smoked with everyone else until we reached Cairo. The trip from Khartoum, a distance equivalent to that separating New York and Chicago, took seventeen hours from the time I'd arrived at the airport. Even for Egyptair this was a little over par, though certainly nothing extraordinary.

"Look on the bright side," the Dane said, as we stood in the passport line at terminal one in Cairo. "We didn't have to fly on Sudan Air."

14

TO BEIRUT
Juʒquʼau Boutiste

*I had thought that danger was the safest thing in the
world, if you went about it right.*
—ANNIE DILLARD,
The Writing Life

Marwan, the young man hud-
dled beside me on the bow, counted loudly as we approached
the Lebanese shore.

"One, two, three, four . . ."

"What are you counting?" It was four in the morning
and I was irritated at being awakened. Marwan pointed at a
geyser shooting straight up from the sea about one hundred
yards to starboard. The water looked rather picturesque,
pluming skyward and fanning out as it cascaded down
through the moonlight.

"What's that?" I asked groggily.

"A one-fifty-five-millimeter shell. Maybe a one-eighty."

There was a muffled roar from the coast and the air
quivered slightly. Marwan started counting again. "One,
two, three, four . . ."

On the fifth beat, another geyser shot up from the sea.
This time it was only fifty yards off our bow. A loud groan
drifted up from the cabin, where the other passengers peered
out through grimy portholes. The pilot spun the wheel.
Guns thudded once more, and Marwan threw his arm across

my back, pulling me flat against the deck. "Home, sweet home," he sighed, crossing himself as he timed the shell's loft once again. "One, two, three, four . . ."

A few days before, I'd received a phone call from a business-man in Oklahoma named Larry who claimed to be a "close personal friend" of the Lebanese Christian commander, General Michel Aoun. The general had been holed up in his East Beirut bunker for weeks, trading howitzer-fire with the Syrians and their Lebanese Muslim allies. Aoun's "war of liberation" against Syria had become one of the worst artillery duels in Lebanon's long civil war, killing or wounding fifteen hundred people.

"Tony, the general has a helicopter waiting in Cyprus to fly you right into the presidential palace," said the Oklahoman, who had gotten my name from an editor in the States. "You'd get an exclusive interview and one helluva story." I found out later that Larry had peddled the same "exclusive" to journalists across the Middle East. But as a free-lancer I was flattered and intrigued.

I was also chicken. On a recent day the Syrians had lobbed twenty thousand shells onto the Christian enclave in East Beirut. Muslim West Beirut was worse; if the bombs didn't get you, the hostage-takers would. Larry's assurance that he felt safer in Beirut than he did in Norman, Oklahoma, and that I'd be greeted by "more bodyguards than you can shake a stick at," wasn't much comfort. Nor was his call the next day, telling me that helicopters had stopped flying because they'd become "sitting ducks" for the Syrian guns. He suggested I go to Cyprus anyway and "hang tight" until the shelling died down.

I called the *L.A. Times* correspondent in Cairo, Michael Ross, who'd been based in Beirut in the seventies. Like other former Lebanon hands, he often waxed nostalgic about Beirut: its nightlife, its beaches, its restaurants, its car bombs. I asked him if he ever got the urge to go back.

"Yeah," he said. "But I wait and it passes."

■   ■   ■

Larry promised there'd be one of "the general's men" to meet me at the airport in Larnaca, on the east coast of Cyprus. There wasn't. He said I should go to a certain hotel and the general's men would contact me there. They didn't. The helicopters still weren't flying. All phone lines to Lebanon were dead. I never did find out exactly who Larry was or why he had a special connection to the general.

The only other way into Beirut was by ferry, across the Mediterranean. The Syrians were shelling that, too, and the boat hadn't left Larnaca for three days. But so many people wanted to flee Beirut that the ferry operators had decided to try again, anchoring outside of artillery range and shuttling passengers to and from shore on motorboats, which presented a smaller target. It had the ring of a dramatic feature, a sort of Lebanese Dunkirk. If I rode the ferry both ways, I could interview the inbound passengers—who goes to Beirut in this mess?—and interview the outbound refugees. I'd be safe. And I wouldn't even need a Lebanese visa.

The Lebanese militiaman at the ferry gate in Larnaca didn't understand. He looked at my round-trip ticket and asked, "Why not you get off in Lebanon?"

"I like boat rides," I said lamely. How do you explain fear to someone who probably traded gunfire as a toddler? "And I don't have a visa."

The militiaman held up his stamp. "I give you visa, no problem." Lebanese, like chain smokers and heavy drinkers, are always trying to thrust their vice on others.

"No thanks," I said. "Maybe some other time, when it's quiet." He shrugged and waved me aboard.

In what passes for "quiet" times in Beirut, the ferry carries six hundred or more passengers to Lebanon on each daily trip. These days, most of the traffic was going the other way; there were fifty people headed to Beirut and nine hundred booked to come out. Fifteen thousand Christians had already fled the shelling, and Larnaca's cafés were crowded with Lebanese waiting for things to "cool down."

"You know, 'cool down,' like a nuclear reactor—from

radioactive to just boiling hot," said the man behind me in the passport line. "These Lebanese are crazy fuckers."

The man extended a sweaty palm and said, "I'm Khatchig Ohannessian." Then he lowered his voice, as if making contact with the one other sane inmate in a madhouse. "I'm American like you, not Lebanese."

Ohannessian was a Beirut-born shopkeeper who had lived in Detroit for thirteen years. He was returning now to sell off two buildings his family still owned in Lebanon. He didn't plan to stick around long. "I'll bribe a few people to get the paperwork done, then get the first boat out," he said, showing me the single small bag he carried as luggage. "This isn't exactly a holiday weekend."

At the start of the civil war, a man had offered Ohannessian's family $750,000 for the property. Now he thought they'd be lucky to get a third that sum. "But if I wait any longer," he said, "there won't be anything left to sell except bricks and scrap metal."

Most of the other passengers were Beirutis working abroad, headed home now to evacuate their families. Unable to phone Lebanon, the men were desperate for news. My short-wave radio, propped on the ferry's open deck, quickly made me the most popular passenger on board.

"Do you mind?" asked a young man named Marwan, picking up the radio as soon as the BBC broadcast finished.

"Please. Go ahead."

He twiddled the dial and picked up, in rapid succession, French Radio, Greek Radio and the Arabic service of Voice of Israel. Then Marwan tuned in Voice of Lebanon, which was judged least reliable of the news services. "It belongs to only one faction, so you get just a piece of the story," he explained. In divided Lebanon, even information was balkanized.

From what I could gather, it was a quiet day in Beirut. "Just sporadic shelling," Marwan said. When the news broadcasts resumed half an hour later, the prognosis changed, like an update in the weather forecast. Sporadic shelling, becoming heavy at times. An hour out of Larnaca, it was raining cats and dogs and ten Lebanese were already dead.

Marwan hit off the radio and lay flat on the deck, unbuttoning his shirt. "I might as well do some tanning now, because I won't get any sun in the bomb shelter," he said.

I lay beside him and we chatted as the ferry steamed out across the azure Mediterranean. Marwan was twenty-four and had been studying architectural engineering in West Germany for two years. "Architecture and engineering—these are two things Lebanon will need a great deal if the war ever ends," he said. This was to be his spring break from school. "Sun and sea for eight hours—then shelling for ten days."

Marwan, like many of the others on board, seemed more European than Middle Eastern. Blue-eyed, with mouse-colored hair, he wore designer jeans and hand-tooled leather boots. He shifted easily from Arabic to French when talking with his fellow passengers, occasionally tossing in a word or two of English. The only Arab thing about him was the string of coral worry beads that he clacked together during the radio reports from Beirut.

"You must understand," he said, "we are Christian Lebanese. Except for the language, I feel nothing in common with Arabs." He closed his eyes, massaging the worry beads. "Of course, some of my best friends are Muslims."

Lebanese I'd met elsewhere in the Middle East were always saying this sort of thing. Beirut, it is a beautiful city—except for the shell craters and shattered buildings. Muslims and Christians and Druze, we can live together in peace—except that we've been killing each other for centuries.

Still, it was hard to resist the Lebanese. There was a lingering whiff of the ancient Phoenicians about them: adventurous and enterprising, mixing easily with East and West. On the plane from Cairo to Cyprus, the woman sitting beside me had introduced herself as Jacqueline Tufenkjiam Davies. I was struck by her name and asked what country she came from.

"Lebanon," she said, then added with a laugh, "which means I'm from all over the place." The child of Armenian traders, she was born in Iran, schooled in Syria and married to an Englishman in Lebanon. She spoke Armenian, Arabic, Farsi, French, English, Greek and German. And she was trying to move back to West Beirut, which she'd fled when Muslim gunmen occupied her house while she was away on vacation.

"Beirut is the only place I feel at home," she said. "Every other city seems, you know, so parochial."

The ferry I was riding was Beirut in miniature, a cosmopolitan stew with at least one person thrown in from every corner of the Lebanese diaspora. Even the boat, a hundred-yard-long cruiser called the *Baroness M*, was a mutt of Mediterranean extraction. It was Greek-owned, Cypriot-flagged and Lebanese-run. And it looked more like a chartered pleasure craft than a ship sailing grimly across the Styx. The wide deck had canvas chairs and a "tropical shower" for sunbathers to cool off in under the hot sun. In the cabin below, there was a bandstand, a well-stocked bar and a casino with one-armed bandits, roulette wheels and blackjack tables bolted to the floor so passengers could gamble on stormy nights. Appropriately, the Greek captain's name was Dionysos.

Escaping the sun, I settled in at the bar beside a muscular man in blue jeans and a tight white T-shirt. He was named Imad. "Usually, it is like *Love Boat*," he said of the ferry ride. "All singing, all dancing, all gambling. Lebanese, they know how to have good times."

Imad looked like a bouncer, which wasn't far off the mark. He worked as a security officer for the Lebanese Forces, a Christian militia that controlled the port at Jounieh, just north of the city. Beirut was carved up, gangland-style, among competing Christian, Muslim and Druze militia, and the ports represented the most lucrative turf. "Guns, drugs, stolen cars—all such things must travel by sea," Imad said, calmly listing the pillars of the Lebanese economy. He

smiled and drained his beer. "The Lebanese, they know how
to make good moneys."

The Lebanese Forces also skimmed profits from gambling, and the casino opened as soon as the ferry pulled out
of Larnaca. I found the casino manager sipping beer behind
a wall of chips at the roulette table. He bet half on black
and half on the number 13.

"It is my lucky number," he explained. "On March thir-
teenth, shells hit every building in the neighborhood except
mine." The wheel spun and the small metal ball stopped at
00. He shrugged and bought another hundred dollars' worth
of chips. "If you may die tomorrow, why not live it up
now?"

Actually, the violence in Beirut wasn't great for business. Usually the boat departed Cyprus after dark and passengers partied until dawn. But because of the shelling, the
ferry now left in the morning so that passengers could shuttle
ashore under cover of darkness. "Everyone thinks too much
about what waits for them at the other end," the manager
said. He was the only gambler. He gave me three free goes
at the slot machine in the hope that clanging tokens would
lure a few more customers into the casino. No one came.
"Business will be better on the boat ride out," he said.

I wandered back on deck in time for the midday news broadcast. It was more of the same. "The Arab League has called
for a cease-fire," Marwan translated, clacking his worry
beads. "The Syrians have launched more bombs." One shell
had hit a power station, knocking out what little was left of
Beirut's electricity supply. There hadn't been water for days.

"We are returning to the Stone Age," said a man named
Hani, who was heading home to Beirut after several days'
respite in Cyprus. He drew a crumpled photograph from his
wallet and passed it around, the way a proud father might
display baby pictures. The snapshot showed the charred
remains of Hani's Mercedes, with its windows and doors
blown out. A shell had hit the car only moments after Hani

climbed from the driver's seat. "I am replacing it," he said, "with a tank."

The others laughed. Hani's photo was a cue for black-humored one-upmanship. One man boasted that he'd survived the civil war by always renting the third floor of tall apartment blocks. In his first residence, a car bomb had taken out the lower few floors, and in his second, an incoming missile had wiped out the floors above. He'd just moved into a new place and taken the third floor again. "It is always best to be in the middle," he said. "That way your neighbors are like armor."

Another man told of visiting a neighbor's house and retreating into the basement when shelling suddenly broke out. After three hours underground, a full bladder finally forced the neighbor upstairs. "He was redoing the cellar and didn't want to pee all over the floor," the man explained. A moment later, a shell hit the house and killed the neighbor in his bathroom. "He didn't even get a last good piss," the man said, shaking his head with a macabre chuckle.

Listening to the stories, I couldn't understand why these urbane, well-traveled men were headed back for more. Couldn't they settle in Cyprus or Paris or New York?

The man who had been blasted out of two apartments shook his head. "Home is home," he said, "even if it is nothing but sticks and stones."

Marwan nodded, adding, "There will be a cease-fire soon. You will see." I thought of the sweaty-palmed shopkeeper from Detroit; crazy fuckers, these Lebanese.

Later in the day, we gathered again to listen to the radio and to hear a story that evoked no laughter. One of the men had just met his neighbor at the bar. The neighbor was returning from Kuwait to evacuate his wife and two kids. The man had to tell him that all three had been killed by a shell that hit their street two days before. "I didn't have the heart," the man said, "to tell him that there was not very much left to bury."

Ten miles off Beirut, the captain pulled up to wait until

dark. I went back to the deck and stood against the rail with Marwan, gazing out at Lebanon. At sunset, the mountains rushing down to meet the sea looked peaceful, a bit like the Côte d'Azur. In more tranquil times—1835—an American missionary named W. M. Thomas wrote of the same approach: "As our steamer came bravely into harbour at early dawn, the scenery was beautiful, and even sublime. . . . You will travel far ere you find a prospect of equal variety, beauty, and magnificence."

As dusk became dark, a few faint thuds resounded from the hills, illuminating the sky with brief bursts of flame, like matches being struck in the distance. Then the thuds became a constant drone and the sky exploded in color. From ten miles out, the shelling had the benign beauty of a fireworks display; I found myself sighing as each rocket and shell streaked through the night. Look at the oranges! The pinks! The display was carefully choreographed, dancing from right to left to right again, with the occasional light flaring straight out across the water and fizzling into the sea a few miles from where we stood.

Marwan leaned across the rail and described the scene with the eerie expertise bred of an adolescence under fire. The thuds from the left were Christian guns. The rapid-fire bursts on the right were the multibarreled rocket launchers of Shiite gunmen in West Beirut. The shells falling in the water were Syrian mortars, positioned on the hills above the city and aimed at us. "It is just a reminder that they know we are here," he said.

The shelling subsided and the captain ordered everyone into the cabin. He was blacking out the ship and shifting position so the Muslim gunners couldn't follow the small boats' path as they wound out from shore to meet us. Below, the casino was still empty but a three-piece band played loudly and the passengers sang along, swigging beer and whiskey. I asked Marwan to translate the lyrics. " 'Fill me up, Lebanon,' this sort of thing," he said, slapping his thighs with the rhythm. A couple got up and gyrated between the tables, shaking their hips and pointing fingers in the air in a lewd parody of Arab dancing. The man was too drunk and quickly slumped back in his seat. But the woman climbed onto the stage, hiked up her blouse and undulated her bare, ample belly. The audience hooted and splashed down more beer. This wasn't how I'd imagined things would be ten miles off the coast of Lebanon.

At midnight we crept back up on the deck. A full moon perched just above the mountains, casting a brilliant beam across the water. Even so, we didn't spot the first boats, their engines muffled and lights extinguished, until they pulled alongside the ferry. The lead craft was a Lebanese Forces gunboat, and just behind trailed two wooden fishing trawlers. All three were crammed to the gunwales, mostly with women and children. We climbed down into the belly of the ferry to watch them come aboard. The first to appear was a young woman. She took two steps and fainted, from relief or exhaustion, it was hard to tell which. The others looked just as bedraggled. Most had been waiting at the dock in Jounieh for three days, with no cover from incoming shells. There were hundreds more still huddled in Jounieh, hoping to shuttle out.

The passengers from Cyprus lined up to board the boat for the ride to shore. "You see how brave the Lebanese are," Marwan said. He was grinding his worry beads. The man beside him lit a Marlboro with the butt of one he'd just finished. I spotted the Detroit shopkeeper near the front, jaw clenched, bag held tightly to his chest. His un-holiday weekend was about to begin in earnest.

Marwan took out a scrap of paper and scribbled his address. "If ever you are in Lebanon," he said, "my home is your home." He laughed. "And my bomb shelter is your bomb shelter." It was one of those uncomfortable journalistic moments I had experienced many times before. After fourteen hours together, we'd become buddies. Now, having milked Marwan for all the quotes I needed, I was headed back to safety and he was headed into hell.

As we neared the front of the line, he grasped my forearm and asked, "Why not you ride into shore with us and then ride back out? It would be good for you just to touch the soil of my country."

It would also be good for my story. If I went in, I could get a much better view of the evacuation—and I could justify a Beirut dateline. Marwan's grip gave me a sudden jolt of peer pressure as well. I felt as I once had as a fourteen-year-old, poised on a lakeside cliff with everyone else jumping in.

We reached the front of the line. Militiamen reached out and half-dragged the last passengers onto the bobbing gunboat. In a moment they'd disappear. I called to the captain and asked him how the ride from shore had gone.

"Fine," he said. "The sea is calm tonight."

"No. I mean the shelling."

He shrugged. "We are here, no?"

Marwan leaped onto the bow of the gunboat. A militiaman unlashed the rope and engines kicked into gear. Marwan reached out his hand. I took it and hopped on board as the gunboat pulled away from the ferry.

Fifty or so people had already crammed into the gunboat's small cabin. We crouched with four other men in the only available space, the narrow bow just in front of the captain's bridge. The boat was so overloaded that we barely seemed to move.

"Moo, moo," went the passenger beside me. He was a middle-aged man named Ali who wore a University of Texas sweatshirt. "In Texas I learned all about cattle," he said, laughing and mooing again. I was wedged tight between Marwan and Ali and buffered from the night wind. The sky was completely black, the sea air soothing. These people lived with danger and knew its contours. If they were unafraid, why shouldn't I be as well? After twenty minutes or so I drifted into a shallow sleep.

The next thing I knew, Marwan was counting aloud and pointing at geysers shooting up from the sea. "One, two, three, four . . ." Whoosh. "One, two, three, four . . ." Whooooooosh. The first shell landed a hundred yards off; the second only fifty. Somewhere in the night a Syrian gunner was shifting his sights, just so. He unleashed another round. "One, two, three, four . . ."

Marwan threw me flat against the deck. Facedown, I couldn't see where the shell came in, but it was close enough to tumble the boat in its wake. Inside the cabin, children began screaming. Marwan clutched his belly. "Never you get used to the bombs," he moaned.

The guns thudded again in the distance. This time we counted in unison. "One, two, three, four . . ." The shell splashed into the water somewhere just to the left, and a fine sea spray sprinkled the back of my neck.

The six of us now lay in an untidy heap on the bow, as if scrambling for a fumble. There was a loud clacking sound, which I took to be Marwan's worry beads. Then I realized it was my teeth.

"I'm freezing cold," I muttered, barely able to get the words out between chattering molars.

"Bullshit," whispered Ali. His University of Texas shirt was drenched with sweat. "You're scared shitless."

Marwan laughed. I laughed. My teeth went clack-clack-clack. My arms and legs jerked wildly. I felt like a ventriloquist's dummy. "Where else in the world," Marwan said, "do you get a welcoming committee like this?"

We laughed again. The cannons boomed, twice in succession. We groaned and huddled closer together. The first shell splashed to the right and we skittered on all fours, crablike, to the left, almost hanging into the water. The captain banged the windshield of the bridge, motioning us back to the center; the weight shift evidently made it difficult for him to steer. He looked little more distressed than when he'd told me back at the ferry that "the sea is very calm tonight."

Whooooosh. The second shell plunged into the sea just ahead of us, and the pilot swung the wheel. My arms and legs flapped in near-convulsions. Can fear bring on an epileptic fit?

The guns thudded. On the fifth beat, water splashed fifty yards off. The guns thudded and the next shell landed a hundred yards off. A moment later, the plumes of water were too far away to be visible in the dim four-in-the-morning moonlight.

"God be praised," Ali said, sitting up and lighting a cigarette. He offered me one. My hands were still shaking so badly that the match kept flickering out before I could light the cigarette. The entire episode had lasted perhaps three minutes.

"How the hell did they miss us?" I asked.

Marwan shrugged. "They were shooting blind," he said. Apparently, the gunners had a rough idea of our course but didn't know our exact location. So they fired down one corridor of sea and then another, hoping to hit the mark.

"Or maybe they didn't want to hit us," Ali said. "The Syrians are brutal people. They would rather torture you than kill you."

I took out my notebook, now soggy, and scribbled to settle my nerves. "Firing blind. Sea corridors. Torture, not kill."

Ali looked at me, wide-eyed. "You a journalist?" he asked.

"Uh huh. Just along for the ride."

He shook his head and said something to Marwan in Arabic, with a French phrase thrown in. The others laughed.

"He says you are like Aoun," Marwan translated. *"Jusqu'au boutiste."*

"What's that mean?"

"You go right to the edge."

"Is that a compliment?"

"Sort of." He punched my shoulder and smiled. "It mean you are very brave. And maybe very stupid."

As shore came into view, my first instinct was to leap onto land and never board a boat again—any boat, anywhere. But I'd be leaping into East Beirut, hardly a safe haven. And the only way out of Beirut was the way I'd just come in.

We pulled up at the dock, and my companions jumped

ashore before the crew had even tied up. Marwan's face was grim; he was already focused on what lay ahead. He forced a smile and shook my hand before disappearing into the night. There was no one waiting on shore for the ride back out to the ferry. Was this it? Was I stuck here in Jounieh?

The crew had disappeared into the embarkation hall beside the dock. The only man in sight was a militiaman patrolling the wharf with what looked like a sawed-off bazooka cradled across one arm. He saw me standing alone on the boat and wandered over to ask why I wasn't getting off.

"I don't have a visa," I said. Under the circumstances, it seemed an inane response.

The soldier shrugged and waved his hand toward the shore, adding in Arabic, "*Etfadil.*" Help yourself. Then he hoisted the bazooka and melted back into the gloom.

I hopped ashore and went into the embarkation hall. The gunboat crew sat in a circle, silently guzzling coffee and wolfing down sandwiches. I asked them why there were no outgoing passengers. The captain pointed at the far end of the hall. There were two jagged holes in the ceiling where shells had torn through.

"Happened at sunset," he said. "Killed a few people." He returned to his sandwich. The passengers had moved to another dock across the harbor, and after refueling we'd head over there to pick them up.

I strolled along the dock as the sky shifted from night-black to a dense, predawn gray. Tall apartment blocks ringed the water and climbed into the hills: shadowy towers of white and beige silhouetted against Mount Lebanon. A few of the buildings were pockmarked by shells. But at five in the morning, with electricity down and the guns momentarily silent, Jounieh seemed peaceful, almost inviting. Thinking of the boat ride again, I wondered if I should stick around.

My doubts disappeared as soon as we reached the other side of the harbor. There were hundreds of people, maybe thousands, almost trampling each other to get onto the gunboat. It would be madness to get off. I felt guilty for occupying a space, though it wasn't much of one. Within minutes the boat was crammed so tight that it was impossible to sit down. A middle-aged woman almost tumbled into my arms as she rushed aboard. *"Mon pays,"* she said, with Lebanese melodrama, *"c'est fini."* Like many of the others, she'd abandoned her luggage at the bombed-out terminal and was fleeing Beirut with nothing but the clothes she had on.

The crew struggled to untie us before more people tried to pile on. As we pulled out, the woman fell asleep on her feet, dropping her head on my shoulder. Then the boat slipped out of the harbor and into open sea. The light was coming up fast; we'd be an easy target for the Syrian guns. And sure enough, half an hour from Jounieh the awful thudding resumed. Babies began crying. A woman vomited on the two people beside her. But the captain had steered us out of artillery range, and the shells weren't very close this time. My teeth barely chattered.

When the shelling died down, I made sympathetic eye contact with a well-dressed young man wedged between the vomiting woman and a mother with two howling babies. He clutched a leather briefcase against his chest and wore the bored expression of a man accustomed to unpleasant travel.

I asked him where he was going.

"Only Cyprus." he held up the briefcase. "It is all Lebanese pounds." He was making a regular run, to buy dollars on the black market. He extracted an arm and handed me a business card. It had Arabic on one side and English on the other, with the words "Currency Exchange" printed neatly beneath his name.

"I go back to Beirut on Tuesday," he said, glancing at his digital watch. "Business is business. Even in Lebanon."

The ferry pulled into Larnaca thirty-six hours after I'd first boarded. No ferries attempted the passage to Beirut again for several weeks. When they did, one of the shuttle boats took a direct hit that killed all the people aboard. By then I was back in Cairo, busy on another assignment. My boat story had made the front page of three papers. DANGEROUS PASSAGE, read one of the headlines. SHIP OF DESPAIR, read another. I pasted them into the looseleaf notebook where I kept all my clips, trying to feel like a *jusqu'au boutiste*. Mostly I just felt stupid. A decision made in a moment of adolescent bravado had almost got me killed.

I came back one night to find a message on the phone machine from Larry, the Oklahoman. He said the helicopters were flying into Beirut again. Did I want an exclusive with the general?

I didn't bother to return the call.

TEHRAN
The Imam Is in the People's Hands

Sorrow, sorrow is this day. Khomeini the Idol Smasher is with God this day!
     —Slogan at the ayatollah's funeral

The plane taxied slowly down the runway in Frankfurt as a Persian-accented voice came onto the loudspeaker. "In the name of God, the merciful, the compassionate, good evening, ladies and gentlemen. In accordance with the laws of the Islamic Republic, ladies must please wear Islamic attire."

Beside me, Geraldine tossed a black chador over her head and clutched it tightly beneath her chin. When she was standing, the black silk cloak reached to her ankles. She scowled in mock Islamic fury, then flashed me a crooked grin.

"Anonymity, I love it," she whispered, as stewardesses in head scarves came down the aisle to check that seat belts and chadors were in place. Geraldine, having endured months of hoots and propositions from Arab males, welcomed her sexless disguise. I found it creepy. With one flick of the wrist, she'd transformed herself from the object of my desire into a forbidding black phantom, a foot soldier of the Islamic Republic. Returning from the airplane toilet a few hours later, I couldn't find my seat. Which form in this sea of black hoods was my wife?

We touched down in Tehran at two in the morning, forty-eight hours after the announcement on Iranian radio that "Imam Khomeini has passed away. From God we come, to God we go." Or, as an editor in the United States put it in a wake-up call to Cairo shortly after, "Khomeini's finally kicked it. Get up and write something."

The news was oddly surprising, despite the fact that the ayatollah was eighty-six and had reportedly been dying for years. Khomeini's failing health was one of those Middle East stories, like civil war in Beirut and the Arab-Israeli "peace process," that had dragged on for so long with so little sign of actual movement that an end seemed unimaginable. The bionic madman would simply live forever.

"I cannot believe he's really dead," said the Iranian standing beside me in line at Tehran's Mehrabad Airport. He was a businessman returning from Germany and had told me on the plane that he hated Khomeini. "But I fear for the future. It is like your saying: 'The devil you know is better than a Satan you have not met.' "

The known devil scowled from a huge portrait on the wall, wreathed now in black crepe. Staring sleepily at the black-turbaned ayatollah, his eyebrows arched in menacing fury, I wondered aloud if Khomeini had ever smiled. Certainly not in any picture I'd seen. "He is not smiling now," said the businessman, shuffling slowly toward immigration. "Not in hell."

The officials at the airport, most of them women, weren't smiling either. Their tightly drawn head scarves made them look both plain and severe, like unfriendly nuns. "Money," demanded one, holding out her hand for my wallet. Confiscating booze and other contraband wasn't enough in Iran. The Islamic Republic also counted dollars to check that visitors changed money legally. The bank sold riyals at seventy to the dollar; the black-market rate was twelve hundred.

We climbed into a taxi and traveled a mile before the headlights shone on a man with a gun, waving the taxi over. He jabbed his Kalashnikov through the window and fired questions at the driver. Who were we? Where were we going? What's in the trunk? It was no different from late-night roadblocks in any of a dozen Middle East capitals, except that our interrogator appeared to be sixteen and wore no identifiable uniform. Not for the last time in Iran, I picked up a whiff of Beirut, a malodorous mix of arms, zeal and anarchy.

It was four in the morning when we reached the Inter-continental Hotel. Following the 1979 revolution in Iran, the hotel had been renamed the Laleh—Farsi for "tulip," the flower of martyrdom—and the words DOWN WITH THE USA! emblazoned on a wall facing the door. A board near registration still advertised several nightclubs and a Polyne-sian bar, even though there hadn't been alcohol served here or anywhere else in Tehran for ten years.

Standards at the hotel had also slid somewhat since the shah's days. Filthy curtains failed to block out the predawn light. In the bathroom a broken faucet dripped. There was crud on the carpet, and coffee-stained butts filled an ashtray on the bedtable.

"Why should they clean it up for the Great Satanists?" Geraldine said, collapsing on the bed. We'd been up for two consecutive nights, filing Khomeini obituaries from Cairo and then flying to Tehran via Frankfurt (Egypt, along with most Arab countries, had no diplomatic or air links with Iran). Geraldine took off her chador, and the sight of her hair aroused me. It was five o'clock when we shut out the light. Lying awake, too tired to sleep, I tried to imagine us years hence, in some First World bed, reliving all the strange places we'd slept together.

A moment later she was asleep. I listened to her soft breathing mingle with the melancholy call to prayer drifting out across the dawn, as it had every day for the two years we'd been in the Middle East—and for thirteen hundred years before that. God is Great! It is better to pray than to sleep!

We were awakened an hour later by a loud thud at the door. A bus was leaving for Khomeini's funeral in five minutes.

Geraldine pulled on her chador and we staggered downstairs to join a hundred journalists boarding the bus. An official from the Ministry of Islamic Guidance—Iran's version of the ubiquitous Information Ministry—hopped on, glanced at his watch and told the driver to go. We looked at each other in astonishment. A government bus in the Middle East leaving on time!

Tehran's streets also surprised me. There was the usual dull sprawl of gray and brown storefronts, interspersed with domes and minarets. But the boulevards were wide, well scrubbed and bordered with trees. The wealthy district through which we were driving was dotted with carpet shops, boutiques and Mercedes-Benz showrooms. To my weary eyes Tehran looked more Western than Eastern, a bit the way Beirut must have seemed before shells and car bombs rearranged the architecture.

We drove north toward the snow-capped mountains overlooking the city and parked at an airfield adjoining a vast prayer ground. It was here that Khomeini's body had lain in state for two days in a refrigerated glass coffin. Now, mourners poured in a black-lava stream down from the hills and into the prayer ground. There were women in black chadors and men in black pants and black shirts to match their black beards. Our group, with its blond heads and khaki clothes, looked like a small crowd of gate-crashers at a very strange party of punks.

A half-dozen Iranians were trying to organize helicopter rides so we could view the gathering from above. But nothing in Iran was that simple. The officials seemed to represent several departments and they shouted at each other in Farsi, gesticulating wildly, as though even the most minor decision demanded theological debate.

After half an hour, with no one yet airborne, Geraldine and I wandered out of the airfield and into the throng of mourners. As we neared the narrow entrance to the prayer ground, the crowd pressed so tightly that I felt myself swept away from Geraldine and into a current of shouting, jostling bodies. The mob funneled fast through the gate, and I grabbed for a vertical iron post, holding tight as the tide swirled past. Then a hand reached down, grabbed my forearm and hoisted me onto a high wall overlooking the prayer ground.

"*Chabar nagar,*" I said, offering the phrase for "journalist." It was the sum total of my Farsi.

The man smiled. He was well dressed in a black open-necked shirt and a black sport coat. "Welcome to Tehran," he said, in unaccented English. "You are American, yes?" I nodded, still catching my breath. "I hate America," he continued. "It is not personal. I like Americans very much. I went to UCLA for four years."

He gestured out at the prayer ground. "Now tell America what you see with your own eyes. Tell America how much we love Imam Khomeini."

The view from the wall caused an odd sort of vertigo. Stretched below us, for a mile in every direction, was a seamless carpet of black tossed over the pink-brown hills. The carpet shifted, rearranging itself, as yet more mourners poured into the prayer ground. A high stand decorated the center of the rug, supporting Khomeini's coffin. The imam's trademark black turban, which denotes descent from the Prophet, rested on his chest. Several other ayatollahs stood beside the dais, and one of them moved to a microphone and shouted, "*Allahu Akbar!*" Mourners paused where they stood and bowed their heads in prayer. Five syllables had sufficed. What had seemed a riot was now an orderly requiem.

"*Allahu Akbar!*" a million voices cried in unison. The crowd had segregated itself loosely by sex, giving the prayers a soprano and baritone chorus. "There is no god but God! Mohammed is the Messenger of God!" Then the Shiite clause, "And Ali is the Friend of God!" The quick switch from near-violence to total discipline was astonishing and a little spooky. I was reminded of Iraqi soldiers I'd spoken to, still scarred years afterward by the sight of Iranian boys surging straight into the Iraqi guns.

The prayers were followed by a few brief eulogies.

Then the mourners filed out of the prayer ground to begin the ten-mile march to a burial site in south Tehran.

"Tell America what you have seen," said the man beside me. He was sobbing. "As a Westerner you cannot understand what this man means to us because you have lost God."

Mesmerized by the crowd, I'd forgotten all about Geraldine. Turning now to find her, I felt the same panic I had the night before on the airplane. Which among this torrent of black hoods was my wife? Luckily I was rather more conspicuous than she and I found her waiting for me near the base of the wall. We struggled back to the airfield to find that our handlers, having failed to organize an aerial view of the prayer ground, were now arguing over how to transport us to the burial site. "No wonder they couldn't win the war," grumbled one reporter, wandering off with several others to watch the funeral on TV in the hotel lobby.

Half an hour later, with little resolved, we sprinted across the tarmac and crammed into whatever helicopter we could enter; ironically, they were all U.S. Hueys left over from the reign of the shah. The overloaded choppers lurched off the ground and swooped in formation toward the south. Tehran is a sprawling city of twelve million and one of the world's smoggiest. But the skies had cleared for Khomeini, and opening up below us was a view that seemed almost hallucinatory. Tehran was wall-to-wall people. Every major avenue had become a dense black river, running south. The main streams were fed by tributaries that wound in from the mountains and plain surrounding Tehran, stretching ten miles or more in every direction. As the helicopter banked for the cameramen, the crowd came into tighter focus. Mourners coursed through the city on foot, on bicycles, on motorbikes, in trucks. Mourners waved banners from rooftops. Fire trucks sprayed water on the people to keep them cool in the 105-degree heat. In some spots the mourners marched in phalanx, men to the right, women to the left, fists raised as they chanted some insult to the West that we were too high to hear.

"It looks like a half-time rally on another planet," shouted the stunned reporter beside me.

Foreign correspondents are a notoriously cynical lot, but even the veterans on board the helicopter stared at each other in disbelief. No regime, however autocratic, could stage-manage a rally of this magnitude. It was the weeping man on the wall writ large: a spontaneous outpouring for a figure Iranians regarded as a saint.

Across from me, a British cameraman just back from Peking began comparing notes with an American who had witnessed Khomeini's triumphal return to Tehran ten years before.

"What do you reckon," the American asked, "three million?"

"Bigger. Double Tiananmen Square, maybe triple. How's it compare to '79?"

"Still bigger."

"Biggest?"

"What do you mean?"

"I mean the biggest bloody crowd ever in history."

It was a bewildering thought. We began a quick thumb backward through history. Hitler. Napoleon. The Crusaders. Genghis Khan. The Roman legions. Jesus Christ. Alexander. None seemed likely to have ever assembled anything close to this many people at one time in one place.

The Brit nodded blankly. "I suspect, gents, that Khomeini takes the cake."

The helicopter set down in a sunbaked field near Behest-e-Zahra, a mammoth cemetery, the centerpiece of which is a cascade of crimson-colored water known as the Fountain of Blood. For reasons that were never made clear, Khomeini's grave lay in the open plain adjoining the cemetery, perhaps because he had already filled Behest-e-Zahra to overflowing with war martyrs. Also unclear was why the helicopter had dropped us in the middle of nowhere, an hour's hike through brambles and dust from the gravesite. The other helicopters were nowhere in sight.

We trudged across the plain and up to a corral composed

of enormous freight containers that were roughly the size and shape of truck trailers. We didn't know it then, but this odd fortress enclosed Khomeini's grave. In fact we didn't know a thing. Our black-shirted escort from the Ministry of Islamic Guidance waved ahead and we followed him through a tunnel and into the corral.

The Iranians were renowned for throwing journalists "into the shit." Trips to the war front had often ended within range of Iraqi guns; a German reporter had died of a heart attack while running for cover. Our leader at the funeral seemed guided by the same kamikaze impulse. At the mouth of the tunnel, a tidal wave of mourners crashed back and forth, tumbling bodies in its wake. Those still standing beat their hands on their heads and wailed, "Khomeini! Khomeini!" One man's forehead was cut open and still he flagellated himself, drenching his palm with blood. Another man was passed from shoulder to shoulder, having fainted or died. The scene was beyond frenzy. The mourners were wild-eyed and oblivious. They didn't seem human at all.

Our guide, followed by a few journalists, edged forward and was swallowed up by the maelstrom. The rest of us hung back, unsure what to do. The day before, eight mourners had been crushed to death while clambering to peek at Khomeini's body. To move ahead now looked like a quick way to become martyr number nine. Or worse, to get trapped in there and miss our deadline. We retreated.

Crouching in a narrow strip of shade, munching cucumbers given to us at the airfield, we waited until the other journalists staggered out of the tunnel, bruised and bewildered, to tell us what we'd missed. A helicopter bearing Khomeini's coffin had set down in the eye of the storm. Mourners mobbed the craft, toppled the casket and tore at the imam's shroud. Most of the reporters hadn't been able to see anything. But one cameraman thought he'd spotted Khomeini's body tossed unceremoniously on the ground. Then the imam was shoved back in his coffin and piled onto the helicopter, which lifted off as revolutionary guards fired guns in the air to clear the crowd.

It took us an hour to hitch a helicopter ride back to Tehran. As Geraldine ran for the aircraft, a blast from the helicopter's rotors blew her chador in the air, revealing the modest black trousers and shirt she wore underneath. The man from the Ministry of Islamic Guidance looked at her with disgust. "Cover yourself!" he shouted. "Cover yourself!"

We reached the hotel in midafternoon, exhausted and sweaty. Meanwhile, the reporters who'd skipped the helicopter ride had seen the funeral much more clearly than we had, on Iranian television. They were already filing their stories while we waited for the TV to replay the scene, hours later, of mourners grasping at Khomeini's legs as a stunned announcer shouted, "The imam is in the people's hands!"

I felt cheated, though a little wiser as to the reality of "historic events." Slumped in the Laleh lobby, watching the funeral on television, I could already hear friends quizzing me in the months ahead, as indeed they did. "You were really there in the middle of that madhouse?" Yes, I was, munching a cucumber and worrying about my deadline, without the faintest notion of what was going on just a hundred yards away.

Islamic law requires that the dead be buried before sunset, and the Iranians accomplished the task by dispersing the crowd and delivering the body in an aluminum casket. The grave was quickly sealed with shipping crates so mourners wouldn't unearth the corpse as they grabbed for handfuls of holy dirt. "Oh stars stop shining!" the Iranian newscaster wailed. "Oh rivers stop flowing!"

"Oh go to hell," a Canadian journalist said, turning down the volume and shouting through the lobby, "He's in the ground!" The crowd of reporters surged toward the telex room, as frenzied as head-slapping mourners, to punch out the news on three antiquated machines which had the keys in all the wrong places:

TEHRAN—In a sceme of astnishing chaos, more than two nillion people thronged . . .

TEHRQAN—Qyatollqh Khomeini went out Tues-dqy the sqme wqy he came in 10 years agop . . .

TEHRAN—Ayxxxatollah Ayqtollxxxxx Ayatollah Ruhollah Khomeini nver ruled Irnaxxxx Iran xxxxx in peace and his grievong followrs wouldn't let him rest in peac either . . .

It was almost midnight before the job was done. "Fuck me!" exclaimed the *New York Times* correspondent, John Kifner, wading through the ankle-deep tangle of telex tape and scan-ning a few dispatches. "This is the worst load of dreck I've ever seen."

In the past twenty-four hours, most of us had had no more than a few minutes' sleep and nothing but cucumbers to keep us going. In another seven hours the buses would reappear at the hotel to carry us to another round of prayers, eulogies and demonstrations. And just so sleep wouldn't interrupt our grieving, a syrupy voice intoned a single word over the loudspeaker, again and again and again: "Imam. Imaaaaaam. Imaaaaaaaaaaaaaam."

16

TEHRAN
Searching for the Twelfth Imam

There is no fun in Islam.
—AYATOLLAH RUHOLLAH KHOMEINI

Over weak tea the following morning, we discovered that we'd gotten the story all wrong. "Those trumpets of arrogance," stated the *Tehran Times*, referring to the Western media, "have tried another clumsy attempt to mislead world opinion." Several arrogant trumpets had been caught "red-handed" by the Iranians, tootling to the world that the funeral crowd had numbered a mere million or two when the actual figure was "over ten million."

We had also erred in portraying the riotous funeral as a macabre embarrassment for the regime. The paper announced with apparent pride that "several people had been killed during the funeral, 438 admitted to hospital and 10,879 given outpatient treatment." The paper printed a picture of trampled corpses as proof.

Another paper, *Kayhan*, reveled in the gore still more. The path laid down by Khomeini, it said, "passes through a sea of blood in order to reach the coast of salvation. Its message is: Islam is nourished with blood."

The reporter reading this aloud put down her stale croissant. "I guess they've got to nourish the people on something," she said.

■   ■   ■

A bus was waiting at the hotel door. The arrogant trumpets were to be given a second chance, this time as witnesses to a massive rally at Tehran University. I opted instead for an unsupervised stroll through the streets. Not that it mattered. The government had declared a forty-day mourning period, closing shops and offices, and the only thing to do was grieve and demonstrate. Five minutes from the hotel I was grid-locked in the morning rush hour. Men marched in tight for-mation, slapping their chests, then their heads, then raising their fists and chanting. It looked like an outdoor aerobics class, with black shirts and black armbands in place of gym clothes.

One of the demonstrators peeled off to rest by the curb, and I edged over to ask him what the mourners were shouting.

"Death to America," he said.

"Oh." I reached for my notebook as self-protection and scribbled the Farsi transliteration: *Margbar Omrika.*

"You are American?" he asked.

"Yes. A journalist." I braced myself for a diatribe against the West and its arrogant trumpets.

"I must ask you something," the man said. "Have you ever been to Disneyland?"

"As a kid, yes."

The man nodded, thoughtfully stroking his beard. "My brother lives in California and has written me about Disney-land," he continued. "It has always been my dream to go there and take my children on the tea-cup ride."

With that, he rejoined the marchers, raised his fist and yelled "Death to America!" again.

Sloganeering was such a fixture of the landscape that it was hard to tell if Iranians heard the words anymore. Since the shah's overthrow, every Western landmark in Tehran had been reincarnated as a symbol of revolution. The Hilton became "Independence" Hotel and a U.S. flag was painted onto the steps so that guests trod on the stars and stripes each time they entered the lobby. Queen Elizabeth Street was renamed Peasant Farmer Boulevard; Los Angeles Boulevard became Hejab Street, the word for Islamic dress. And the former Israeli embassy had originally been turned over to the PLO (though Iran later fell out with the organization, considering Arafat too moderate).

Fleeing the demonstrations, I took shelter in a lush park near the city center. Once named for the shah, it was now known as People's Park. Men sat on benches in the shade, and I walked from group to group, looking for English speakers. Of the first dozen I approached, three spoke English and two had attended university in America; Iran's anti-Western venom was of very recent vintage.

Most of the men quickly declared their devotion to the deceased imam, but one young technician spoke up and said, "Khomeini too much bad and I am more happy he dead." This was translated into Farsi—presumably, with syntax corrected—for the huddle that had formed around our bench. The others shook their heads in disagreement, but they heard the man out. I asked him if another group could govern Iran better.

"Of all the organisms I like Mujahadeen," he said, referring to the most militant of the underground movements in Iran. "Mujahadeen use bombs."

Two armed men edged over from their post by the gate. This didn't seem to bother anyone. When we'd finished chatting, I asked the technician if I could quote him. He shrugged and said a name that began and ended with Z, with six unpronounceable syllables in between. No doubt a common Iranian name. I asked Mr. Z if the eavesdropping soldiers caused him any concern.

"We scared, but only some little," he said. "Persians too much proud to scare." I tried to imagine another country in the Middle East where someone would speak so openly to a foreign journalist in front of security forces. Egypt on a good day. I couldn't think of any others.

Of course, talk was one thing, action quite another. Members of the Mujahadeen and other "organisms" were routinely imprisoned and executed. Shooting and hanging were the preferred methods. Iran's penal code also included crucifixion, as a punishment for the "corrupt on earth," which was a catch-all phrase for enemies of Islam. There were no recorded instances of crucifixions being carried out, although stonings and floggings were not uncommon.

Even so, the regime was unable—and, to a degree, unwilling—to muzzle its citizens to the same degree as other Middle East autocracies. In the seven days that followed, wandering the streets of Tehran, I collected more on-the-record comments than I would have gathered during a month in most Arab countries.

Not that the comments were always straightforward. Persians, like Arabs, are fond of frustrating journalists by substituting long-winded parables for simple, juicy sound bites. One student said he'd once thrown Molotov cocktails at the shah's tanks and subsequently become disillusioned with the revolution. He illustrated his feelings with a story about two men in adjoining hospital beds. One patient, whose bed is by the window, passes each day telling the other man about all the fantastic things he can see through the glass. Trees. Beautiful women. Spectacular night skies. Gradually, the other man wishes his companion dead so he can inherit the bed by the window. His wish comes true. Then, drawing aside the curtain, he finds that the window looks out on a wall. Then he dies.

"Before the revolution, we were like this man, filled with dreams," the student concluded. "Now we have seen the wall."

There was another wall, ten feet high and made of brick, which explained a good deal about the revolution. The wall ran for several city blocks and enclosed what had once been the U.S. embassy. Inside the wall were grounds vast enough to accommodate a suburban shopping mall, with space left over for parking. The embassy building itself was at least three times larger than any other American mission in the Middle East, and it dwarfed every other structure in downtown Tehran.

"You see how America controls everything," said a young man named Ibrahim, who guided me to the embassy. We had met on the street twenty minutes before, and he'd spent the intervening time reciting a catalogue of U.S.-inspired conspiracies. America started the Iran-Iraq war to divert Arab and Persian attention from Israel. America and its allies perpetuated the war to enrich their arms merchants and drain the two sides of manpower. America engineered Khomeini's death, just as it had once controlled the shah's every breath.

"You seem like nice man," he told me, "but you probably CIA." Standing before the massive edifice of the U.S. embassy, it wasn't hard to see how such notions had taken root.

The Iranians had revenged themselves, of course, first by holding U.S. hostages in the embassy and then, with characteristic perversity, by turning the mission into a training center for Revolutionary Guards, the cadres of the Islamic Republic. They had also transformed the embassy wall into the world's biggest billboard for anti-imperialist graffiti.

"We Will Make America Face a Severe Defeat!"

"This Century Will be the Period of Victory of the Oppressed over the Oppressors!"

"The Superpowers' Law Is Worse Than the Law of the Jungle!"

We followed the man-high letters for fifty yards before coming to one of the compound's gates. Several soldiers stood guard beside a sign that said "The Center for the Publication of the U.S. Espionage Den's Documents." The documents had been pieced together from shredded cables left behind by the Americans and published in a set of slim volumes, the book jackets of which were displayed on the embassy's wall. A sample title: *Leaders of the Arabian Peninsula: Puppets of the Great Satan.*

Ibrahim chuckled, and so did I. There was an exuberant, "in-your-face" quality to Iranian propaganda that resembled the lyrics of incendiary black rap groups. Here, the street revolution had come and the formerly oppressed were determined to have some fun.

Fun wasn't a word that otherwise came much to mind in Tehran. In addition to banning booze, the Islamic Republic had outlawed popular music. A nine-year ban on the sale of most musical instruments had recently been lifted—so long as the tunes they produced "don't make you tingle," said an official from the Ministry of Islamic Guidance. Dancing also was prohibited; at weddings among Iran's small Christian community, even the bridal waltz was off-limits. The two-station television system, called Voice and Vision of the Islamic Republic, offered such a monotonous diet of Koran readings and fundamentalists that irreverent Iranians called it Mullah Vision, Khomeini 1 and Khomeini 2, or Fiberglass (glass for the box, fiber for the beard of almost everyone on it). Even the Iranian national passion, chess, had been banned. Chess, like cards and other games, offered an occasion for gambling, and its pieces flouted the Islamic prohibition on image-making.

Policing of the sexes was severe. A man and a woman alone together—in a restaurant, in a car, or just walking on the street—could be accosted by roving revolutionary enforcers, called Komitehs, and asked to show proof of marriage. The Komitehs also harassed and occasionally imprisoned women who wore bad *hejab*—clothes too tight, too colorful, or revealing of anything other than their face and hands. Nor were visiting Westerners exempt from these restrictions. One female journalist had her nail polish rubbed off at the airport, and Geraldine was confronted at the entrance to a bank because the three inches of stocking showing beneath her chador were judged too sheer.

"Believe it or not," an Iranian dissident later told us, "Khomeini was a feminist compared to the most conservative mullahs." Other clerics, for instance, believed that veiling wasn't sufficient; women should also stick coins or fingers in their mouths when speaking, lest their voices distract men from spiritual thoughts. "If these mullahs had their way," the dissident added, "they'd drag Iran back to the seventh century instead of the eleventh."

But nothing in Iran was quite as medieval as it first appeared. One afternoon a twenty-four-year-old student named Payon took me to a coffee shop in north Tehran, a neighborhood of leafy boulevards where signs such as "Piaget" and "Patisserie" still clung to Parisian-style shopfronts. Millions of Tehran's *taghoutis*, the "idle rich," had fled since the revolution. But the regime, desperate to retain the money and skills of those who remained, turned a blind eye to remnants of shah-era high life.

At first, the coffee shop appeared subject to the same strictures as every other public place I'd visited in Iran. A sign on the glass door showed the outline of a woman's head with an X through her hair and proper *hejab* superimposed. "Sister," the sign said, "please be quiet about yourself." Cafés whose patrons wore bad *hejab* risked closure by the Komitehs.

Inside, couples sat at tables well spaced from one another, speaking in virtual whispers. The women wore calf-length coats with long sleeves and head scarves tied beneath their chins. The costume was less severe than the tentlike chadors common among the poor, but it was, if anything, even more uncomfortable in the hammering heat of midsummer.

Payon scanned the café and glanced at me meaningfully. Iranians were always glancing at me meaningfully. "Do you see?" he whispered.

"See what?" The scene seemed as anonymous and depressing as that in every other café I'd visited.

He nodded his head in the direction of a woman at the next table, who wore a floral head scarf. "She is not so Islamic," he said. "If she was, she would be wearing brown or black."

He tipped his head at the woman sitting beside her. "What do you see?"

I saw a belt wrapped at the waist, giving her otherwise shapeless coat a slight hourglass effect.

"The belt," I said.

"Very good. Keep going."

The coat ended at mid-shin, and from beneath it poked tight blue jeans and Reebok running shoes. Her companion wore black lace stockings and high heels.

I nodded meaningfully. "Now look at the man," Payon said. "See how one of the women leans close and the other does not? The second woman, she is only for cover, so the others can flirt."

A waiter arrived with coffee, and Payon paused before decoding the rest of the café. One woman—very risqué—allowed her bangs to slip out from beneath her head scarf. The men were all clean-shaven. If they were real believers in Khomeini—real "Hezbollahis"—they'd sport at least three days' stubble, a symbol of Islamic humility. At another table, a man and woman glanced furtively into each other's eyes, an intimacy not normally permitted in public. Through Payon's expert lens, the innocent coffee shop was gradually revealing itself as a den of illicit seduction.

"You see, we have learned a few tricks in ten years," he said. There were other deceptions, which he ticked off on his fingers:

Sitting away from the window to avoid detection by passing patrols.

Borrowing a baby when going on a date to ward off demands for marriage certificates.

Buying tickets separately at the movie theater, then slipping beside each other when the lights went down.

Masquerading as a taxi driver so you could cruise the streets in search of single women.

Periodic crackdowns made it risky to attempt even such oblique contact between the sexes. But Payon felt confident, after scanning the scene in the coffee shop, that the atmosphere was loosening up.

"Perhaps soon," he said, "I will take a chance and come here with my girlfriend."

■   ■   ■

The coded scene in the coffee shop became the leitmotif of our week in Tehran. Arab countries had made me accustomed to indirection. But Persian subtlety was of another order of magnitude. Shiite theology holds that the world will be redeemed by the return of the twelfth imam, a religious leader who vanished in the ninth century, without a successor. Shiites believe the imam never really died; he is in "occultation"—hidden but present. Understanding Iran was like finding the twelfth imam; the truth was there, somewhere, if only you could peel away the onionskins of obfuscation.

Persian invitations typified this obscurity. As in Arab countries, Iranian hospitality was immediate and abundant. Except that offers rarely led to anything. A man who invited me to dinner didn't show up, as planned, to drive me to his home. A student we invited for coffee didn't appear.

Fear was a factor, but not the only one. "In Iran, an invitation must be repeated three times," explained a dissident whom I will call Sharam, one of the few people I met who honored our rendezvous. "It's proper to say no the first two times and then if it's offered again to say yes."

Sharam had gone to college in the United States and been mystified by blunt American ways. "I was surprised to find in the United States that yes means yes and no means no," he said. "This seemed very rude to me." The problem was particularly acute with women. If she immediately said yes to an invitation or advance, what did this mean? "And if she said no, well, I'd assume it was really a deep yes. She actually wanted me."

Sharam offered to take us to a party in north Tehran. As usual, the invitation was cryptic. "I think," he said, "you will find it interesting to see what goes on behind closed doors." Sharam picked us up at the hotel just after nightfall. His wife sat beside him in the front seat, hooded and silent. We drove to north Tehran and parked in front of a brown stucco duplex. Sharam knocked lightly on the door and it opened just enough for us to slip inside.

"Sharam! Maryam!" the hostess cried, kissing them each

on the lips. She was wearing a silver miniskirt, which matched the streaks in her carefully permed hair. A coatrack in the foyer was draped in black; in north Tehran, women left their chadors at the door. Maryam peeled hers off instantly, as a child might discard an itchy sweater. "Ah, much better," she sighed, shaking out long curls. Like the hostess, she wore a short skirt and a sleeveless, low-cut blouse. Turning to take Geraldine's chador, she smiled broadly and gave us each a kiss on the cheek. "In the car I could not greet you properly," she said.

There were twenty guests arrayed around the living room, nibbling pistachios and tapping their feet to a Madonna cassette. The music played at low volume. Thick dark curtains were drawn tightly across the windows.

"Let me offer you some of Iran's finest," the host said, handing me a glass of clear alcohol. The vodka was raisin-based and made by Christian Armenians, who were permit-ted to drink at home and used the privilege to produce bath-tub booze for other Iranians. In the four days since we'd boarded Iran Air in Frankfurt, I hadn't tasted alcohol or seen the hair, neck, arms or legs of a woman other than Geral-dine. Now, taking it all in at once, I felt an exaggerated intoxication, as though I'd walked into a drunken orgy instead of a weeknight cocktail party in the suburbs.

The same overblown naughtiness infected the guests. The women, most of whom were in their mid-thirties, wore tight, frilly skirts, none of which reached as far as the knee. Some added black lace stockings and spike heels—the sort of vampish, costumey getup a sophomore might have worn to a campus disco at a Midwestern campus, circa 1975. Far-rah Fawcett hairdos and blood-red lipstick completed the effect.

The male guests looked much as they would have on the street, except they were all clean-shaven and one wore a loud plaid tie (most Iranians disdained ties as an emblem of the decadent West). Male modesty in Iran required only long sleeves and loose trousers.

"For us, it is not so liberating to dress up," explained

an engineer named Farshad. "So we drink too much instead." He drained his vodka and winced. "In the West I would pour such stuff in the sink."

Farshad had studied engineering at a Baptist college in North Carolina and returned just before the revolution. "I didn't think it was possible for people to be so ignorant and backward," he said of his American classmates. "Until I came home." He started a consulting company, but after Khomeini seized power, four of his six partners fled overseas. Farshad stayed, he said, because the exodus of trained Iranians and foreign technicians put a premium on the skills of those who remained. "In the West, I would be nothing special," he said. "But here I am a big fish." He chuckled. "A big fish in an ocean of crazy people."

Most of the guests had known each other since high school, and they met at each other's homes about once a week. It was relatively easy for wealthy Iranians to travel abroad, and holiday souvenirs littered the coffee table; a German tennis magazine, Italian fashion catalogues and a photo album showing the party's host and hostess in Japan. The guests took turns devouring the pages with almost pornographic pleasure.

"It is a little sad, no?" Farshad said, following my gaze. "It becomes a little boring like this, week after week. But what else is there to do? Go to the mosque?"

Our conversation was interrupted by a little girl running into the room and leaping into Farshad's lap. She wanted her father to change the videotape she was watching. I followed the two of them to the back of the house, where four children sat on a bed, eyes riveted to a cartoon on the television screen. It was Popeye, dubbed into Farsi. Most Western programs were prohibited in Iran, usually because they showed women with their heads uncovered, or couples kissing.

"Things are getting better," Farshad said, changing Popeye to Pink Panther. An actress had recently appeared in a Tehran theater wearing a wig instead of a veil. And he'd seen a Bogart movie aired on late-night television. "This, for us, is glasnost."

Farshad's daughter was nine and had already assumed a dual personality. At home, her parents drank vodka and watched bootleg videos smuggled from the West. At school, she wore *hejab*, sang Khomeini songs and said nothing of her parents' behavior. But Farshad worried about her approaching adolescence. Would she rebel against us or against them? Which would make life more difficult for her? And for the first time he was thinking of taking his family out of Iran for good. "You cannot spend your whole life behind closed curtains, drinking bad vodka and listening to low-volume Madonna."

We returned to find the others digging into a vegetable stew spiced with mint and thyme. Home-cooked food in Iran was the best I'd yet sampled in the Middle East. Over dinner, the guests quizzed Geraldine and me about the funeral. They seemed surprised by our account of the size and sincerity of the crowd, and also depressed. "I thought they were using wide-angle lenses," Farshad said of the Iranian television broadcasts. "The crowd seemed much too big."

The conversation confirmed the impression I'd begun to form while wandering Tehran's streets—that there were two completely separate cities, one poor and devout, the other bourgeois and disenchanted. North Tehranis were frozen in time, like White Russians or French monarchists, left on the sidelines by revolution.

But as usual in Iran, nothing was as clear-cut as that. Most of the guests said they'd originally supported the revolution, and although they came to hate Khomeini, they found it hard to rejoice at news of his death.

"I cried and had to take a Valium," Maryam confessed. Farshad had reacted similarly. "I poured myself a glass of vodka and said a private toast. But mostly I just felt hollow."

Khomeini, for all his fanaticism, hadn't abused power to enrich himself or advance his family. But the guests' grudging respect for the imam had another source. They felt the same pride as other Iranians when Khomeini thumbed his nose at the rest of the world. The imam had even issued one last rage from the grave, bequeathing on the United States and moderate Arab states a final benediction in his will: "May God's curse be upon them."

"The superpowers thought they owned us, and he stood up to them," Maryam said.

Sharam nodded. "Imagine someone telling you for decades that you should wear Western clothes, have Western values, think Western thoughts," he said. "Then someone stands up and says, 'Fuck you! We have a culture and history of our own.'" He paused, gazing into his vegetable stew. "Khomeini gave Iran some self-respect. It was a very exhilarating ten years."

The room went silent for a moment. Then the hostess came in from the kitchen, bearing cups of Turkish coffee. "Don't forget to read your fortune in the grinds," she said gleefully. "It's un-Islamic!"

The others laughed, draining their vodka. I caught Geraldine's eye. Is this place confusing, or what?

Iranians, like Arabs, eat late and don't linger long once the dinner is done. It was midnight when the guests got up and said their goodbyes. The women stopped at the door to collect their chadors; miniskirts and streaked blond curls disappeared beneath anonymous hoods.

"We will see you next week, yes?" the hostess asked Maryam. She nodded, pulling the veil tightly beneath her chin and heading into the night.

The rules of everyday commerce were as veiled as those regulating social life. A few days after our arrival, when shops began to reopen, I lost myself in the dingy maze of covered streets that run through Tehran's Bazaar-e-Bozorg, the Grand Bazaar. At first glance the market resembled an Arab souk, with each cramped alley devoted to a different product: metalware, plastic goods, clothes, carpets, nuts and spices, worry beads, watches, chadors. Motorcyclists raced between the stalls, adding exhaust fumes to air already ripe with saffron and incense. In the carpet bazaar, old men crouched by ancient looms, working thread by thread on silks from Isfahan and Qum so finely wrought that there were five hundred knots to each square inch of rug.

But the surface bustle concealed a curious absence of actual buying and selling. There were almost as many merchants as shoppers, and most storeowners showed little interest in luring passersby into their shops. Instead, they sat clustered together, smoking and sipping tea, and chatting in lowered voices.

I navigated out of the bazaar and stopped at a building labeled "Chamber of Commerce." It seemed a curious, shah-era dinosaur. Since I was on assignment for *The Wall Street Journal*, I decided to pay a visit.

"Always we are happy to talk with Wall Street," declared an amiable official, showing me into his office. He wore aviator glasses and a frayed seersucker suit, and proudly showed me his graduate degree in systems analysis from MIT. Waving out at Tehran's smoggy skyline, he added, "this city is bursting with opportunities."

I took out my notebook, and the official chatted nonstop for an hour. About his years in Cambridge. About foreign business prospects in Tehran. About an upcoming trade fair. About the gluttony of the West. About the prevalence of bestiality in Europe. And about America's sick attachment to material things. "If you want spiritual peace, it is enough to have one television set," he said. "Iran wants your technology but not your promiscuity."

As the conversation degenerated, I decided that the prospects for foreign business in Iran were not so good.

But the official did offer one insight. I told him about my visit to the market and asked how it was that the *bazaaris* survived.

"Survive?" he said. "They thrive. The bazaar is the healthiest sector of the Iranian economy."

Most of the shops were fronts for the *bazaaris'* actual business: loan-sharking, black-marketeering and currency speculation. All those men who appeared to be idly sipping tea were actually cutting deals worth millions of riyals. As usual, the truth about Iran was in occultation, hidden but present.

"You must remember," the Chamber of Commerce man said, seeing me to the door, "that 'bazaar' is a Persian word."

"Bizarre" seemed a more appropriate word for Iran. On our last day in Tehran, I was tapping out a story when the telephone rang at the Laleh Hotel.

"Hello," I said. There was nothing at the other end. "Anyone there?"

A woman's voice came on the line and said timidly, "Hello. What your name?"

"Tony. Who are you?"

"Merced."

Had I met a woman named Merced?

"Toady," she continued, "what are you doing?"

"Tony. T-O-N-Y. I'm sitting on the bed."

"Sitting on the bed," she repeated. "Toady, what color your eyes?"

"Do I know you, Merced?" Silence again. "Who are you?"

"I am student of economics. I just begin university."

"Why are you calling?"

"Just to talk. With a foreigner." She paused. "With a man."

"Merced, how did you get my number?"

She giggled. "This is secret."

"Where do you live?"

"This is more secret." She giggled again. "Toady, you are married?"

"Yes."

"What her name is?"

"Geraldine."

"This is very beautiful name. She is beautiful?"

"Yes."

She paused. "Toady, what color your eyes is?"

"Blue. Bluish-green."

"What color your hairs is?"

"Blond. What color is yours?"

"This is secret." The giggle again. "Toady, you come to Iran more?"

"I hope so."

"I must go now."

The phone line went dead. I lay back on the bed. The conversation gave me an odd sense of *déjà vu*. It took me a moment to locate the memory. It was the black-veiled woman in the Empty Quarter: "I love you," she had said. "I love you always." Two years later, I was lying on a lumpy bed in the Laleh Hotel, still fielding conversations I could not begin to comprehend.

17

EXODUS FROM EGYPT
Metal Fatigue

I believe in doubt. I believe in keeping clear of believers.
—DONALD HAYS,
The Hangman's Children

In the cool of the Cairo day, when the sun lay low across the desert, I liked to pull on a pair of tired sneakers, strap a Walkman to my waist and run around a track circling the soccer field beside my apartment. The track was a pleasing ocher, the field a soothing splash of green amid miles of ferroconcrete. Teenage Egyptians pole-vaulted over a five-foot-high wire and onto a mattress that exhaled dust each time they landed. Except for a mosque abutting one corner of the oval, and women in Islamic veils resting their elbows on the fence, I could have been jogging around a high school field in Lubbock, Texas, or Butte, Montana.

The only Western cassette on offer at the local music shop was a bootleg disco tape with pulsing beats and songs such as "Sexual Healing" and "Ring My Bell." Heading out at sunset, I usually hit the track just as the evening call to prayer wafted out from the mosque's minaret.

"God is great!" came the muezzin's call.

"Get up! Get up!" Marvin Gaye growled through my headphones.

"There is no God but God!"

"That's the way, uh huh uh huh, I like it, uh huh uh huh."

By the time I'd made my third or fourth turn around the track, men in turbans had fallen to their knees, bowing toward Mecca.

"Mohammed is the messenger of God!" the muezzin cried as Patti Labelle cooed in my ear. *"Voulez-vous coucher avec moi, ce soir?"*

When buildings fall down in Cairo, as they frequently do, Egyptian engineers often blame the collapse on "metal fatigue," as though the structural beams simply give out from accumulated exhaustion and stress. I returned from Iran feeling the journalistic equivalent. I had turned thirty at an Arab summit in Algiers, waiting for a midnight press conference with Colonel Quaddafi. I had turned thirty-one at Khomeini's grave, amid a sea of head-beating Shiites. I wasn't sure what to do for an encore. I wasn't sure I wanted to find out.

Midnight flights to Baghdad and boat rides to Beirut were losing their thrill. Cairo had once seemed exotic and abrasive. Now it just seemed abrasive. I was weary of peeling, disinfecting and voodooing the bacteria from bruised fruit and limp carrots; weary of bribing the mailman so he wouldn't toss our mail in the gutter; weary of the heat, the dust and most of all the noise. In between flights, I'd taken to shutting the city out, wrapping myself in a cocoon of *Herald Tribune*s and long-distance phone calls. And by the end of my second year it had become a ritual, that sunset run, as the faithful prayed and "Boogie Oogie Oogie" thundered through my headset.

Soon after our trip to Iran, I returned from a run one hot night to find Geraldine at the door with a bubbly grin on her face and a flat Egyptian beer in her hand. While I'd been boogy-oogying around the track, she'd been phoning friends and gathering intelligence. She had heard word of a job opening in London that I might apply for, and a chance for her to transfer there as well.

I slumped in front of our Middle Kingdom air conditioner to consider the news. Free-lancing had worked out much better than I'd originally dreamed possible, carrying me to fifteen countries—usually at someone else's expense—and into the pages of a half-dozen newspapers. But there had been plenty of sand traps and double bogeys along the way: long evenings spent hanging on a crackly phone line from Khartoum or Algiers or Tripoli while a secretary in New York or Washington or Atlanta put me on hold so editors could search through their desks for some forgotten story I'd filed weeks before.

I turned the air conditioner to "high cool" and bathed my head in the lukewarm breeze, trying to clear my brain.

"Don't start thinking about a shower," Geraldine said. "The water's down."

"*Malesh*," I said. We'd taken to tossing Arabic phrases into our conversation; *malesh*—"never mind"—was the one that came most often to our lips.

"Plenty of showers in London," Geraldine said. "Indoor and outdoor."

"Trees. Grass. Edible vegetables."

"Harrods' food hall."

"Mmmm."

During a recent six-hour layover in London, we'd managed to spend three hundred dollars at Harrods, all of it on food to carry back to Cairo. I'd felt like applying for citizenship at the checkout counter.

"Should we go for it?" she asked.

I shrugged. "Why not?"

The air conditioner wheezed and blew hot. We shared the last inch of beer. I went to type up my résumé. Another Major Life Decision, made on the soundest of grounds.

It wasn't until we began packing that I felt the first flicker of nostalgia. Where else in the world would I collect the odd trinkets I'd gathered in Arabia? There was the curved dagger I'd secured after endless haggling with the Jewish merchant in Yemen; it had since rusted stuck in its scabbard. There was the PLO keyring I'd been given by an aide to Yassir Arafat, during a four-hour wait for a press conference in Tunis that never happened. I had a Saddam Hussein watch from Iraq and a Khomeini watch from Iran, though neither one told

time. And I had a going-away present from Mr. Mahn at the
Information Ministry in Baghdad: a small glass globe containing an inch of dirt and a tiny Iraqi flag, commemorating Iraq's
"liberation" of a strategic peninsula called Faw. The globe's
wooden base bore an inscription that read: "The Earth of Faw
Mixed with Blood of Iraqi Martyrs." It was destined for the
mantelpiece in London.

I hit on the television to keep me company while I packed.
The English-language news began as it always did, with a
crude Mercator projection of the Middle East and an off-speed
medley of Arab tunes. An anchorman began reading the AP
wire in halting English. There was shelling again in Beirut.
Something about hostages in the Bekaa Valley. A new American plan for Middle East peace. And the Israelis had shot dead
two more Palestinians in Gaza. I wondered for a moment if
Egyptian TV, through oversight or impoverishment, had simply rebroadcast a tape of the news from two years before. Or
five. Progress in the Middle East was measured in grains of
sand.

Just before midnight, my Nubian friend, Yousri, showed
up to wish me goodbye before heading to work at the hotel.
He repaid most of the money I'd lent him eighteen months
before to wheedle a visa out of one of a dozen Western
embassies. It hadn't done him any good.

Yousri perched on the edge of a suitcase, guarding the
crease in his trousers, and smoked Cleopatra cigarettes as I
finished packing. "You know the old saying," he said. "He
who drinks of the Nile always comes back. *Insha'allah*." God
willing. It was the same line Egyptians gave every departing
Westerner.

"I only drink bottled water," I said.

Yousri smiled. "Don't kid yourself, man. Most of those
bottles are filled from the Nile, too."

He went silent for a moment, then asked, "What's
England like?"

"Cold and wet. Nothing like Egypt."

"Must be a good place, then."

I looked up. Yousri seemed on the verge of tears. In

twenty-four hours I would be back in the First World, reading about the Middle East on the Underground. Yousri would be back working the graveyard shift at the hotel. Probably forever.

"I cannot wait much longer," he said, having waited his whole life already. "I will shortly go out of my mind."

I reflected, not for the first time, on the accidents of birth and place that had landed Yousri here and me on a plane out the following day. I responded, reflexively, with a material offering.

"Here, your pick from the summer collection," I said, gesturing at my frayed wardrobe of shirts and jackets. It wasn't much. But I couldn't see that Yousri would have much use for a Yemeni dagger or a watch with Saddam Hussein's face on the dial.

"Tony. I can't take those."

"Why not? You think I'm going to wear short sleeves in London?"

Reluctantly, he picked through the pile, plucking out the three items with faded designer labels. He left the rest. "Too much synthetic," he said, casting a discerning eye across the discards. "I prefer one hundred percent cotton."

Yousri, like Egypt, had nothing to lose but his pride.

Months later, on a raw November day, I received a letter from Cairo. It was carefully typed in capital letters on a small page of hotel stationery.

HI TONY MAN!
HOW ARE YOU IN COLD RAINY LONDON!
ABOUT ME I'M STILL LOOKING FOR AWAY TO
    BREAK. I HAVEN'T LOST HOPE YET!
MAN IT'S SO BORING HERE NO THING HAPPENED
    AND EVERY DAY IS THE SAME!
I STOPPED READING NEWSPAPERS I DON'T KNOW
    WHERE THE TRUTH IS!
BUT LIFE GOES ON AND TIME IS THE INVISABLE
    ENMY FOR ME!

I'M TRYING NOW TO IMPROVE MY FRENCH SINCE
    I SEE SO MANY FRENCH LADIES!
IF YOU WANT ME TO COME TO LONDON LET ME
    KNOW AND MAYBE I CAN GET VISA!
WELL TAKE CARE MAN AND WRITE SOON!
YOUSRI

I put the paper in my pocket and headed out into the drizzle, composing a letter in my head. I would tell Yousri about the cold, about the pasty English women, about the bad food and warm beer. And I'd tell him to come to London, just the same.

Insha'allah, we'd find a way.

No One Makes Love
to Iraq

Yousri was right; I *would* be back, though it was the Tigris, not the Nile, to which I returned. One morning a year after leaving Egypt, I switched on the BBC to learn that Saddam Hussein's tanks had overrun Kuwait. Twenty-four hours later, I'd been deployed by my editors to the Middle East for what was to become a months-long journalistic seige.

After a year of writing features in Europe—most recently about elf-worship in Iceland—I was badly out of shape. The submachine guns poking through taxi windows made me uneasy. My Arabic was so rusty that I was reduced to making small talk with toddlers ("My name is Tony, what's yours?"). And I'd failed to pack key Middle Eastern accessories, such as stacks of hard currency and an album's worth of passport-sized photos.

So it was that I found myself one sweaty afternoon, crouched outside the Iraqi embassy in Jordan, mutilating my Scotland Yard pass and London library card to get at plastic-coated mug shots. The Iraqis had finally granted me a visa;

all they wanted in exchange was two more photos to add to the dozen I'd already given them. At a nearby pharmacy, I scored an anti-dysentery drug with the reassuring French name "*Arret.*" And through a friend of a friend I made contact with a wan money changer named Ali H. Ali, who agreed to cash a personal check—at a fee of ten percent. Cashed up, passport-stamped, and stomach in a tenuous state of *arret*, I was as ready as I ever would be for another expedition to Iraq.

It was a dicey time to be flying into Baghdad. All week, hawks in America had insisted the moment was now ripe to "make the rubble bounce" across the blistered Mesopotamian plain. The Iraqis, meanwhile, were scooping up Westerners to sequester as their "special guests" at strategic locations, as a human shield against U.S. bombs. Breadlines wrapped around the block in Baghdad, and Saddam Hussein had declared that foreigners would be last in line for whatever crumbs remained.

I had another reason to feel edgy. Earlier that week I'd written about Iraq's ruthless leadership in the gray flannel pages of *The Wall Street Journal.* On the morning of my departure for Baghdad, without warning, a London tabloid splashed a reprint of the story across its two-page centerfold beneath a seven-column headline that read "SADDAM: THE ULTIMATE BARBARIAN." Beside the subhead—"MURDER . . . EXECUTION . . . TORTURE"—and photos of two of Saddam's victims—captioned "DOSSIER OF DEATH"—was my byline, in bold, twelve-point type.

"Special guest suite waiting for you, mate," said the British cameraman seated beside me at the airport terminal in Amman. "Strapped to a Scud-B missile."

He chuckled grimly as the Iraq Air 727 taxied toward the terminal. Several hundred passengers poured off, wearing the dazed smiles of prison parolees. Baghdad, I realized then, was a city I'd never dreamed of revisiting, except in nightmares.

■　　　■　　　■

On arrival at Saddam International Airport, apprehension gave way to astonishment. The customs man glanced at my laptop computer, short-wave radio, and pocketful of batteries—all seizable contraband during the Iran-Iraq war—and lazily waved me through. Whereas before, Big Brother had stared down from all four walls of the terminal, there now hung abstract murals. On the drive into the city, intersections that I remembered displaying four huge paintings of Saddam were down to only one.

"It is normal," a Ministry of Information official assured me. "They need to be cleaned."

Many of the portraits had in fact vanished soon after the revolution in Romania, an event which seems to have spooked Saddam Hussein. The parallels between his own police state and that of Nicolae Ceausescu's were discomfiting. Saddam had also lifted a long-standing prohibition on overseas travel by Iraqis. Even the weather report was back on the airwaves after a six-year ban, announcing with withering regularity that the midday temperature in Baghdad was 110 degrees.

But Iraqi *perestroika* had its limits. When I optimistically asked for a map at the desk of the Baghdad Sheraton, the receptionist looked at me as though I'd dialed room service and ordered a gun. "I am so sorry," she said, pointing me to an Information Ministry desk in the lobby. "I am sure they can tell you where to go."

Wandering out of the hotel, it also became obvious that Saddam's personality cult hadn't really waned, despite my first impression. It was true that there were fewer portraits of the president. But hewing to the architectural axiom "less is more," new likenesses of Saddam were grotesquely bloated, as though some pituitary disorder had infected the paint and clay.

One fresh sculpture rivaled the Colossus of Rhodes, four stories high, with Saddam's outstretched arm casting a shadow the length of a football field. Even Iraqis seemed stunned by its size. "Normally you must be dead before they put up something so big," a cabbie confided, stalled in traffic beneath the statue's promethean gaze. A much smaller statue that had once graced an adjoining lot, title "ARAB HORSE-MAN," had been yanked down so as not to obstruct the view of Saddam's shins.

On a nearby parade ground, a new monument called Hands of Victory soared one hundred fifty feet into the air. The hands—pharaonic in scale and modeled on those of Saddam's—clutched enormous crossed sabers, their hilts draped with nets of Iranian helmets. In the same complex an Eiffel Tower-like structure was going up, topped with a giant clock. Its base was to be decorated with scenes from the president's life. This was Baghdad's answer to Big Ben, though it wasn't destined to become a tourist attraction. The clock lay inside one of Baghdad's many "restricted areas," where cars were forbidden to stop and pedestrians to enter.

Back at the hotel, the Information Ministry had arranged its usual "program" for visiting journalists. We could watch Iraqi volunteers shouting "Death to America" at a training camp outside Baghdad. There was a spontaneous demonstration by Iraqi three-year-olds, waving empty milk bottles at the U.S. embassy—the time of which was posted two days in advance. And there was the obligatory trip to the ministry headquarters, the only audience we'd get with Iraqi officials.

Arriving at the ministry, it seemed once again that encouraging changes were in the air. My old friend Mr. Mahn—he of the red pen and vigorous red flyswatter—had moved upstairs to an office with only one modest portrait of Saddam. "Mr. Tony, by God!" he exclaimed, suppressing the urge, I think, to ask, "Why the hell did they give *you* a visa?" There was no mention of the "Ultimate Barbarian" featured that week on London news stands, though the ministry received faxes of almost everything we wrote. A veteran correspondent later hypothesized that some officials in Iraq—as in other iron-fisted states—secretly welcomed hostile press reports as a way of undermining a regime they themselves were unable to condemn. Someday, I hoped, it would be possible to sit down with Mr. Mahn and find out if this was so.

Also startling was the metamorphosis of Latif Jasim, the Minister for Information and Culture. When I'd interviewed him two years before, Jasim had been a scowling, pistol-toting ogre who offered only the stiffest of pronouncements in Arabic. Now he grinned ear to ear and made small talk in exuberantly bad English. The only echo of my earlier visit was the minister's careful choice of couches; he still sat with his back to the wall, facing the open door.

He also remained rather reticent about his background. When a reporter asked about the minister's birthplace, Jasim replied, "Kuwait." He waited a moment, then laughed awkwardly. "This is a joke," he added, as though it were the first he'd ever attempted. Kuwait, of course, no longer existed. A man in the Information Ministry showed the sheikdom as the nineteenth province of Iraq, with one section of the annexed territory already renamed Saddamiyat. The ministry also had rushed into print a book called *End of Fragmentation*, which laid out the historical roots of Kuwait's "return to the Motherland" just four weeks before.

Jasim rambled on for an hour, producing the usual Iraqi absurdities. He said he had "documents" proving that George Bush was a partner with Gulf sheiks in several oil companies; hence the president's decision to send troops. A week before, Jasim had said that any U.S. airmen shot down over Iraqi airspace would be eaten; this time he said only that "your soldiers will go down in the sand. You will not find them."

Still, I was encouraged by Jasim's friendly manner, and on the way out I asked one of his minions, a slick, fluent English-speaker named Hadithi, if I needed a permit to visit Babylon, a trip that would let me eyeball the countryside. Hadithi's calm face curled into a chilling smile. "To follow the line of Bazoft?" he asked. "You are free." Farzad Bazoft, a London-based journalist, had been hanged by the Iraqis a few months before, accused of spying during a drive south from the capital.

In the elevator, a reporter from *The New York Times* fired a few follow-up questions about food shortages. Again, Hadithi's smooth veneer vanished. "Do you have another card other than the press card?" he snapped, staring the *Times* reporter in the eye. "Your questions are put the same way as FBI people."

It was the paranoid and thuggish Iraq I remembered so well from previous visits. And as the elevator doors swished open, I decided I could live without seeing the Hanging Gardens of Babylon again.

Unfortunately, the safe confines of Baghdad didn't offer much fodder for stories. Street reporting was, as always, a frustrating and rather futile exercise. I quickly came upon a long line of old men and women in black *abayas*, queued in front of a bakery. When I inquired how long they'd been waiting for bread, a man looked at me blankly and said, "We are lining up to volunteer to fight America."

The few Iraqis I could engage in conversation seemed oddly detached, as though the crisis in Kuwait were some distant sandstorm that would quickly blow away. At an open-air teahouse, an engineer named Abdullah pulled up his trouser leg to reveal an ugly shrapnel wound he'd received during Iraq's long war with Iran. "My friend," he said, returning to his dominoes game, "we know about war. We are ready. Is America?" In the souk, a young merchant named Tariq showed me his last bottle of imported shampoo and said, "My father was bedouin, he washed his hair with camel's urine. So what if we do the same?"

Wandering down to the U.S. embassy, I found myself in the midst of one of the daily, stage-managed rallies against "American-Zionist colonial oppression." When I took out my notebook, a psychiatrist named Ali Harchan quickly volunteered a quote. "Really, ninety-nine percent of Iraqis despise America," he said. "My patients are filled with hate."

But as the demonstrators dispersed after a token ten minutes of chanting "Down! Down! Bush!" Dr. Harchan fell to chatting about his affection for *The Bob Newhart Show* (prime time in Baghdad) and about the beautiful blonde women he'd met while studying medicine in the West. "Please write that Ali says hi to all his friends in Detroit," he said with a gay wave, melting away into the shimmery midday heat.

There was one man, I knew, who could show me the cracks in this facade of defiant normality. Saleh, the lone Iraqi dissident I'd met two years before, was still there in his dusty downtown office, though he looked grayer than I remembered and kept popping pills for what he called his heart sickness. A few months before, the army had furloughed his son after eight years at the Iranian front—only to call him back again to serve in the trenches in Kuwait.

"I think," Saleh confided in a sarcastic whisper, "his Excellency and Field Marshal, the Water of the Two Rivers, has finally gone too far."

As before, Saleh waited for the office to empty for lunch before talking freely. "If America kills Saddam," he said, turning up the air conditioner, "many people here will think the Prophet Mohammed is alive and well in Washington."

Immediately after the invasion of Kuwait, terrified Iraqis had hoarded food and loaded their families into cars to pay unscheduled visits to relatives in the countryside. Saddam Hussein quickly decreed the death penalty for hoarding and black marketeering, and Baghdadis had filtered back to the city. But Saleh said grumbling about food shortages and army service was getting loud.

I asked Saleh who among Saddam's brutal ruling clique he'd prefer to see in power.

"Who cares?" he exclaimed. "Let us have the devil. Even he would be better than this madman."

Earlier in the year, when the travel ban had been lifted, Saleh had visited Europe for the first time in ten years. What struck him most was the hotel newsstand, stuffed each morning with a dozen different newspapers. "Half of them were in languages I could barely read, but I bought them all just the same," he said.

Sighing wistfully, he unfurled an Iraqi paper to show

me the thin gruel to which he'd returned. Gone was the staple of two years before—Orwellian war communiques about victories on some distant front of a never ending war. But in an even eerier echo of *1984*, history had been hastily rewritten. Iran, the millenial foe, had become a "fraternal" ally and the Gulf sheikdoms that had bankrolled Iraq were now the "backward agents" of America. A front-page story reported that the Kuwaiti royal family was riddled with syphilis. On the inside pages, readers learned that rabbis were ministering to U.S. troops inside the holy Muslim shrines of Mecca and Medina.

Saleh chuckled and tossed the paper in the trash. Opening his desk, he drew out smuggled copies of *Newsweek* and *Time*, wrapped in brown bags as though they were pornography. "Without this," he said, "I would be a sheep like everyone else."

Two co-workers returned from lunch. Saleh's face assumed its impassive, public mask. "Isn't the weather dreadful?" he asked me in a booming voice before seeing me to the door.

Back on the street, I realized I'd forgotten to ask Saleh if he still kept his Saddam carpet rolled up in the closet as security against visitors in the night.

There was one other person I wanted to see. Down by the river, I found Mohammed the fishmonger where I'd left him two years before, in a bloodstained smock, clubbing fish and propping them against an open wood fire. Thrashing around in their tiled tub of water, the unsuspecting fish looked fat and happy. Mohammed didn't. "Business no good," he said, waving his monkey wrench at the sole customer in the restaurant. "No one have money anymore."

He seemed pleased to see me, though his long list of Iraq's enemies now included America. "And Egypt and Saudi and England and France and Russia," he said, ticking them off on his fingers. I pointed out that Iran, at least, was off Iraq's hit list.

"Persians be enemies again someday," he said, shaking his head. "No one makes love to Iraq."

I offered Mohammed a consoling beer at the neon-lit club where he'd taken me one midsummer's night two years before. I was curious to see if the quality of the bar girls had improved, as Mohammed had hoped.

For the first time Mohammed's mood brightened. "I only go out with Allah now," he said. He pointed to a picture of Mecca that now hung above his fish tank, beside a dusty picture of Saddam. Mohammed had found religion.

"Nine years I throw my dinars away at ugly women and bad beer," he said. "Why I do this?" Clutching his monkey wrench, he smiled and nodded suggestively at the fish tank. "Stay here, Mr. Tony, I make you nice dinner."

I declined the offer and ducked across the street to visit the nightclub without him. The joint was closing early for lack of customers, but the doorman said I could poke my head in for a quick look round. The scene inside was even more tattered and depressing than before: two Iraqis hunched over a half-empty bottle of whiskey as a lone dancer shuffled back and forth across the stage. Months-old tinsel hung from the rafters, cigarette burns scarred the tablecloths. One amplifier had blown out, bombarding half the club with deafening warbles and feedback.

The doorman, a glum Egyptian named Omar, said the club would probably close for good now that the free-spending Kuwaitis no longer came to town. "Kuwaitis paid, got drunk and paid some more," he said. Even Egyptians—the club's other large clientele—were fleeing Iraq in the mass exodus of foreign workers. "I think the happy days are all done in Baghdad," Omar said.

I walked back past the shuttered stores on Sadoun Street, Baghdad's main shopping drag. A few days before, the government had closed ice cream parlors to conserve milk, and pastry and chocolate shops to nurse Iraq's dwindling store of sugar. Restaurants were scheduled to shut over the weekend, since meat, rice, and other staples now were subject to rationing. At one A.M., the only other person on the street was a soldier snoozing over his submachine gun.

Cutting back down to the riverside, I found a bench and gazed out at the anti-aircraft emplacements on the other bank. The guns, taken down after the end of the Iran-Iraq war, had been resurrected now that enemies threatened Baghdad once again. A small boat with an unmuffled engine puttered toward me and then turned around. It was forbidden to continue downriver, past the Tigris-side presidential palace.

A night out in Baghdad had never been my idea of a good time. But it depressed me that what little vitality the city once possessed was now draining away so fast. War or no war, Iraq seemed destined to become a desert Albania: destitute and lifeless, forever armored against the outside world.

But then, anything was possible. Ten months before, on a raw Christmas night in the Romanian town of Timisoara, I'd seen ill-clad and crooked-toothed mobs rush into the street to celebrate the news that the dictator Ceausescu was dead.

Walking back to my room at the Baghdad Sheraton, with its dim light and tapped phone, I made a silent wish that I would be back again some starry Arabian night to watch Baghdad dance on the banks of the Tigris.

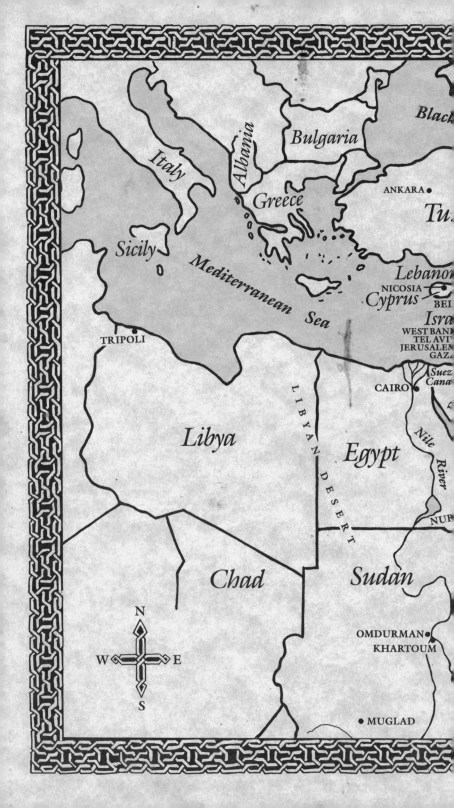